AF716179

THE IMPORTANCE OF MONEY

To my friend
and colleague
Hal Hill

The Importance of Money

Essays in domestic macroeconomics, 1949–1999

H.W. ARNDT
The Australian National University, Canberra

Routledge
Taylor & Francis Group
LONDON AND NEW YORK

First published 2001 by Ashgate Publishing

2 Park Square, Milton Park, Abingdon, Oxon OX14 4RN
605 Third Avenue, New York, NY 10017

Routledge is an imprint of the Taylor & Francis Group, an informa business

First issued in paperback 2021

A Library of Congress record exists under LC control number: 2001086753

ISBN 13: 978-1-138-72073-2 (hbk)
ISBN 13: 978-0-367-24946-5 (pbk)

Contents

Preface

This is the third collection of essays written over 50 years, following *50 Years of Development Studies* (ANU 1993) and *Essays in International Economics1944–1994* (Avebury 1996). Since Keynesian income theory and monetary and fiscal policy were my main interests in the 1940s and 1950s, before I turned to development and international economics, most of these essays are older and, like the earlier ones in previous volumes, mainly of historical interest. The title essay represents second thoughts about the subject of my inaugural lecture of 1950. The most recent ones, on aspects of political economy, fit into the collection only by courtesy.

I would like to thank Professor C. P. Kindleberger and Professor T. Wilson who supported this project, my publisher, Ashgate who again took it on and to May Stinear and Karen McVicker who prepared the camera-ready copy.

H.W.A.

Part I
THEORY

1

Keynes's Theory of Wages

This essay formed part of a review article on *The New Economics: Keynes's Influence on Theory and Public Policy,* edited by Seymour E. Harris (Knopf 1947). The essay drew on six chapters of the book to sum up the prolonged discussion of the theory of wages implicit in Keynes's *General Theory.*

Originally published as "Recent Discussion of Keynes's Theory of Wages: A Review", in the *Economic Record,* December 1949.

In a symposium on "Keynes' Influence on Theory and Public Policy"[1] which was published in the United States in 1947 both to mark the occasion of the tenth anniversary of the *General Theory* and as a Memorial to Lord Keynes, one aspect of Keynesian theory receives, apparently by accident rather than design, an unexpectedly large amount of attention. Of the twenty-five or so new essays of substance contained in the volume, at least six deal wholly or in part with Keynes's theory of wages.[2] These six essays do not in themselves form a well-arranged symposium. But if one takes the trouble to piece the arguments together, one finds in them a useful starting point for a summing-up of the prolonged discussion which this part of the *General Theory* provoked.

The task which Keynes set himself in his treatment of wage theory in the *General Theory* was to refute the implication of classical theory that general wage deflation was an appropriate remedy for general unemployment. His special problem was to perform this task while retaining one of the basic assumptions of classical theory, the assumption that employment is inversely related to the level of real wages (from which it follows that unemployment is involuntary only if labour is willing to accept work at a lower real wage). His solution was expressed in two propositions. First, wage deflation is difficult because labour resists cuts in money wages even though it would be prepared to accept an equivalent reduction in real wages through rising prices (and would, therefore, qualify as "involuntarily unemployed" in the classical sense). Secondly, even if labour were willing to accept reductions in money wages, this would not increase employment since prices would fall proportionately, leaving real wages (and therefore output and employment) unchanged.

1 *The New Economics: Keynes' Influence on Theory and Public Policy.* Edited by Seymour E. Harris (New York: Alfred A. Knopf), 1947. All page references in this Note are to this volume.

2 Wage theory is the subject of Dr J. Tobin's essay on "Money Wage Rates and Employment" and, from a rather different angle, of Dr A. Smithies's essay on "Effective Demand and Employment." It also forms the main theme of one of Professor S.E. Harris's introductory essays ("Keynes' Attack on *Laissez Faire* and Classical Economics and Wage Theory") and of Professor Leontief's essay on "Postulates: Keynes' General Theory and the Classicists." Finally, it is one of the parts of Keynes's theory which is criticised by Professor Haberler and defended more briefly by Professor Hansen.

Both propositions and particularly the more far-reaching second one, were qualified by Keynes himself in the *General Theory* and have been subject to criticism ever since. Much of the discussion in these essays summarises and elaborates these qualifications and criticisms.

Keynes's own qualifications of the second proposition related to four main points. (a) The argument applies only in a closed economy. In an open economy, a reduction in money wages will improve the balance of trade and thus increase employment, although these effects may be nullified by similar wage reductions (or tariffs) abroad or by changes in exchange rates. (b) A general fall in money wages and prices, by releasing cash balances from the transaction sphere, may reduce the rate of interest and thus stimulate investment. But this effect, on which Keynes—one cannot help feeling, with his tongue in his cheek—placed chief emphasis, is likely to be nullified either by the "liquidity trap" (at low interest rates) or by the tendency for investment to be interest-inelastic. At best, "monetary management by the Trade Unions" would be a singularly clumsy solution. (c) A reduction in money wage rates may have a favourable effect on business confidence. But if the general thesis is correct, any additional investment stimulated by the favourable impression made by cost reductions is bound to lead to losses, even if the wage cut is expected to be once-for-all and permanent. If, as is more likely because of resistance of labour, it is merely one stage in the process of a "sagging wage level" the effect will certainly be unfavourable. (d) Lastly, Keynes considered possible effects on the propensity to consume, through redistribution of income from wage-earners to other prime factors or from entrepreneurs to rentiers. The second of these Keynes thought doubtful and unimportant, while the effects of the first would be unfavourable.

At least four of the six contributors to the "symposium" on Keynes's wage theory seem prepared to follow Keynes up to this point. The chief exception is Professor Haberler who is his generally critical essay makes a root-and-branch attack on Keynes's position.[3] Professor Haberler is primarily concerned to demonstrate that Keynes's theory of under-employment equilibrium depends on his postulate of (downward) rigidity of money wages. He has little difficulty in showing that a completely unstable Wicksellian system could hardly be said to be in under-employment equilibrium; though, as Professor Hansen points out, that is hardly relevant to Keynes's main problem. Professor Haberler also advances two arguments against the thesis that employment is independent of the level of money wages. The first, to the effect that a continuous rise in the value of money would increase the real value of cash balances held in the form of gold and may thus raise the consumption function, is not taken very seriously by himself. The second would seem to be a mere reassertion of the classical position against Keynes. No Keynesian denies that "a reduction in the cost of certain consumption or investment goods may well stimulate demand for them"; but when Professor Haberler adds "and for consumption and

3 Professor Leontief does not deal with this aspect of Keynes's theory directly, but his generally unsympathetic position suggests that he would side with Professor Haberler rather than with the Keynesians.

investment as a whole" he surely begs the central question. The argument which he advances in support of this proposition is little more convincing. "Assume that the elasticity of demand for some of these things, and therefore incidentally for labour, is unity. Then the wage bill remains unchanged and there are no adverse effects through a fall of consumption demand of the workers. Then employment will clearly rise" (p. 172). This assumes that the additional output (investment) will generate equivalent additional income before cost reduction has any effect on consumption; it is merely one hopeful version of the argument that cost reduction will increase business confidence, the marginal efficiency of capital and investment. Professor Haberler's further point that the additional output must be interpreted as due to a rise in the marginal efficiency of capital or the consumption function, according as to whether the newly produced goods are consumption or investment goods, is even more difficult to accept. Professor Haberler's oblique claim, later in the essay (p. 175), to have shown that Keynes was unable to reconcile "a competitive system (flexible money wages) with the existence of unemployment" can hardly be substantiated.

Even those, however, who broadly accept Keynes's argument so far, and Dr Tobin and Dr Smithies in particular, insist that it is acceptable only on the special assumptions on which the whole model of the *General Theory* was worked out, especially the short-period assumption of constant techniques and equipment, the assumption that consumption is entirely a function of real income, the assumption of perfect competition, the neglect of variable factors other than labour, of changes in relative prices and wages, and of the role of Government, and finally, the predominantly static character of the model. Their further elaboration of the argument proceeds primarily by an analysis of the consequences of relaxing these assumptions.

Dr Tobin is led by his analysis to add two further qualifications to Keynes's thesis. First, Keynes's neglect of prime factors other than labour led him to ignore the possibility of substitution of labour for other factors in the event of a reduction in money wages. Substitution will take place, and thus increase employment, unless the other prime factors are totally immune to the "money illusion" which, according to Keynes, is a characteristic of labour. Dr Tobin's subtly developed argument is unexceptionable. One may yet doubt whether the technical obstacles to substitution in the short period in most modern industries do not deprive this qualification of any very serious significance.

Secondly, Keynes's definition of the consumption function in real terms led him to ignore the possible effects of falling money incomes (with stable real incomes) on the propensity to consume. Dr Tobin argues that these effects may be expected to be favourable to employment (a) because, if wage-earners in their capacity as consumers are subject to the same money illusion as afflicts them in their capacity as sellers of labour, a decline in their money incomes should make them feel worse off and thus tend to raise their propensity to consume; (b) because, if consumers' price expectations are inelastic, a rise in the value of money will lead them to anticipate purchases; while, if they are not, the increase in the real value of past savings will tend to depress wage-earners' propensity to save. Here again, the net effect is probably (though not so obviously)[4] in the direction which Dr Tobin indicates; but it is hard to believe that this effect would be of practical importance.

As against these two favourable effects of wage deflation, Dr Tobin points out that, once the assumption of pure competition (or at least a constant degree of monopoly) is abandoned, price rigidity may lead to a redistribution of income in favour of (monopoly) profits which would have an unfavourable effect on the consumption function and employment.

Dr Smithies, incidentally to his main argument, adds two further points. First, if the role of Government is taken into account, a general fall in money incomes will automatically reduce the yield of progressive income tax and, since some parts of Government expenditure are fixed in money terms, is likely to bring about a budget deficit with favourable effects on effective demand. Dr Smithies, however, would probably agree that this effect is likely to be more significant in the reverse case of wage inflation (which is the context in which he raises the point) than in the case of wage deflation with which we are here concerned. Secondly, changes in relative wages between different industries which Keynes's aggregate analysis ignored may have important effects on the propensity to consume though, in the nature of the case, their direction cannot be determined in advance.[5]

It is doubtful whether analysis of this often analysed question can fruitfully be carried further than it has been in these essays. What then are we to conclude? On the one hand, there is no question that the bold thesis of Keynes' formal system that real income and employment are independent of the level of money wages is untenable even in a closed economy. There is a large number of ways in which changes in money wages can, and are likely to, bring with them consequential changes in real wages, real income and employment. What cannot be said to have been shown by Keynes's critics is that these effects will necessarily yield a negative correlation between money wages and employment, or, if they do, that they will be sufficiently certain and significant to justify a policy of wage reduction in a depression. As a theoretical foundation for the "presumption against wage-cutting" Keynes's simplification would seem to emerge remarkably unscathed from the ordeal.

What of the other part of Keynes's wage theory, the proposition that "labour stipulates (within limits) for a money-wage rather than a real wage"?[6] This is a question of fact, not of economic analysis; a matter for empirical verification rather than for

4 To mention but one point, the fact that nowadays a large proportion of (institutionalised) saving is fixed in money terms may well outweigh the factors mentioned by Dr Tobin.

5 In a further argument, Dr Smithies seems to get close to Professor Haberler's position. He argues that statistical evidence suggests that in 1937 money wage increases increased labour's share in the American national income and that this contributed to the subsequent depression, (partly) because prices adjust themselves only with a lag and because during that lag "lower profit rates may become reflected in investment plans and a lower rate of investment in future" (p. 568). This effect, which could only be expected to follow a quick and drastic change in wage rates, is less unlikely in the case of wage inflation than in the case of wage deflation; but in either case, the probability that the new favourable (unfavourable) expectations will be disappointed as prices catch up surely sets narrow limits to the chances of a decisive effect on the rate of investment.

6 *General Theory*, p. 9.

theoretical reasoning. The contributors to the symposium seem, on the whole, agreed that Keynes's hunch was sound.[7] As Dr Tobin puts it, "his denial of the 'homogeneity postulate' for the labour supply function constitutes a belated theoretical recognition of the facts of economic life" (p. 581). Here, too, however, the symposium clarifies a number of issues. It also stimulates one or two doubts about the soundness of the traditional formulation of the thesis.

The most interesting contribution is Dr Tobin's demonstration that the acceptance of Keynes's postulate about the behaviour of labour does not, as has commonly been held, require the assumption that labour behaves irrationally, that labour is "naively deceived by the 'money illusion.' Judged by labour's consciousness of the cost of living in the United States in 1946, this explanation, if it ever was important, is not now significant" (p. 581). Dr Tobin mentions at least three major rational (or at least institutional) reasons which would explain a tendency of labour to resist an equal reduction of real wages through rising prices.[8] First, in a system of sectional wage bargaining, a cut in money wages for one section means a relative *reduction* in real wages. Secondly, "the cost of living is a remote phenomenon, apparently beyond the control of organised labour, certainly beyond the control of any single bargaining unit" (p. 581). It is obviously easier to organise strike action against a definite decision by a definite employer to cut wages than for a demand for higher money wages to catch up with a creeping, at best roughly measurable, rise in the cost of living. Thirdly, workers fear that wages will not rise again when prices rise in future. In other words, it is on the whole easier in the face of public opinion to resist a cut than to obtain a rise in money wages.[9]

Here is a convincing rational explanation of Keynes' postulate about the apparently irrational behaviour of labour. Yet it does not altogether allay one's uneasy feeling that Keynes overstated the extent to which labour pays attention to money as contrasted with real wages. Undoubtedly labour does, probably for the reasons just given, resist money wage cuts more strenuously than equivalent reductions in real wages with stable money wages. But is this more than a perhaps slight matter of degree? To Keynes the validity of his postulate was matter of great theoretical importance. For on it depended his demonstration of the possibility of "involuntary unemployment."

7 Except Professor Leontief. He attributes Keynes's thesis to the fallacy of short-term interpretation of a time lag which "leads easily to treatment of the lagging variable as if it were a constant. A dynamic relationship between money wages and the cost of living, considered from the point of view of supply of labour, implies the existence of a definite lag between the former and the latter. Hence the short-period assumption that the wage rates are constant" (p. 239). If this means that labour will concede reductions in money wages following a fall in the cost of living, it may be right but is irrelevant to the problem with which Keynes was mainly concerned. Keynes's question was whether labour would be willing to accept wage cuts in the hope that these would be *followed* by an equivalent reduction in the cost of living – a very different proposition.

8 Dr Tobin's list is here rearranged, with some change of emphasis.

9 Dr Tobin mentions two further, less plausible, explanations. (a) Wage-earners have obligations fixed in money terms (i.e., to some extent they share the attitude of debtors to deflation). (b) If their price expectations are inelastic, workers will resist money wage cuts because the expected future price rise would diminish the real value of current savings out of reduced money incomes. One wonders whether workers are even unconsciously influenced by such subtle calculations.

Having accepted the classical doctrine that employment if a function of real wages, he had to show that labour, despite its resistance to money wage cuts, was prepared to accept lower real wages. That doctrine, however, as Keynes later conceded,[10] depended on the assumption of short-period diminishing returns and, therefore, on the two further assumptions of absence of excess capacity and perfect competition. As soon as one abandons these unrealistic assumptions, the dependence of "involuntary unemployment" on the willingness of labour to accept a lower real wage falls to the ground. Since an increase in employment is possible without a fall in real wages, labour cannot be denied the right to demand jobs for the unemployed without cuts in current levels of real wages. "Involuntary unemployment" can legitimately be defined, without any reference to changes in the level of money or real wages, as any unemployment which could be absorbed by increasing the aggregate level of effective demand.

A similar point might be made about Keynes's formulation of the labour supply function. Here, too, he retained a "classical" concept without inquiring very seriously whether it was reasonably realistic. Take Dr Tobin's paraphrase of Keynes' thesis: "Labour does attach importance to the money wage *per se* and more labour will be supplied at the same real wages the higher the money wage" (p. 580). It is one thing to insist that labour resists money wage cuts; it is quite another thing to postulate a smooth supply curve of labour with a certain elasticity in terms of money wages. To reinterpret labour's resistance to money wage cuts in terms of a labour supply schedule which is "perfectly elastic with respect to money wages below the current level," as is commonly done in theoretical models of Keynes's theory, obscures the fact that, after all, wage-earners cannot afford to withdraw their labour from the market as a whole indefinitely. They may resist wage cuts by withdrawing their labour (striking) for a time; but if their resistance is broken they willy-nilly work at the reduced wage. Similarly, it is surely a little unrealistic to represent a situation of mass unemployment in a depression as one in which the supply of labour would increase with increasing money wages. The outstanding fact is that the unemployed are "in the market" regardless, within limits, of the level of money wages. No doubt, the aggregate supply of labour always has a certain elasticity (though, if war experience is anything to go by, this elasticity is rather more likely to be with respect to real than to money wages). But if a bold generalisation is wanted, the assumption that the labour supply schedule (representing what happens to the supply of labour when money wages change, rather than the fact that it may be difficult to change them) is highly *inelastic* would seem to fit better into the general framework of Keynesian theory than the conventional assumption of an elastic labour supply schedule. But here theorising had better stop and make way for further empirical study of how labour really behaves.

10 "Relative Movements of Real Wages and Output", *Economic Journal*, March, 1939.

2

Hicks's Trade Cycle Theory

In 1950 J. R. Hicks published *A Contribution to the Theory of the Trade Cycle*. He argued that "Keynesian economics has left at least one major thing quite unexplained, and that thing is nothing less than the business cycle itself". This essay was an attempt to compare Hicks's trade cycle theory with Kaldor's in his 1940 *Economic Journal* article "A Model of the Trade Cycle".

Originally published as "Mr Hicks's Trade Cycle Theory", *Canadian Journal of Economics and Political Science*, Vol. 17, No. 3, 1951.

In quiet moments, most Keynesians have suspected what Professor Hicks has now blurted out. "Keynesian economics, in spite of all that it has done for our understanding of business fluctuations, has beyond all doubt left at least one major thing quite unexplained; and that thing is nothing less than the business cycle itself."[1] Of course, there have been numerous Keynesian "models of the trade cycle." But none of them has seemed completely convincing. One agreed that this or that mechanism *could* produce an endogenous cycle; but one was left wondering whether some of the tricks were not a little far-fetched, whether the theoretical props were not rather thin to support the solid and complex trade cycle of the real world.

Hicks now makes his "Contribution." He has given it a handsome start by devoting a book to it, not a mere article. While original theoretical work is usually most economically presented in article form, each field from time to time needs a book to survey the ground systematically and put enough flesh on the theoretical skeletons to enable the reader to judge whether they bear a reasonable resemblance to real life. This book has all the skill of exposition, lucidity, and elegance which we have come to expect from the author. The style makes reading a pleasure, though it has its dangers. The reader is firmly taken by the hand, warned of difficulties here, of weaknesses there, so disarmingly that he has to pull himself up now and then not to be hypnotized into complete acquiescence. Though much of the analysis is based on mathematics, Hicks has mercifully relegated the latter to a Mathematical Appendix on which the author of this review is unfortunately incompetent to offer critical comment.

The main features of Hicks's model of the trade cycle are easily indicated because, as he says, "its constituent parts are all of them fairly familiar." The mechanism of cyclical upswings and downswings is explained, following Frisch and Samuelson, in terms of the interaction of the multiplier and acceleration principles; the downturn,

1 J. R. Hicks, A *Contribution to the Theory of the Trade Cycle*. Oxford: At the Clarendon Press. 1950. Pp. vii, 201. Cf. also, for a summary of the theory, J. R. Hicks, "Mr. Harrod's Dynamic Theory," *Economica*, May, 1949.

following Harrod, by the effect on investment (via the accelerator) of the "full employment ceiling" to expansion of output; and the upturn partly (following Keynes, Kaldor, and others) by the growing need for replacement investment, but also (taking up hints by Harrod) by an assumed rising trend of "autonomous" investment. So crude a summary does, of course, much less than justice to the subtlety and originality of Hicks's synthesis. In particular, the approach to trade cycle analysis through fluctuations around a rising long-term trend, corresponding to a progressive economy, transforms the picture; it is the "new and penetrating light" which "descends on the spectacle" on this occasion.

Hicks's Model

The first two chapters of substance are devoted to a reworking of multiplier theory designed to follow out the implications of consumption lags and the effects on the multiplier process of a uniformly rising trend of investment. Their primary purpose in the scheme of the book is to bring out the damping, and therefore stabilising, effect on economic fluctuations of consumption lags.

Chapter IV introduces the acceleration principle, under the heading "Induced Investment." It provides an opportunity to explain the reinvestment cycle, because of the tendency of replacement investment to reflect "humps" in original investment. But the chief novelty is the demonstration that the accelerator works differently in expansion and contraction, at any rate for investment in fixed equipment. In an expansion, the successive humps of new investment induced by successive increases in output may overlap and reinforce each other, leading to a rapid increase in the rate of induced investment. In a contraction, a strict limit is set to the rate of induced disinvestment in fixed equipment by the rate at which equipment wears out. Successive declines in output, therefore, cannot increase the rate of induced disinvestment beyond that limit: they can only prolong the process of disinvestment. This "transformation" of the accelerator, which is at the root of the phenomenon of excess capacity, plays a considerable part in Hicks's model of the downswing and depression phases of the cycle.

The next three chapters complete the preliminaries by developing the analysis of the interaction of the multiplier and acceleration principles in a progressive economy. The first adopts Harrod's concept of a "regularly progressive economy" to establish the equilibrium conditions of a growing economy with induced investment. Equilibrium is possible if, but only if (assuming constant saving and investment coefficients) autonomous investment grows at a constant rate. Subject to these conditions, "it is the rate of growth of autonomous investment which determines the equilibrium rate of growth of the whole system; and it is its level which (through the 'Super-Multiplier' of induced investment) determines the equilibrium level of output" (p. 61). The equilibrium path is a theoretical, not a practical possibility, but it serves as the point of departure for the study of displacements from equilibrium operating through the interaction of the multiplier and accelerator. This study is the subject of the next chapter where the familiar mathematical analysis of the various possible movements of output for different combinations of the saving (s) and investment (v) coefficients is summarised, with reference to a stationary economy, and elaborated to allow for investment and consumption lags. Chapter VII shows this analysis to be applicable, with only slight modifications, to a regularly progressive economy.

The construction of Hicks's model of the cycle actually begins in this chapter with the rejection of the idea that such a model could be built on the regular fluctuations or the damped oscillations which can be shown to result, for certain values of the investment coefficient, from the interaction of multiplier and accelerator alone. The case of regular fluctuations must be ruled out because it depends on a very special value of the investment coefficient; "it would be an extraordinary thing if we lived in a world which had got stuck for two centuries with an investment coefficient which was always equal to this precise value" (p. 89). The possibility of explaining the cycle in terms of damped oscillations (implying a lower value for v), set going by erratic shocks to the economy, is also ruled out, though less firmly, on the same ground; for it could explain the *periodicity* of the trade cycle only if v remained fairly close to the improbable "middle point" which would result in regular fluctuations. That leaves only one further possibility; the investment coefficient in the real world must normally be *above* the middle point, implying an "explosive" system (whether in the form of ever widening fluctuations or a relentless movement away from equilibrium). The apparently absurd conclusion becomes acceptable once it is realized (chap. viii) that expansion of real output cannot in fact "explode"; it is constrained by the "full employment ceiling." Together these two factors provide Hicks with his explanation of the downturn. The acceleration principle implies that, once output can no longer expand at the boom rate, it must inevitably decline sooner or later.

The downswing is dominated by the "transformed" accelerator. The system cannot "explode" in a downward direction. Once net induced investment has been reduced to a (negative) rate equal to depreciation of fixed equipment, it ceases to depend on output, i.e., it ceases to behave like induced investment. The system, therefore, will converge gradually to depression equilibrium which is an upward path determined by the rate of growth of autonomous investment, but lies below "normal" equilibrium because the "super-multiplier" has temporarily been demoted to the ordinary multiplier. The upswing begins when, with the gradual elimination of excess capacity by depreciation and the growth of autonomous investment, the accelerator comes into action again.

These are very much the bare bones of the argument. The remaining chapters of the book elaborate the model by analysing the factors which will determine the periodicity of the cycle; by allowing for fluctuations in autonomous investment; by conceding the possibility of a limited inflationary extension of the boom beyond the full employment ceiling; and by introducing, in the last two chapters, the monetary aspects of the cycle. While Hicks admits that a purely monetary cycle is theoretically perfectly conceivable, and that some cycles in the past may have been primarily monetary in origin, he resorts to monetary influences in his own model only to explain the rapidity of the slump which his own model cannot otherwise account for. Further detail on some of these aspects of the theory, however, is best given in examining its central features more closely.

Hicks *vs.* Kaldor

Hicks, in a footnote, makes a passing reference to an older model of the trade cycle, by Kaldor.[2] It is a curious commentary on Keynesian trade cycle theories that, but for their Keynesian background, the two models have virtually nothing in common. Kaldor's explanation of the cycle rested almost entirely on two factors which, on the face of it, play no part at all in Hicks's model: (a) systematic variations in the saving and investment coefficients over the period of the cycle, and (b) the process of capital accumulation. On the other hand, Kaldor (c) made no explicit distinction between autonomous and induced investment and (d) did not explicitly treat the cycle as fluctuations around a rising long-term trend.[3]

These four contrasts will prove useful pegs on which to hang some comments on Hicks's model. It will be convenient to deal separately with the stability of the saving coefficient and the investment coefficient; to turn then to the question of capital accumulation; and finally to discuss the closely related points (c) and (d) together.

The Saving Coefficient

Kaldor presented an ingenious argument for expecting the saving curve (saving as a function of income) to be S-shaped, with high marginal propensities to save at boom and depression, relatively to intermediate, levels of income. Hicks, on the contrary, assumes throughout his model a constant marginal propensity to save equal to the average propensity to save, i.e. that the saving curve is a straight line through the origin. Nor is this merely a preliminary simplifying assumption which is later relaxed. Hicks suggests that this assumption is as likely to be realistic as any alternative hypothesis: "I do not know of any convincing theoretical reason why the proportion in which income is divided between consumption and saving should change in one way or the other with a change in income" (p. 36).[4]

In general the question whether the marginal propensity to save does or does not change significantly over the period of a trade cycle is probably not very important. As Hicks shows, the character of the cycle depends far more on the investment than on the saving coefficient; if the investment coefficient is large enough to make the system "explosive," quite substantial changes in the saving coefficient will make little difference even to the duration of the upswing or downswing. But there is one aspect of his model where the question is distinctly relevant. It is the very aspect in connection with which Hicks raises the question.

2 N. Kaldor, "A Model of the Trade Cycle," *Economic Journal*, 1940.

3 Kaldor's model also used the *ex ante* concepts of saving and investment in contrast to Hicks's period analysis; it was this, rather than the shape of the saving and investment functions, which gave his model its "distinctly esoteric" (p. 9) character.

4 The notion of the "diminishing marginal utility of income" is certainly not, in itself, a convincing reason; but it rests in part on the recognition of certain facts about social behaviour which, as we shall suggest presently, cannot be overlooked.

"One of the most noticeable features common to nearly all actual cycles is the relative stability of the consumption goods trades; consumption seems to fluctuate less than investment" (p. 32). Two alternative explanations are available. One is that, as incomes fall to very low levels, the saving curve becomes more and more elastic, which implies that aggregate saving, or at least a substantial portion of it, becomes negative. The other is that consumption lags behind income, so that, as income falls, consumption (dependent on higher income of earlier periods) falls less. Kaldor accepted the first explanation; Hicks puts the second in its place.

We can readily accept Hicks's insistence on the importance of consumption lags on which his views closely parallel recent American work;[5] and we can admit that consumption lags can go a long way towards explaining the relative stability of consumption in a slump. But it is difficult to feel altogether happy about this explanation. What is at issue is the validity of the concept of a "bedrock of consumption," the idea that, regardless of normal saving habits, aggregate consumption cannot really fall indefinitely below or near subsistence level in a civilized community. In the last resort, peaceful or violent pressure for government action underpins consumption.[6] This, one feels, is too fundamental a fact about any economic system to be explained merely in terms of technical, institutional, or even psychological "consumption lags,"[7] i.e., in terms of delay in people's adjustment of consumption to falling income. Nor is Hicks's reason for rejecting the Kaldor argument altogether convincing. It may be true that "large-scale negative saving must surely be of necessity a transitory phenomenon" and that a situation of this sort can hardly be regarded as one of static equilibrium (p. 32). But the situation may be sufficiently prolonged to outlast a depression.

Since either of these explanations explains the facts reasonably well, it would not be worth arguing about them were it not for one point at which the question directly affects Hicks's model. In his theory, the bottom to a slump is set by autonomous investment and the (ordinary) multiplier, and by nothing else. What if there is no autonomous investment? Or if, in consequence of the slump,[8] autonomous investment is even temporarily reduced to a very low level? Can we really dispense with some such concept as the "bedrock of consumption"? This, perhaps the least satisfactory, feature of his model follows necessarily from his decision to treat the saving coefficient as constant.

5 E.g., apart from work cited by Hicks, J. S. Duesenberry, *Income, Saving and the Theory of Consumer Behaviour* (Cambridge, Mass., 1950).

6 Such government action could be treated as induced investment with a negative coefficient; but such treatment, appropriate for some purposes, would go particularly badly with Hicks's concept of induced investment.

7 Hicks relies exclusively on institutional and technical consumption lags and makes no use of the psychological lag which operates chiefly in a downward direction (because of reluctance to lower living standards that have once been achieved) and which plays the major role in Duesenberry's hypothesis.

8 See p. 20 below.

The Investment Coefficient

Hicks claims for his model that it shows the trade cycle to be explicable "in terms of simple reactions, by entrepreneurs and by consumers, which are not in any mysterious sense psychological, but are based upon the technical necessities of a capital-using economy" (p. 117). The claim is very largely, perhaps entirely, justified (subject to one or two queries which will be raised presently); and to have shown this is undoubtedly an important achievement. The mysterious psychological factors too easily serve as substitutes for genuine explanations. But when this is conceded, there remains the fact that the real behaviour of the economy, as Hicks has himself always been at pains to stress, depends very much on complex, if not mysterious, psychological reactions of individuals. If his model is to be accepted as a reasonable approximation to a realistic picture, instead of a mere demonstration of a theoretical possibility, there is no special merit in neglecting psychological factors in favour of technical necessities.

These considerations are relevant to the contrast between Kaldor's and Hicks's treatments of the investment function. The two main points of contrast are, first, that the former treated induced investment as a function of the absolute level of output, while the latter takes a stand firmly on the acceleration principle, according to which induced investment depends on the rate of change of output; and secondly, that Kaldor's model relied on the assumption of systematic changes in his investment coefficient over the period of the cycle, while Hicks assumes his investment coefficient to be constant. On the first point we have no wish to defend Kaldor's position, though it is worth noting that, when psychological reactions as well as technical necessities are borne in mind, the current rate of profit which is largely a function of the absolute level of economic activity might be conceded a substantial influence on the inducement to invest. It is the second assumption which makes one feel uncomfortable. The acceleration principle, as Hicks says, is not new, and it has been shot at from many sides. He refers specifically to only two exceptions to the general rule that "any rise in the level of output which businessmen regard as 'normal' will tend to induce an investment in new capital to support that increased output" (p. 51). One is that the increase in output may be regarded as temporary (p. 43); the other, the existence of excess capacity (p. 52). In these two cases, the accelerator will not operate at all. Where it does operate, the resultant investment coefficient is assumed to be constant, the only qualification relating to the possibility of changing returns to scale (p. 58).[9]

Will this really do? The mere fact that there are certain conditions in which the accelerator does not operate at all suggests that, if these conditions exist partially and

9 In the *Economica* article, Hicks adds two further conditions upon which he believes the assumption of a constant v to be reasonably justified; they are (a) given conditions of technique, and (b) a given rate of interest (p. 107). Neither changes in techniques nor changes in interest rates, however, would seem as likely as some of the factors mentioned in the text to cause changes in v. In fairness, it should also be mentioned that Hicks admits his assumption of constant coefficients to be a "serious limitation" on his theory (p. 170).

in changing degree, we would expect to get changes in the investment coefficient.[10] Two other factors come to mind which might render the accelerator partially inoperative and might be responsible for short-term changes in the investment coefficients. One is monopoly. Hicks conducts his formal analysis, as in *Value and Capital,* on the implicit assumption of perfect competition.[11] It is at least arguable that changes in the extent of monopoly in capital goods industries might have significant effects on the investment (although these effects are most likely to show themselves during the later stages of the slump when, as he shows, the accelerator does not operate anyhow). The second factor is the mysterious confidence reactions which cannot be neglected altogether in a realistic picture and which manage to creep even into Hicks's discussion at a less formal level. In explaining the way in which monetary restriction might speed the slump he adds: "It is also conceivable that the sharp application of the monetary brake would induce a sharp revision of expectations in a downward direction" (p. 125). Could not such a revision of expectations result from the downturn itself, quite independently of monetary measures? Whatever the cause, a revision of expectations of this sort surely implies a change in the investment coefficient.[12] There seems no obvious reason why Hicks spurns this explanation, and relies so exclusively on monetary factors to fill the gap in his model.[13]

These considerations, in turn, suggest two others which throw some slight doubt, not so much on the realism of Hicks's model, as on his claim to have explained the cycle in terns of "simple reactions of entrepreneurs based upon the technical necessities of a capital-using economy." With reference to induced investment, the claim must presumably be interpreted to imply the assumption that entrepreneurs undertake no more induced investment than is "technically necessary," in the sense of providing the necessary additions to capital equipment, to support a given increase in output. Let us call the value of v which is "technically necessary" in this sense $\emptyset$.

The first question which naturally suggests itself is whether $\emptyset$ can normally be expected to lie above the middle point. Hicks must assume that it does, if he is to get an "explosive" system based on no more than "technically necessary" induced investment. Yet he nowhere raises the question, and the answer is by no means obvious. It would require empirical investigations to establish whether the amount of investment needed to support a given increase in the rate of final output over a period

10 For instance, in analysing the recovery (p. 105) Hicks writes as if the accelerator came into operation simultaneously all over the economy at the moment when excess capacity had been absorbed. In practice, of course, the absorption of excess capacity will be "completed" and the accelerator come into action, at different points of time in different industries; the investment coefficient for the economy as a whole will, therefore, increase gradually. Similarly, businessmen's views about the temporary or permanent character of an increase in output may not be unanimous and may change.

11 There is a fleeting reference, in a later chapter (p. 128), to "deliberate price stabilisation (cartels, valorisation schemes, and so on)."

12 Even if, owing to "transformation," there is an upper limit to induced disinvestment in fixed capital, that does not apply to disinvestment in stocks, and there may, as we shall suggest, even be repercussions on "autonomous" investment.

13 G. V. Marrama, "Short Notes on a Model of the Trade Cycle," *Review of Economic Studies,* no. 35, 1946–7.

is normally sufficiently large, relative to the increase in final output, to make ø exceed the middle point, on reasonable assumptions about consumption lags.[14] The answer to this question would make little difference to the acceptability of his model of the trade cycle. While his argument that v must normally lie above the middle point if we are to be able to explain the periodic cycle of the real world at all may not be quite convincing,[15] we could still grant that v will frequently be large enough to make the system "explosive." But if ø should normally be found to lie below the middle point, the "explosive" character of the upswing would have to be attributed to a normal tendency of investors to react excessively to changes in final output, a very plausible but distinctly "psychological" explanation.

Secondly, it is clear that induced investment does not become "technically necessary" so long as there is excess capacity of capital equipment. The "technically necessary" accelerator, therefore, does not come into action in the upswing until excess capacity is eliminated; and it ceases to function when the economy hits the full employment ceiling. One wonders how much scope there would be for the accelerator to operate at all. On Hicks's assumptions, the accelerator could operate in the upswing only within the interval between the two points of (*a*) elimination of excess capacity of capital equipment and (*b*) "full employment" (i.e., elimination of excess capacity of labour); and there are only three factors which would assure that there would be any such interval at all: depreciation, autonomous investment, and growth in the labour force. It is true that either depreciation or autonomous investment can be relied upon to eat into the excess stock of capital equipment, since the former will do its work unless the depression is cut very short by rapidly growing autonomous investment, in which case the latter takes its place. On the other hand, we have to remind ourselves that point (*a*) is not really a "point" at all—excess capacity will be eliminated gradually in industry after industry; and the same is true, as Hicks emphasizes (pp. 129 ff.), of point (*b*)—the "ceiling" must really be envisaged as broken up into "sectional ceilings" which do not all become effective at the same time. The interval during which v would have the full value of ø for the economy as a whole would, therefore, be shorter than appears at first sight.[16] As an objection to his explanation of the cycle, this second query is no more serious than the first. We can easily get over the difficulty by making the realistic assumption that investors will normally anticipate increases in demand; the accelerator will generally begin to operate before point (*a*) is reached in any one section of the economy. But this again would be assuming something more than "simple reactions based on technical necessities."

14 In his *Economica* article, Hicks points out that "if only part of consumption is lagged, we can manage to work our model with much smaller values of [v]. The value of [v] can be appreciably less than unity and we can still get the required instability of output" (p. 119 f.).

15 Two reviewers have pointed out that Hicks's rejection of the possibility of explaining the cycle in terms of damped oscillations (implying that v lies below the middle point) is not necessary if the transformation of the accelerator, in effect, makes each cycle "the first of its kind"; cf. J. S. Duesenberry, "Hicks on the Trade Cycle," *Quarterly Journal of Economics*, Aug., 1950; and T. W. Swan, "Progress Report on the Trade Cycle," *Economic Record*, Dec., 1950, p. 197 ff.

16 This of course corresponds closely to Kaldor's assumption of an S-shaped investment function.

Capital Accumulation

A good half of Kaldor's explanation of the trade cycle rested on the phenomenon of capital accumulation. In particular, the effects of capital accumulation (primarily) on the marginal efficiency of capital provided him, like other trade cycle theorists, with his explanation of the downturn. In Hicks's book there is virtually no explicit discussion of capital accumulation at all. (The two references in footnotes, pp. 40 and 123, have the appearance of afterthoughts, one with a specific acknowledgment to a reminder by Professor D. H. Robertson.) Now this omission is not necessarily a serious defect in a model of the trade cycle. There has always been something unconvincing in attempts to derive the swift and violent movements of the cycle from the slow and gradual process of capital accumulation.[17] It is, nonetheless, a little remarkable that a book which is so largely concerned with the investment process should, on the face of it, not concern itself at all with (to appropriate Professor Higgins's terminology)[18] the "product" effects, as contrasted with the "process" effects, of investment.

The "product" effects of investment might be expected to impinge on Hicks's model at three points: the movement of the "ceiling"; the investment coefficient of induced investment, and the rate of growth of autonomous investment.

The movement of the ceiling Hicks's footnote references to product effects relate almost entirely to the movement of the ceiling. While he explains apologetically that his mention of the effects of investment on the movement of the ceiling "poses questions without answering them," his impression that they "cannot (as far as I can see) make any decisive difference to the results obtained" (p. 123 n.) is probably correct. Any changes in the ceiling which are due to changes in the rate of investment (i.e., to changes in productive capacity brought about by changes in the capital stock) would merely represent changes in the real output associated with full employment of labour. They would not, on this aggregative level of analysis, affect the process of the trade cycle in any other way.[19]

This question of the product effects of investment on the movement of the ceiling is nonetheless of some interest and deserves a further word of comment. Hicks assumes that the ceiling (i.e., full employment output) grows at the same rate as autonomous investment and believes this assumption to be "approximately" valid provided

17 Cf. E. D. Domar, "Capital Accumulation and the End of Prosperity" (abstract), *Econometrica,* 1948, 191, III (*a*).

18 International Labour Office, *Public Investment and Full Employment* (Montreal, 1946). Professor Higgins devised the two terms to distinguish between the effects of investment on the level of economic activity ("process" effects) and on welfare, i.e., full employment output ("product" effects). They will be used rather differently here, to differentiate between the effects on income of the *process* of construction of capital equipment ("process" effects) and the effects of the *products* of construction of capital equipment (in the form of increases in effective productive capacity) both on the level of economic activity and on full employment output ("product" effects).

19 Whether this would still hold if allowance were made for specificity and immobility of resources, with the resulting possibility that sectional ceilings might be due to scarcity of fixed equipment or raw materials, is another matter.

population is increasing (p. 96). The assumption that the (percentage) rate of growth of full employment output will bear a close relation to the rate of growth of the capital stock, and therefore to the rate of growth of net investment is not unreasonable, particularly if the labour force grows at much the same rate. But autonomous investment, in his model, accounts for only a portion of net investment. The question may be raised whether the rate of induced investment has no effect on the ceiling at all.

Even if we make the difficult assumption that the rate of induced investment does not in any way affect the rate of change of techniques of production, it must necessarily, over the period of the cycle, be responsible for part of the increase in the stock of capital equipment. That this is so is apparent from the fact that, of the total increase in capital stock which would be associated in one way or another, for example, with a growing population, a fair proportion is bound to be in those fields of investment which must be classed as sensitive to changes in current output and, therefore, as falling in the category of "induced" investment. The rate of growth of the ceiling, from one cyclical peak to the next, must, therefore, be in part a function of the average level of induced investment (or, more precisely, of the average annual increase in the capital stock due to induced investment) during that period.[20] Whether this would ever significantly modify Hicks's assumption about the movement of the ceiling is difficult to say *a priori*; and, as we have seen, the question does not really affect his model of the cycle. But the distinction may be relevant to other problems of the theory of growth.

The induced investment coefficient But this does not in itself mean that the product effects of investment are irrelevant to trade cycle theory. Hicks makes no explicit reference to the product effects of induced investment of one period on the investment coefficient in later periods.[21] Formally, these product effects are allowed for in assuming a finite investment coefficient; but the point might deserve less formal treatment. In considering it, we can again make use of our symbol ø. For vy = øy indicates that rate of induced investment which will just meet the additional demand for capital equipment resulting from a given increase (y) in income. If v ø, more capital equipment will be produced than is necessary to support y; if v ø, less than is necessary. In other words, if entrepreneurs are aware of the limited nature of the investment opportunity presented by y, they will respond with øy induced investment; if not (and we have already seen reason to believe that v may have to exceed ø if there is to be an "explosive" upswing) the rate of induced investment will be excessive in relation to

20 Strictly speaking, a fall in the rate of net investment below zero would lead to a temporary absolute reduction of "full employment output" owing to depreciation; but by the time the ceiling became again effective at the peak of the following upswing, the dip in the ceiling would have been more than made good.

21 In fact, in his first reference to the product effects of induced investment, Hicks insists that it is "not directly relevant" to the discussion of "effects on changes in the demand for output"; it is to the discussion of the ceiling that "it belongs" (p. 40 n). In the second reference, however, he admits the possibility that "the movement of the ceiling (that is to say, of full capacity output) has more effect upon actual output, when that is below the ceiling," than he has allowed (p. 123 n). This is not quite how we would put it; but it may refer to the same point.

the increase in output which called it forth. This will not necessarily have a depressive effect on v at the end of the gestation period of the induced investment, when the increase in capacity becomes effective. Whether it does so, depends on the effects on demand for final output of the income generated by the extra induced investment. Even if it is not entirely true that "optimism that is consistent over time necessarily justifies itself for the economy as a whole,"[22] any such depressive effects would probably be swamped in a rapid upswing. But it would be surprising if they never asserted themselves.

Autonomous investment Finally, there are the product effects of autonomous investment on the future rate of autonomous investment. They show themselves in the exhaustion of opportunities of autonomous investment and are touched on by Hicks in his discussion of fluctuations in the trend of autonomous investment (p. 121 f). While he mentions that a "relapse of autonomous investment" (after a prolonged hump), coinciding with the cyclical downswing, would deepen the depression, he does not specifically raise the question whether a decline in autonomous investment, due to the exhaustion of major opportunities of autonomous investment, could end a cyclical boom and precipitate a slump.[23] His answer would probably be that a slow decline in autonomous investment would hardly interfere with a really "explosive" cyclical boom until the latter hit the ceiling of its own account; and that, in any case, no theory of a *periodic* cycle could be built on fluctuations in autonomous investment which, *pace* Schumpeter, he treats as exogenous for purposes of trade cycle theory (p. 95).

Autonomous Investment and the Rate of Growth

There is no question at all that the setting of Hicks's model in the framework of a progressive economy represents a major advance in trade cycle theory.[24] It not only throws new light on the mechanism of the cycle, but also makes the whole picture more realistic and brings us nearer the long overdue integration of trade cycle theory with the theory of economic development. On this aspect of the theory we wish to make only two comments. One relates to the distinction between "autonomous" and "induced" investment. The other to the relation between Hicks's trade cycle model and the stagnation thesis.

Hicks distinguishes between the "quite large proportion of the net investment which goes on in normal conditions [which] has been called forth, directly or indirectly, by past changes in the level of output" and that portion of current investment "for which this effect is so small as to be insignificant" (p.59). The distinction though,

22 W. J. Fellner, *Monetary Policies and Full Employment* (2nd ed., Berkeley, Cal., 1947), p. 22.

23 While some such explanation of the downturn has been popular, it is not Kaldor's. Although he did not distinguish clearly between autonomous and induced investment, in his model the downturn resulted from the product effects of what was essentially induced investment. This was, in fact, one of the least convincing features of Kaldor's model.

24 But see Professor T. W. Swan's claim for priority for Harrod's *Trade Cycle* ("Progress Report on the Trade Cycle," *Economic Record*, December 1950, p. 193 ff.).

as he points out, "not in practice a sharp one," is an analytical device which helps him over a number of difficulties. But the distinction raises difficulties of its own. If "autonomous" investment were rigidly defined as investment unrelated to changes in income, it is doubtful whether any investment could ever be said to be "autonomous." Even pure deepening investment will normally be affected in its timing by income changes; and all other investment, however long-range, must be called forth at least by expectations of income changes, since all investment must be expected to justify itself sooner or later. On the other hand, Hicks's definition of induced investment, as investment "called forth by *past* changes in the level of output," if interpreted rigidly, is clearly too narrow even for his own purposes; in practice some allowance must be made for anticipation by investors, however short-term. The line which is relevant for his model should probably be drawn somewhere between widening investment undertaken in response to past changes in output and changes in output expected to take place in the near future (where "near future" may be defined roughly in terms of a phase of the trade cycle), on the one hand, and all other investment (including most characteristically deepening and long-range developmental investment), on the other. Even this distinction fails to meet the difficulties in differentiating sharply between net and replacement investment;[25] and it does not permit us to take for granted that different fields of investment will invariably fall into one or the other class.

It may be added that in Hicks's model the distinction derives some of its clarity from the aura of technically conditioned precision in which the accelerator is presented. Once it is admitted that the volume of induced investment depends on entrepreneurial reactions into which all sorts of psychological elements may enter, the distinction gets further blurred at the edges. For it is not entirely clear that the portion of total investment which, for most purposes, may reasonably be regarded as autonomous may not, at times, be subject to similar disturbances. If this is so, it makes some difference to the model at two points at least. One, the significance of which in this model has already been pointed out, is the possibility that "autonomous" investment may be reduced to very low levels in the depression. The other is that the downturn, even without "financial stringency" or "breakdown" (pp. 118, 120), may, at least temporarily, exercise a depressive effect on "autonomous" investment, and that this may function as a further "accelerator" of the slump.

The other point is less directly relevant to Hicks's model. Throughout the book, there is no hint of stagnation until the last page but one, when we are quickly transported into an "overemployment" economy. Nor is this perhaps a reasonable ground for complaint. Stagnation may, after all, be a "bogey." But just in case it is not, it would be interesting to see how the theoretical concept of stagnation could be fitted into Hicks's model. And that turns out to be quite difficult. The difficulty arises chiefly from the fact that the stagnation theorists, even when they have transformed the problem into one of "increasing underemployment," have not (at least explicitly) distinguished between autonomous and induced investment.

25 Cf. G. A. D. Knox, "On a Theory of the Trade Cycle," *Economica*, Aug., 1950, p. 321 f.

At first sight one might be tempted to identify the secular trend (whether of stagnation or long waves) in the degree of underemployment with Hicks's trend of autonomous investment. But a trend towards increasing underemployment, as Professor Higgins has emphasized,[26] does not imply a declining or even constant secular trend of investment. Strictly speaking, it implies a growing gap between the ex *ante* rate of saving and the rate of total (induced *plus* autonomous) investment. If the investment coefficient could be assumed to be reasonably stable over long periods, a decline in the long-term rate of growth of autonomous investment could, at best, be isolated as a probable (though not necessary) contributing factor towards stagnation.

But this is still rather vague and unsatisfactory. We can more effectively come to grips with the problem when we recall that a "secular trend" of increasing underemployment can only show itself, from year to year, in weaker (and shorter) short-term booms and in longer (and deeper) short-term depressions. Now there is no difficulty about the long and deep depressions. Abstracting from long-term changes in the propensity to consume, Hicks agrees with the stagnationists that a long-term trough (or, presumably, decline) in the rate (or rate of growth) of autonomous investment would tend to prolong and deepen short-term depressions (p. 122). The position is more complicated in relation to weak (and short) booms. His model allows for the possibility of weak booms which do not hit the full employment ceiling and thus permit "chronic" unemployment. But both his types (those due to damped oscillations, and free cycles made possible by the "transformation" of the downward accelerator) essentially depend on low values of the investment coefficient and it is, at first glance, difficult to see any connection between a secular trend towards stagnation and small investment coefficients.

In Hicks's model, a decline in the rate of growth of autonomous investment would not, as such, make for weak booms. Provided the rate of growth (reinforcing the recovery of replacement investment) remains strong enough to bring the accelerator into action at all, and provided the investment coefficient is large enough, it will carry the economy to full employment, however low the level of autonomous investment.[27] And that, Hicks would probably argue, has hitherto been, and is likely to remain for any foreseeable future, the normal case.

Weak booms The same does not apply to Hicks's "weak booms." Weak booms would be made still weaker by a low level and/or a small rate of growth of autonomous investment. Both a low level and a small rate of growth of autonomous investment would increase the degree of underemployment corresponding to the equilibrium path of the system (in his model, the distance between the equilibrium path and the trend of the ceiling); the former by increasing the degree of underemployment represented by the level of autonomous investment alone, without any multiplier effects (i.e., the

26 B. Higgins, "The Concept of Secular Stagnation," *American Economic Review*, March, 1950.

27 This might need to be qualified to allow for possible effects of the rate of growth on the investment coefficient. Once it is realised that v depends on entrepreneurial expectations the possibility that "stagnation" may have a depressive effect on v cannot be ruled out altogether.

distance between the trend curve of autonomous investment and the ceiling trend), the latter by reducing the "super-multiplier" for any given value of the investment coefficient. But weak booms, in his view, would be relatively rare.

If we have interpreted Hicks's view correctly, he would argue that stagnation (or secular depression) would tend to prolong and deepen cyclical depressions and weaken still further any occasional weak booms that may occur; but that it would not turn "full" into "weak" booms or make "weak" booms any more frequent than they would otherwise be.[28] While this does not correspond to all formulations of the stagnation thesis, it seems a reasonable conclusion, in harmony with the available historical evidence.

Conclusion

What then can we say, by way of general conclusion, about Hicks's contribution?

There can be little doubt that his hope, to have presented "something which may have a better claim to be regarded as *the* theory of the cycle than any which have preceded it" (p. 2), is amply justified. He himself would be the first to insist that it is "neither the beginning nor the end" of trade cycle theory. His central thesis that the trade cycle, as a species of economic phenomenon, is due to the sort of mechanism which he analyses carries conviction. That, even as a species, the trade cycle of the real world is a more complex thing than his simple model, he would readily agree. That his theory still leaves us the choice between a number of possible explanations of downturns and upturns, besides the two "Harrod effects"—monetary, exogenous, and perhaps even psychological explanations remain among the "also-rans"—represents no more than due recognition of differences between historical individuals of the trade cycle species.

28 This conclusion would, of course, need to be substantially modified if, as Duesenberry and Swan suggest, "free" cycles may be the rule rather than the exception; cf. note 15 above.

3

Deliberate Saving and the Consumption Function

Keynes thought it best to think in terms of "decisions to consume (or to refrain from consuming) rather than of decisions to save". This article, written jointly with a graduate student, J. R. Wilson, suggested that this negative or residual conception of saving had been carried too far. The level of spending and therefore of economic activity is influenced by deliberate saving decisions of which the increasingly institutionalised forms of contractual saving are the most important example.

Originally published in *Economic Record*, June 1951.

"Clearness of mind on this matter is best reached, perhaps, by thinking in terms of decisions to consume (or to refrain from consuming) rather than of decisions to save."[1]

Keynes's insistence on the desirability of treating saving as "not spending" was one of the most fruitful ideas of the *General Theory*. It concentrated attention on spending as the dynamic determinant of the level of income and economic activity. It helped to overcome the confusion between allocation of income and distribution of assets which had bedevilled earlier thinking. And it emphasised the role of income changes in the automatic adjustment of saving and investment.

But like most fruitful ideas, this negative or residual conception of saving has been carried too far. There has been a tendency in Keynesian literature to forget that some saving, after all, is planned and deliberate. It is the purpose of this article to suggest the need for a more careful distinction between deliberate and residual saving, and to point to deliberate saving as a minor, but not necessarily negligible, determinant of the allocation of income, and thus of the consumption function and the level of economic activity.

In order to elucidate the distinction between "deliberate" and "residual" saving, it will be convenient to consider first, two extreme assumptions about saving behaviour; one which makes all saving "deliberate"; another which makes all saving "residual."

The first is the neo-classical theory which treated the allocation of income between consumption and saving as merely a special case of the general theory of rational choice. Each individual has a multitude of future as well as present wants. If he behaves rationally he will allocate his limited income by equating at the margin the satisfaction he expects to derive from each future and present wants. In this view, there is no place for residual saving. Income is thought of as exhaustively allocated by deliberate spending and saving decisions.

1 J. M. Keynes, *General Theory of Employment, Interest and Money*, 1936, Macmillan, London, p. 64 f.

At the other extreme, it could be assumed that the rate of saving always results as a residual from the level of income and consumption decisions. This is necessarily the case in some degree whenever income changes unexpectedly. If saving is defined as unspent income, any unexpected change of income is bound to give rise, in the first instance, to saving (or dissaving) which is purely residual. This, the only pure type of "residual" saving is, in the nature of the case, temporary. It continues only until individuals find time to adjust their plans to the new level of income.

But, by departing from the neo-classical assumption of exhaustive rational allocation of income, one can conceive a situation in which all personal saving whatever, including even saving out of expected income, would, to all intents and purposes, be residual. This would be the case, if the only plans and decisions which people made concerning the disposal of their incomes were plans and decisions to spend. If people could be assumed to dispose of a given income by budgeting for, or simply making from day to day, certain consumption expenditures and to leave the rest of their expected income unallocated; and if, similarly, in the event of changes in their incomes, people determined the reallocation of their incomes solely by adjusting (or failing to adjust) their consumption decisions, all saving could be said to be residual. Such residual saving could not perhaps be said to be altogether unintentional. If people did not consider saving worth while at all, they would presumably plan to spend the whole of their expected income (unless the effort of finding objects on which to spend the last pound of income outweighed the satisfaction they expected to derive from the expenditure). But all that needs to be assumed is a general willingness of people to save what they do not choose to spend. This willingness to save would not in any way affect the level of their consumption expenditure. Their level of saving (or dissaving) would be determined entirely by their consumption decisions and their income (though it should be noted that the level of income effectively restrains consumption expenditure only to the extent that people are unwilling to bear the cost—in every sense—of dissaving).[2]

Of these two extreme assumptions, it is the second towards which Keynesian thinking has leaned. Nor can there be much doubt that it is the more realistic of the

2 The distinction between "deliberate" and "residual" saving here suggested is not identical with the distinction between ex ante saving and the excess of *ex post* over *ex ante* saving in the Swedish terminology since it includes, in addition, an element of residual saving out of expected income. The Swedish school, at any rate as represented by Ohlin ("Some Notes on the Stockholm Theory of Savings and Investment," *Economic Journal (E.J.)*, 1937; reprinted in *Readings in Business Cycle Theory* (esp. p. 108), followed classical thinking in assuming that individuals exhaustively allocate (expected) income as between (planned) consumption and (planned) saving though it pointed out the occurrence of unplanned (residual) saving due to unexpected income changes. In other words, Ohlin assumed that $Y_a = C_a + S_d$ stands for the expected income, where Y_a stands for expected income, C_a for planned consumption, and S_d for deliberate saving. If, as we suggest, it is more realistic to assume that even expected income is not necessarily exhaustively allocated, i.e., that the sum of planned consumption and planned or deliberate saving may diverge from expected income, $Y_a = C_a + S_d \; S_u$, where $S_u$stands for the unallocated or residual part of expected income, and ex ante saving, $S_a = S_d \; S_u$. It follows, incidentally, that, whereas in the Swedish terminology, the system is in equilibrium if $S_d = I_a$ (provided income is expected to remain unchanged), in our terminology the equilibrium condition is $S_d \; S_u = I_a$.

two. It is probably realistic to assume, by and large, with Katona, "that expenditures and not amounts saved represent people's primary concern. It is much more usual for people to meet their expenses first and save what is left than to consider saving as the first charge on their income."[3]

But people are, after all, not merely willing to save; they also often actively desire and plan to save. Their saving plans must, therefore, at least in principle, be conceded some influence on the allocation of their incomes. And that means that, in principle, aggregate deliberate saving must be one of the factors determining the position and shape of the consumption function, and, through its influence on consumption expenditure, the level of economic activity.

Deliberate saving decisions, plans and habits may be relevant both to shifts in, and to the shape of, the consumption function.

In relation to shifts of the consumption function, the distinction between shifts brought about by changes in consumption plans and shifts brought about by changes in (deliberate) saving plans has probably no great significance, though it should help to clarify analysis. Slow secular changes (e.g., changes in social attitudes to thrift) are probably adequately represented by thinking, in neo-classical terms, of a single decision to allocate income, since all complications due to adjustment lags can be ignored; and for most short-period shifts, e.g., those induced by a war-time savings appeal, it matters little whether we attribute them to decisions to spend less or to save more. On the other hand, it is worth bearing in mind that all shifts due to increases or decreases in the attractiveness of holding assets necessarily result from changes in saving plans. Thus, in so far as changes in interest rates affect the consumption function at all, they do so by inducing people to save, not to spend, more or less. Similarly, a "flight into goods" in inflation mainly represents decision to dissave, rather than change in consumption plans.

In relation to the problem of the shape of the (historical) consumption function, the common failure to allow for deliberate saving may be rather more serious. All recent studies of the problem seek to explain the empirical data in terms of consumption plans and habits. The tendency for the propensity to save to rise in cyclical upswings, and to fall in cyclical downswings, is explained in terms of lags in adjustment of consumption plans to changes in income.[4] Duesenberry and Modigliani have stressed the influence on the consumption function of cyclical peaks of consumption levels, due to people's reluctance to adjust downwards consumption levels once attained.[5] And Duesenberry has tried to explain the empirically observed linearity of the secular consumption function by the hypothesis that people's spending habits are determined by their relative position in the income scale, rather than by the

3 G. Katona, "The Effect of "Income Changes on the Rate of Saving," *Review of Econ. and Stats.*, May, 1949, p. 99 n. The second part of this quotation is supported by a reference to empirical studies.

4 E.g. M. Ezekiel, "Statistical Investigations of Saving, Consumption and Investment," *American Economic Review* (*A.E.R.*), 1942; J. S. Duesenberry, *Income, Saving and the Theory of Consumer Behaviour,* 1949; J. R. Hicks, *A Contribution to the Theory of the Trade Cycle*, 1950.

5 J. S. Duesenberry, *op. cit.*; F. Modigliani, "Fluctuations in the Saving–Income Ratio", *Studies in Income and Wealth*, NBER, Vol. XI.

absolute level of their incomes.[6] None of these studies have considered the possibility that saving plans and habits may have any significance.[7] Yet on the face of it, all the considerations which have been adduced to explain consumption behaviour might be equally relevant to deliberate saving behaviour.

If people tend to be slow in adjusting their consumption plans to changes in income, are they not also likely to be slow in adjusting their deliberate saving plans to changes in their income? Such lags in adjustment of deliberate saving plans would not affect the consumption function in the case of rising incomes, since the lag would merely substitute residual for deliberate saving. But in conditions of falling incomes, lags in downward adjustment of deliberate saving plans could do so, since they might occur at the expense of consumption rather than of residual saving. In so far as deliberate saving lags did occur at the expense of consumption, their significance for income analysis would, of course, be exactly the opposite of that of consumption lags; if the latter are stabilising, the former would be destabilising.

Much the same applies to the Duesenberry–Modigliani effect: if previously attained peaks of consumption are significant, why not, for analogous reasons, previously attained peak rates of deliberate savings? Again, there seems no conclusive reason why Duesenberry's hypothesis about the social conditioning of people's consumption standards could not be extended to people's deliberate saving habits.[8]

It may be argued that it is precisely their much greater flexibility which distinguishes saving habits from consumption habits, because people's desire to save tends to give way before their much more insistent demand for consumption. Even when we abstract from all short-run complications of adjustment of plans to changes

6 J. S. Duesenberry, *op. cit.*

7 A survey of the extensive literature on the consumption function reveals few references to deliberate saving, and scarcely any to its possible influence on the propensity to consume. Indeed, so ingrained has the habit of thinking exclusively in terms of consumption expenditure decisions become that, when authors do stumble on forms of saving which refuse to behave as mere residuals (e.g., contractual saving commitments), they tend to treat them, solely for that reason, as forms of expenditure. One, in discussing expenditure rigidities and other factors which will influence the rate of dissaving, mentions among others "the extent of their firm commitments (such as mortgage, insurance premiums and instalment loan payments)," seemingly oblivious of the fact that these very rigid "expenditure" commitments are in fact saving commitments (G. Garvy, "The Role of Dissaving in Economic Analysis," *Journal of Political Economy* (*J.P.E.*,) October, 1948, p. 426). Another goes so far as to refer to the net saving, caused (in periods of falling incomes) by the fact that instalment credit repayments exceed new purchases of durable goods on credit, as "negative expenditure." (M. Ezekiel, *op. cit.*, p. 45) No doubt, policyholders themselves often think of their premium payments as part of their spending budget; but premia do not thereby cease to be a form of saving.

8 Duesenberry agrees that saving plans, like consumption plans, will be socially conditioned, but argues that this social influence will be indirect, via consumption standards. "We can safely assume that a consumer's choices between present and future are not strongly affected directly by the actions of other people. Most people do not know how much their neighbours save or what their assets areBut choices between present and future consumption will be indirectly affected by the interdependence of desires for current consumption" (J. S. Duesenberry, *op. cit.*, pp 33 f). As a general picture, this description is certainly valid, but direct social conditioning of saving behaviour is not inconceivable. Is not life insurance behaviour, for example, significantly influenced by the social standards so shrewdly played upon by aggressive insurance salesmen?

in income or tastes, this is at best a generalisation which, though generally valid, needs to be qualified. In the average individual's scale of preferences, certain minimum consumption needs no doubt stand higher than any saving whatever. But once these needs are met, some forms of saving probably take priority over any less essential consumption; and as one goes down the scale, objects of spending and saving probably alternate in their degrees of urgency. Even when we allow the necessary time for full adjustment of plans, therefore, individuals may frequently give priority to some saving over much consumption expenditure.

When we are concerned with the adjustment of plans to short-period changes, there are special reasons for expecting much personal saving nowadays to be relatively inflexible.[9] One is the growing institutionalisation of personal saving, which is likely to impart some degree of rigidity to such institutionalised forms of saving, both upward and downward. While it would be incorrect to identify all relatively inflexible deliberate saving with saving through institutional channels (such as insurance), and all residual saving with non-institutional saving, the two divisions probably overlap to a large extent.

A second reason which is relevant only to downward adjustment, is the fact that much personal saving is contractual in the sense that individuals have committed themselves to a given rate of saving, and that any reduction in that rate of saving involves them in serious loss or inconvenience. The two most important categories of contractual saving which comes to mind are insurance premia and payments into retirement funds, on one hand, and debt repayment, including especially home mortgage and instalment credit, on the other. Since these forms of contractual saving constitute the largest, most inflexible and statistically most easily identifiable portion of deliberate saving, it will be worth concentrating attention on them, although much of the analysis should apply also to other forms of deliberate saving.

The degree of flexibility of contractual saving with downward changes in income will depend on four factors: the duration of the contract; the cost of breaking the contract (e.g., loss on lapse of insurance policies, or the consequences of default on consumer credit); the flexibility which the contract itself may provide; and the flexibility of the rate at which new commitments are entered upon (corresponding to the income elasticity of demand for the services which involve the assumption of new commitments to save).

If the contract permits no variations in the rate of saving, and the cost of breaking the contract is prohibitive, the individual is forced to save until the contract ends.

9 Discussion in this article is confined to personal saving. An analogous distinction between "deliberate" and "residual" corporate saving could be developed in terms of different dividend policies. A policy which made dividends a first charge on profits (e.g., rigid dividend stabilisation) would make all corporate saving residual; a rigid reserve policy which distributed only the residual net profits after meeting planned reserve requirements, would make all corporate saving deliberate. But the relative insignificance of consumption out of dividend income renders the distinction less interesting, despite the much greater volume of corporate saving. The relevant issues are, in any case, easily derived by analogy with the analysis of personal saving, although, in this case, possible effects on the availability of funds for investment would also have to be borne in mind.

Aggregate contractual saving of this type would be maintained in the face of a fall in incomes until the contract is fulfilled (e.g. debts repaid). After a lag corresponding to the length of the outstanding contracts, the rate of saving would fall, the extent of the fall depending largely on the income elasticity of demand for new commitments.

If the contract permits no variations and is indefinite in duration, but the cost of breaking it is not prohibitive, the rate of saving will fluctuate with income with little or no lag, but the fluctuations will be more or less strongly damped. The degree of damping will vary directly with the cost of breaking the contract and inversely with the income elasticity with the income elasticity of demand for new commitments.

If the contract explicitly provides for adjustments of the rate of contractual saving to changes in savers' incomes, but, subject to such provision, the cost of departure is prohibitive, the duration indefinite, and the income elasticity low, the rate of contractual saving will fluctuate with income to the degree provided for by the contract.

These three cases have been differentiated because they exemplify the most important types of contractual saving. The first case represents repayment of consumer credit, except for the fact that the cost of departure from the contract is not usually prohibitive, so that a fall in income will affect the rate of saving (debt repayment) through delinquencies even during the interval of the lag. The length of the lag will be not much more than a year for most consumer instalment credit, but much longer for home mortgage repayments. Since the income elasticity of demand for durable consumer goods, such as cars or household goods, is probably greater than for new houses, the decline in instalment credit repayments, when it comes, will usually go further than in the case of mortgage repayments. Those forms of consumer credit which leave the debtor much discretion about the timing of repayment, such as charge accounts and personal loans by banks or insurance companies, do not in effect involve any commitment to save regularly; repayments of such credit, therefore, are not likely to show any significant rigidity.

The second case represents all private and personal insurance premium payments, particularly life insurance, but also private accident and health insurance.

The third case represents compulsory social insurance, both contributions by the insured to state health, old-age, etc., schemes, and most compulsory retirement or superannuation schemes. Most such schemes tie the rate of contribution in some degree to the contributor's income, while, in so far as they are compulsory, the contributor's "income elasticity of demand for new commitments" is in effect zero.[10]

The graph shows how closely the cyclical behaviour of the first three types of contractual saving corresponded to expectations in the only case for which we have adequate data, the period 1929–40 in the United States.

10 Such schemes, in fact, constitute borderline cases between private and voluntary saving and compulsory saving through taxation. This merely emphasises the fact that the effect of contractual saving on the consumption function approximates to the effect of taxation in changing disposable incomes.

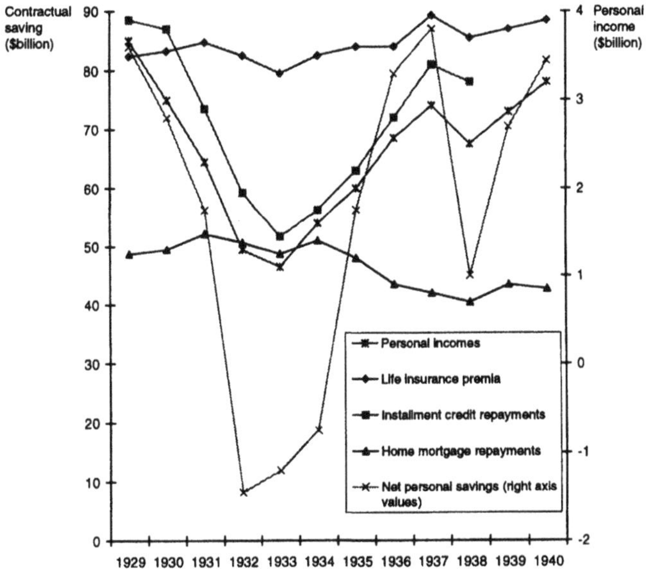

Figure 3.1 Personal incomes and selected forms of contractual saving, USA, 1929–40

Note: Installment credit payments data for 1939 and 1940 not available.

Sources: Life insurance premia: *Statistical Abstract of the United States*, 1947, p. 448. Home mortgage repayments: series represent new mortgage loans made *minus* net change in mortgages outstanding at end of year, for operating savings and loan associations only: *Statistical Abstract of the United States*, 1949, p. 453. Instalment credit repayments: Holthausen, D. *The volume of consumer instalment credit*, 1929–38, NBER Studies in Consumer Instalment Financing No. 7, 1940, p. 75. Net personal saving and personal incomes: US Department of Commerce.

The evidence of the graph gains in significance when the magnitude of contractual saving in advanced countries is appreciated. The available data do not permit any precise statements. But it appears that in 1948 contractual saving in the United States in the form of insurance premia and home mortgage repayments alone amounted to about $15.5 billion.[11] If instalment credit repayments and social insurance and retirement fund contributions (both of which, for reasons already given, are likely to be less inflexible) are added, the total amounted to about $27 billion, as compared with $212 billion personal incomes, $179 billion consumption expenditure, and $12

11 Premium income of life insurance companies amounted to $7,131 million (*U.S. Statistical Abstract*, 1950); premium incomes on other private life, health and accident insurance to $1,323 million (*ibid.*), and non-farm mortgage repayments (1–4 family non-farm houses) to $7,097 million (*ibid.*, p. 409). In the light of these figures it is difficult to understand the much lower estimate if $10 billion for contractual saving in the form of "payments on home mortgages, life insurance policies and retirement funds," given on the basis of "rough calculation" in the 1949 *Survey of Consumer Finance* (Distribution of Consumer Saving, 1948," *Fed. Res. Bulletin*, Jan. 1950, p. 26).

billion net personal saving.[12] Available information is not sufficient to indicate any secular trend in the relative importance of contractual saving, but it is not unlikely that it has increased in recent decades, with the rapid and continuous growth of private and of social insurance and instalment and mortgage credit, and there are signs that this trend is continuing.[13]

A number of considerations, such as the growing institutionalisation of society in general and of saving in particular, the redistribution of income from high income groups, most of whose saving is residual, to low income groups, most of whose saving is deliberate, and the increasing relative importance of durable consumer goods, and, consequently, of consumer instalment credit, with rising consumption standards, suggest that a secular upward trend in the relative importance of deliberate saving is not improbable.

In order to demonstrate that deliberate saving plans and habits affect the consumption function, it is, of course, not enough to show that some important forms of deliberate saving exhibit rigidity and lags in the face of falling incomes. It is also necessary to show that the maintenance of deliberate saving occurs at least in part at the expense of consumption expenditure, and not wholly at the expense of residual saving.

On this point it is difficult to obtain any empirical evidence. There is ample evidence of a tendency to maintain contractual saving in the face of declining incomes by reductions in residual saving, whether in the form of reductions of other forms of positive saving (bank or savings bank accounts, etc.), or by dissaving (realisation of assets or borrowing). The tendency for emergency borrowing by loans on insurance policies and other forms of personal loans to increase in depression partly reflects a desire to maintain consumption standards, but a fair proportion of such borrowed funds (dissaving) is used to maintain contractual saving.[14] Evidence of the opposite effect—maintenance of contractual saving at the expense of consumption—is, in the nature of the case, hard to obtain, since the effect would show itself merely as a

12 Premium income of life insurance companies $7, 131 million, and premium payments on other personal insurance $932 million (*Stat. Abstract*, 1950); home mortgage repayments $7,097 million (*Home Loan Bank Report*); instalment sale credit repayments about $7,000 million (*Fed. Res. Bulletin*, April, 1949, p. 335); social insurance, etc, contributions $4,751 million (*Social Security Year Book*, 1950); personal incomes, consumption and personal saving from Department of Commerce series (*Fed. Res. Bulletin*, Oct, 1950). The comparison with net personal saving is misleading, because most contractual saving is directly associated with a corresponding volume of preceding or subsequent dissaving. The proper comparison would be with gross positive personal saving, but since most personal saving estimates are derived from data on net changes in assets, no suitable estimates of that magnitude are available.

13 Cf. G. Garvy's discussion of the new developments in private industrial pension plans in the USA and his estimate that projected further developments of social insurance and private pension plans may, within a few years, raise saving in these two forms alone to a rate of 2 per cent of gross national product in the United States (*op. cit.* p. 223).

14 Cf. G. Haberler, *Consumer Instalment Credit and Economic Fluctuations*, NBER Studies in Consumer Instalment Financing No. 9, 1942, pp. 110 ff. and references given there; cf. also, for evidence from household budget inquiries, C.D. Hyson, "Notes on Savings in Relation to Potential Markets", *A.E.R.*, Dec., 1946, p. 892.

shortening of the lag, or decrease in the damping of fluctuations, of consumption in conditions of falling income. Even the individuals concerned will not usually be able to say how far the reduction in their consumption expenditure, which a fall in their incomes forced them to make, was aggravated by their decisions to keep insurance policies going or to maintain other forms of contractual saving.

That, there will be some effect on consumption expenditure, is, however, highly probable. Between the lowest income groups who cannot afford to cut consumption at all and who must therefore, abandon contractual saving rather than starve, and the high income groups who can maintain contractual saving entirely by corresponding reductions in positive residual saving that is not contractual,[15] has few assets which it could easily realise or on which it could borrow,[16] and which yet maintains a sufficiently comfortable standard of consumption to enable it to cut its spending in order to avoid the cost of breaking its contractual saving commitments. Professor Haberler's statement that "in periods of general contraction people would probably spend more on consumption if they were not compelled to use part of their current income for repaying debts that they had contracted in the past upswing,"[17] is applicable to all forms of contractual saving, and probably to much deliberate saving that is not strictly contractual.

We have no wish to claim too much significance for this effect. Normally, the lag in adjustment of saving plans will, even in times of falling incomes, not be sufficient to invalidate the general presumption that the propensity to consume moves inversely with short-period fluctuations in income. But saving rigidities and lags should be recognised as possible offsets to the well-known and obvious consumption lags. As a minor determinant, deliberate saving would seem to deserve some attention in future empirical studies of the consumption function.

15 Cf. G. Haberler (*op. cit.* p. 46): "The fact that many instalment debtors have no saleable assets, and that those who do have wish to retain them, suggests the most plausible answer. The more institutionalised saving is, the stronger is the presumption that repayments are made by cutting down current spending; if savings are made mainly through the various types of insurance, saving habits are relatively rigid and are not likely to be influenced by the demands of debt repayments." Cf. also A. H. Hansen, *Fiscal Policy and Business Cycles*, 1941, p. 243.

16 "In a sense, ability to dissave is proof of a certain financial strength, because in order to dissave one must have accumulated savings to draw upon or have sufficient income or collateral or both to qualify as an acceptable credit risk"; and "contractual saving was a larger proportion of total positive and net saving in the lower and middle income groups than in the upper income groups...The uppermost income group (highest third) invests a larger proportion of its savings on the basis of current decisions than do other groups. The highest third can, of course, also suffer a greater cutback in saving owing to declines in income or other reasons before a conflict arises with its contractual saving obligations" ("1949 Survey of Consumer Finance: Distribution of Consumer Saving, 1948," *Fed. Res. Bulletin*, Jan., 1950, pp. 20, 26). The high cost of "emergency borrowing" will encourage cuts in consumption even by those who could obtain credit; cf. G. Haberler, *op. cit.*, p. 109.

17 *Op. cit.*, p. 135.

4

An Australian Consumption Function

In Australia the ratio of consumption to personal disposable income was found to fluctuate with incomes of farmers. This 1951 article, written jointly with Burgess Cameron, suggested that for Australia a stable consumption function was best derived by relating consumption to non-farm disposable income.

Originally published in the *Economic Record*, April 1957. We are indebted to Dr C. E. V. Leser, who kindly carried out the statistical computations for this note.

The favourite child of Keynesian econometrics, the consumption function, has everywhere let down its admirers. In Australia, the ratio of consumption to personal disposable incomes (at current prices) has varied in the post-war years between 79 per cent and 90 per cent. The year-to-year variations have been much too large to make this functional relationship a reliable tool for forecasting. Conversion of the function into real terms, with all the price-index snags which this encounters, does not appreciably improve the situation. Can anything be done about this?

It has frequently been noticed that the variations in the ratio of consumption to personal disposable incomes in Australia are closely related to year-to-year fluctuations in the incomes of farmers. This appears to reflect a tendency of farmers not to adjust their current consumption expenditure to the large short-term fluctuations in their incomes. Perhaps the simplest hypothesis on these lines is to assume that consumption (C) is related, not to total personal disposable incomes (PDI) but to *non*-farm disposable incomes (NFDI).[1]

Table I compares the ratio of C to NFDI with the ratio of C to PDI for the post-war years. It appears that the ratio of C to NFDI not only is a good deal more stable but also happens to be very close to unity. We are tempted to proclaim, as an empirical law for the Australian economy, that consumption equals non-farm disposable incomes. More soberly, the regression line for the function (data from Table I) is

$$C = 67.9 + 0.9598\ (\text{NFDI}).$$

1 In either case, *disposable* income is here obtained by subtracting from income the relevant personal income taxes (excluding estate and gift duties)—in the one case all personal income taxes are subtracted to obtain PDI, in the other personal income taxes paid by the non-farm sector are subtracted to obtain NFDI. No breakdown of personal income tax between farmers and non-farmers is published. Non-farm income tax for the post-war years has been estimated from data published in the *National Income White Paper*, the *Reports* of the Commissioner of Taxation, and (for 1954/5 and 1955/6) from the Commonwealth Budget Papers. It has been assumed that the shares of the two sectors in total income tax paid in any year are proportionate to the ratio of the incomes of the two sectors in the preceding year weighted by the average tax rates applied to each sector (in the preceding year). For the pre-war years, the data needed for this method of estimate are not available. Since income tax rates were lower and varied less, it has been thought sufficient to divide total income tax paid in the ratio of farm to non-farm incomes given by H. P. Brown, *Economic Record*, 1949.

Table I

£m	1946–47	1947–48	1948–49	1949–50	1950–51	1951–52	1952–53	1953–54	1954–55	1955–56
1. Personal income	1,345	1,622	1,900	2,204	2,897	3,214	3,501	3,643	3,827	4,079
2. Personal income tax	154	162	198	194	351	399	388	394	361	387
3. Personal disposable income	1,191	1,460	1,702	2,010	2,546	2,815	3,113	3,249	3,466	3,692
4. Income of farmers	165	261	323	423	700	526	594	532	453	(406)
5. Non-farm incomes	1,180	1,361	1,577	1,781	2,197	2,688	2,907	3,111	3,374	(3,673)
6. Personal non-farm income tax	132	131	145	128	154	236	287	263	255	304
7. Non-farm disposable income	1,048	1,230	1,432	1,653	2,043	2,452	2,620	2,848	3,119	(3,369)
8. Personal consumption	1,069	1,261	1,464	1,661	2,018	2,380	2,545	2,815	3,079	(3,324)
C ÷ PDI	.894	.864	.86	.826	.793	.845	.812	.866	.888	.9
C ÷ NFDI	1.02	1.025	1.022	1.005	.987	.971	.971	.988	.987	.987

Note: Figures in general are from the *National Income and Expenditure White Paper*, 1955–6. However, data for 1946–7 and 1947–8 are from the 1954–5 White Paper. Personal consumption includes private remittances overseas. Refer to footnote 1.

The rest of this note deals briefly with five questions about this consumption function which suggest themselves:

(a) How can we account for it?
(b) How stable is it?
(c) Does it hold for the pre-war as well as for the post-war years?
(d) What is its form in real terms?
(e) Of what practical use is it?

(a) A stable relationship between total consumption and non-farm disposable incomes can plausibly be rationalised by asking what determines consumption expenditure by farmers if it is not governed by current farm incomes. It is not unreasonable to suppose that farmers' consumption levels are in various ways (such as direct personal contacts, availability of goods and services, advertising) influenced by consumption levels in the rest of the community.[2] If farm consumption is a function of non-farm consumption, which in turn is a function of non-farm disposable incomes, total consumption will be a function of non-farm disposable incomes.

It has sometimes been suggested that farm consumption follows farm incomes with a time lag. Various lags have been tested: that current farm consumption is a function of last year's farm incomes, of the average of this year's and last year's farm incomes, or

2 J. G. Crawford has pointed out to us another possible influence of non-farm on farm consumption standards. Government measures of aid to farmers during the 1930s were explicitly based on the principle that farmers were entitled to an income which would enable them to maintain a standard of living (excluding luxury expenditure) comparable to standards prevailing among city people.

of the average of this year's and the preceding two (or three) years' farm incomes. Each of these gives a distinctly less good fit than the thesis that farm consumption is a function of current non-farm disposable incomes. It seems not unlikely, however, (though the available data are inadequate to test this) that farm investment, including expenditure on durables such as cars, moves with current farm incomes, or follows them with a lag.

(b) How good a fit does the proposed function give, compared with say the PDI function? Since each of the series C, NFDI and PDI rose rapidly after 1946/7, it is clear that the correlation between any pair of them will be high. We can overcome this difficulty by taking the regression of year-to-year changes in consumption on year-to-year changes in income. Here the relation between changes in C and changes in NFDI yields a correlation coefficient of 0.36 for the relation between changes in C and changes in PDI.

Chart I

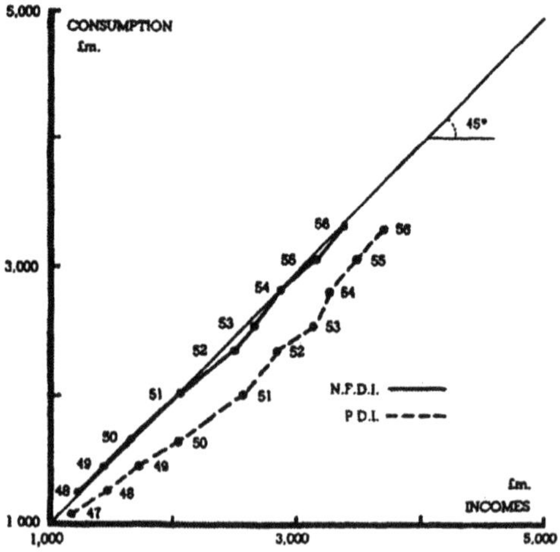

The correlation of C with NFDI, though very good, is not perfect. As Chart I shows, consumption was relatively high in 1946/7, 1947/8 and 1948/9 and relatively low in 1951/2 and 1952/3. On the principle of econometric gamesmanship that one improves the fit of a curve by "explaining" the deviations,[3] one might point out that 1946/7, 1947/8 and 1948/9 were post-war years in which liquid asset holdings were still abnormally high, while the low figures for 1951/2 and 1952/3 might be accounted for on the hypothesis that Australian consumers as a group spend less, out of a given income, if their income is falling than if it is rising.[4]

3 Cf. R. Dorfman, "The Nature and Significance of Input-Output", *Review of Economics and Statistics*, May 1954, p. 129.

4 Such a hypothesis also fits the low *real* consumption levels of 1929/30 and 1930/1 (Chart III). It is only fair to add, however, that the observations for 1951/2, 1929/30 and 1930/1 might also be explained by the hypothesis that the income of farmers *does* exercise some influence on farm consumption – for farm incomes were falling in these years relatively to other incomes.

(c) The hypothesis that consumption in Australia is a function of non-farm disposable incomes fits the data for the pre-war decade (1928/9–1937/8) as well as for the post-war decade (Table II, Chart II). But the result is less impressive because, for the 1930s, the conventional consumption function also works well. (The correlation coefficients, even for the relation between year-to-year changes, are almost identical: 0.99 for changes in C on changes in NFDI; 0.97 for changes in C on changes in PDI.) The approximate post-war equality C = NFDI, however, does not hold for the pre-war decade,

Chart II

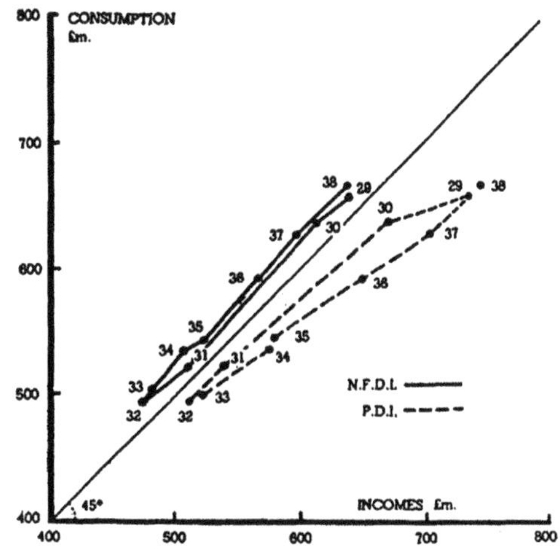

Table II

£m	1928–29	1929–30	1930–31	1931–32	1932–33	1933–34	1934–35	1935–36	1936–37	1937–38
1. Personal income	748	681	557	531	542	593	600	670	725	768
2. Personal income tax	12	12	19	21	22	20	20	22	23	24
3. Personal disposable income	736	669	538	510	520	573	580	648	702	744
4. Income of farmers	99	60	30	40	45	70	60	85	111	107
5. Non-farm incomes	649	621	527	491	497	523	540	585	614	661
6. Personal non-farm income tax	10	11	18	19	20	18	18	19	19	21
7. Non-farm disposable income	639	610	509	472	477	505	522	566	595	640
8. Personal consumption	657	636	522	494	500	534	544	591	627	666
C ÷ ΠΔI	.893	.951	.970	.969	.962	.932	.938	.912	.893	.895
X ÷ NFDI	1.028	1.043	1.026	1.047	1.048	1.057	1.042	1.044	1.054	1.041

Note: Personal incomes are from H. P. Brown in *Economic Record (E.R.)*1949, and personal consumption is from an ms by H. P. Brown. Income of farmers is obtained by using % figures in H. P. Brown *E.R.*1949 for farm income. Personal income tax is obtained from an analysis of government accounts. Refer also to footnote 1.

as the regression line of consumption on non-farm disposable income shows

C = 0.8 + 1.0473 (NFDI)

The ratio of consumption to non-farm disposable incomes was stable at about 1.05 rather than unity, suggesting that the function has since shifted downwards (or is curvilinear).

(d) In order to explore this apparent downward shift further, it is necessary to convert the C = c (NFDI) function into real terms, since the slope of the function in money terms will have been distorted by the post-war inflation. Chart III shows the relation between consumption and non-farm disposable incomes, both deflated by the C-series index. (There is no need to enter here upon the merits and demerits of alternative deflators; almost any alternative deflator available will give a rather lower marginal propensity to consume since other indices, such as the wholesale price index, have risen more sharply than the C-series in the post-war period.) The pre-war decade gives a regression line of

C = -40.8 + 1.071 (NFDI).

The post-war period gives a regression line of

C = 288.2 + 0.8875 (NFDI).

By comparison, the regression line for the twenty years is

C = 160.8 + 0.9342 (NFDI).[5]

These relations support the suggestion that the consumption function has shifted downward, a shift for which post-war pressures towards voluntary and involuntary personal saving may be the explanation.

Chart III

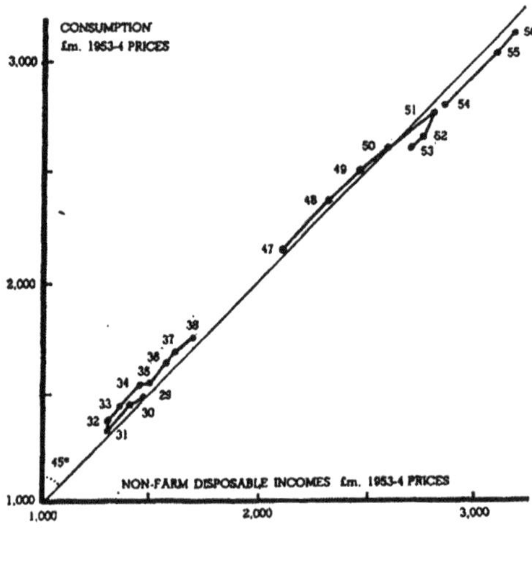

5 The correlation coefficients for these three regression lines (*not* first differences) are 0.9952, 0.9926 and 0.9988 respectively.

(e) Of what practical use is an Australian consumption function of the form C = a + c (NFDI) (or, more boldly, C = NFDI)? Consumption has hitherto proved one of the most precarious components of market demand to forecast from year to year. The hypothesis here put forward does not solve the problem. But if confirmed it would mean that, given an independent estimate of market supplies, and of gross private investment, government expenditure and exports, the large residual component of consumption (small errors in the forecast of which make a great deal of difference to the result) can be fairly accurately forecast provided we have a reasonable idea of non-farm incomes (from our estimate of domestic full employment output and wages rates) and of income tax on these non-farm incomes.

5

Radcliffe Monetary Theory: A Comment

The revival of interest in monetary policy in the 1950s gave rise to a controversy about monetary theory. The Report of the UK Radcliffe Committee (1959) argued that the decisions that determine the level of total demand depend on the whole liquidity position of spenders, not upon immediate access to money, and that therefore monetary policy must focus on the structure of interest rates rather than on money supply. This article sought to elucidate the implications for monetary theory.

Originally published in the *Economic Record*, September 1962.

Professor Rowan's admirable exposition of Radcliffe Monetary Theory (RMT)[1] goes a long way in sorting out the confusion created by the ambiguities of the report itself and worse confounded by the discordant chorus of critics. But even Professor Rowan has left some loose ends. To attempt to tie up some of these is the object of this paper.

"Acts of Spending" and "Decisions to Spend"

Much of the air of paradox which surrounds RMT is due to the combination of its emphasis on availability (as contrasted with costs) of finance and its strident playing down of the importance of money supply. As several critics have pointed out, if monetary policy operates primarily by influencing the *ability* rather than the *desire* to spend, it would seem to be the availability of money proper, i.e. means of payment, that matters; "for *acts* of spending (as distinct from decisions to spend) unquestionably require the possession of money here and now, the promise of money very soon will not do".[2]

Professor Rowan's defence of the logic of RMT against this line of criticism runs mainly in terms of the inefficacy of cuts in money supply in conditions where the effects of such cuts on availability are readily offset by activation of idle balances (although he also seems to feel uncomfortably that RMT's playing down of the money supply is rather overdone).[3] In all his discussion of this aspect of RMT he seems to

1 D. C. Rowan, "Radcliffe Monetary Theory", *Economic Record*, December 1961. This article will be cited as "Rowan"; Professor Rowan's earlier article, "The Radcliffe Report: A Distant View", *Economic Record*, March 1961, as "Rowan, March 1961".

2 M. Gaskin, "Liquidity and the Monetary Mechanism", *Oxford Economic Papers*, October 1960, p. 277.

3 Rowan, p. 440.

miss the crucial point which is also perhaps the only original contribution of RMT to monetary theory: its insistence on the subjective character of liquidity.

When Professor Rowan paraphrases RMT in two propositions: "(a) the ability to spend is not circumscribed by the amount of money an individual possesses; (b) it is circumscribed by the amount he can get hold of on 'tolerable terms'",[4] he seems to lay it wide open to the objection quoted above. The reason is that Professor Rowan fails to distinguish between "acts of spending" and "decisions to spend". "Acts of spending", in the sense of actual payment, require money proper, here and now. But "decisions to spend", in the sense of commitments to spend or placing of orders, do not require money here and now; they merely require confidence that money will be available when payment falls due. RMT is emphatic that what matters for the level of economic activity are the "decisions to spend" (placing of orders), not the "acts of spending" (payment).

> Decisions to spend on goods and services—*the decisions that determine the level of total demand*—are influenced by the liquidity of the spenders... It is the whole liquidity position that is relevant to spending decisions, and our interest in the supply of money is due to its significance in the whole liquidity picture. A decision to spend depends not simply on whether the *would-be* spender has cash or 'money in the bank'... There is the alternative of raising funds either by selling an asset or by borrowing; and the *prospect of* a cash flow from future sales of a product both encourages *commitment* beyond immediately available cash and makes borrowing easier. The ease with which money can be raised depends on the one hand upon the composition of the spender's assets and on his borrowing power and on the other hand upon the methods, moods and resources of financial institutions and other firms which are prepared (on terms) to finance other people's spending... The *decision to spend* thus depends upon liquidity in the broad sense, not upon *immediate* access to the money. This is most clearly seen in the giant industrial firms, making plans for their constructional developments *two, three or four years ahead of much of the actual spending*; but this is merely an extreme example of what is being done throughout the economy, by spending units great and small, all the time.[5]

It is clear that when RMT continues "the spending is not limited by the amount of money in existence; but it is related to the amount of money people think they can get hold of",[6] spending means "decisions to spend (in future)" and the emphasis is on the amount of money people *think* they can get hold of.

Professor Rowan painstakingly discusses the distinction between effects of monetary policy on the "desire" (or "willingness") to spend and effects of monetary policy on the "ability" to spend.[7] He broadly equates the former with the "incentive effects" of higher or lower rates of interest and the latter with effects of monetary policy (and especially of rising or falling interest rates) on "availability". He rightly points out that RMT, sceptical of the short-run interest-elasticity of consumption and investment, puts its hopes on the availability effect. But Professor Rowan's discussion almost entirely misses RMT's emphasis on the crucial importance of effects of

4 Rowan, p. 426.

5 *Radcliffe Report* (Cmd. 827), 1959, paras. 389f; my italics.

6 *Ibid.*, para. 390.

7 Rowan, pp. 423ff.

monetary policy on *decisions* to spend taken in the light of spenders' *expectations*.[8] In discussing effects on the "willingness" to spend, Professor Rowan at least refers to "real *planned* expenditure", although, curiously, his whole discussion relates to consumption, not to investment expenditure.[9] But when he refers to effects on the ability to spend, he always seems to have in mind objective liquidity, the possession (or ability to get hold) of money here and now.[10]

In a sense, RMT here merely spells out one of the central points of Keynesian theory. Keynes emphasised that the level of economic activity depends on spending (and especially investment spending) decisions. (It was part of his case against the quantity theory that what matters is not the possession of money but the decision to spend it.) We have come to treat it as self-evident that the "desire" to spend (especially to invest) depends on expectations, the expected yield or the marginal efficiency of capital. Changes in the cost of finance, such as the incentive effects of higher or lower interest rates, can, as Professor Rowan points out, be regarded as affecting the "desire" to spend since they change the net yield to the spender, though the effect here, too, must be thought of as operating on the *expected* net yield. The new contribution of RMT is to extend this argument to availability: what matters is not merely or primarily actual availability of money here and now but spenders' expectations about the amount of money available to them when payment falls due. For it is these expectations that will influence their spending decisions.[11]

It is worth noting in passing that this emphasis on expectations does not eliminate the distinction between effects of monetary policy on the "desire" and on "ability" to spend. The "desire" to spend depends on the expected net yield of the expenditure, after allowing for the costs of finance. Monetary policy can influence this by changing

8 Some confusion is liable to arise from the fact that in one place (p. 423) Professor Rowan uses "decision to spend" as synonymous with "desire" or "willingness" to spend.

9 Rowan, p. 424.

10 It should be mentioned that the Radcliffe Report itself is explicit in its emphasis on the subjective aspect of liquidity only in the two paragraphs that have been quoted.

11 At one point, RMT distinguishes three points of time at which monetary policy may affect "spending": "It was therefore not surprising to find, in evidence we received from industry, that the blow fell not on projects already in train but on capital projects in their earliest planning stages—implying an effect on spending not immediately but many months later. It was not, that is to say, the current level of demand that was affected; rather, action was upon possible prolongation and development of the boom" (para. 460). Monetary policy, therefore, may impinge on (a) the planning stage (and thus affect demand some months later) or (b) the placing of orders (and thus affect current demand) or (c) acts of payment (which are not significant for the level of demand).

The emphasis on spending *decisions*, rather than on *acts* of spending, has one implication of considerable practical importance in countries like Australia which use the overdraft system of bank advances. It suggests that the important statistics for policy control of bank credit may be the statistics for overdraft limits rather than the statistics for advances outstanding. The issue is not clearcut; for it depends on whether decisions to spend precede and motivate applications for a new or higher limit (the subsequent *use* of these limits, which shows up as a rise in advances, merely reflecting the unimportant lagged acts of spending or payment) or whether unused limits are held in reserve, much like an idle cash balance, and drawn upon—possibly with a lag—as and when spending decisions are made. The question which of these two alternatives more nearly represents the actual situation is one on which more knowledge is urgently needed.

the cost of finance (the "incentive effect"); Professor Rowan's "financial assets" effect (on the marginal propensity to save) would be another effect on the "desire" to spend;[12] any effects of monetary policy on general business confidence (i.e. on the marginal efficiency of capital) would be a third. RMT's "availability" effect is not of this kind, even if it is interpreted as an effect on spenders' expectations. For it operates, not on the expected yield of planned expenditure, but on the spender's ability to finance (and therefore undertake) the expenditure.

RMT is undoubtedly correct in saying that, since the level of economic activity depends on the decisions to spend, rather than on the subsequent acts of spending, the efficacy of monetary policy must be judged in terms of its effects on these decisions to spend and on the expectations of spenders in the light of which these decisions are made. This shift of emphasis certainly renders RMT less open to the charge of inconsistency in stressing the general liquidity position rather than money supply. How much difference it makes to one's judgment of the efficacy of monetary policy is another question. The main difference would seem to be that the nature and magnitude of "availability" effects of monetary policy at once become much harder to assess. Some spenders *may* be inhibited from placing orders if the authorities take steps which make it seem likely that credit will become less readily available (whether through direct restraints on money supply or through measures which impede the activation of idle balances). But there is no telling how significant such effects on spending decisions via expectations are likely to be. For those spenders who are not deterred but go ahead and try to raise the money, the issue becomes, once again, one of "objective liquidity", i.e. actual availability and/or terms of finance. Just as the "desire to invest" will be determined the more nearly by objective determinants of the actual yield of investment the more rational and better informed the profit expectations of investors, so the effects of monetary policy via expectations of spenders will diverge the less from those via actual availability and/or terms of finance the more rational and the better informed are the expectations about these matters of would-be spenders.

"Availability" and "Incentive" Effects

The significance of the distinction between effects of monetary policy on the "ability to spend" and effects on the "desire to spend" obviously depends on the degree of prevalence of credit rationing in the capital market. In a perfect capital market, spending would never be limited by lack of availability of money since money could always be obtained *at a price*. By definition, therefore, monetary policy would always operate through its effects on the desire, not on the ability, to spend. Conversely, if one could imagine a financial system in which all finance is distributed by rationing at a fixed rate of interest, monetary policy would operate exclusively[13] on the ability to spend.

12 Rowan, p. 424.

13 Even in such a system, changes in monetary policy might affect the climate of business confidence.

The trouble is that the distinction is liable to evaporate when one tries to apply it to the real world where rationing is a matter of degree. As Professor Rowan points out, when RMT says that "if the money for financing the project cannot be got on any tolerable terms at all, that is the end of the matter",[14] everything turns on what is meant by "tolerable terms". "'Intolerable terms' which (by definition) check borrowers, cannot mean 'high interest rates'—for that would imply the very interest elasticity of investment which is decried."[15]

An interesting answer to the puzzle has been given by Professor Tew.[16]

> When a firm seeks finance from outside, there are a number of considerations that may limit the total amount available, or at any rate worsen the terms of finance, the larger the amount required...The net effect of these different considerations is that the typical firm has access to outside finance in a series of tranches, differing from one another in the interest rate charged and/or in other terms (voting rights, security, repayment period, etc.) imposed by the lender or subscriber. These tranches, together with (perhaps) a tranche of internal finance, may be conveniently considered as arranged in order of increasing cost, the first tranche available to finance an investment project being the one having the least burdensome terms of finance, and the last, or marginal, tranche the one with the most onerous terms.
>
> If this is a fairly realistic description of the way in which a typical firm finances an investment project, it follows that a change in monetary policy can impinge on the *marginal* terms relevant to the finance of the project in two distinct ways, which in my view correspond respectively to the Radcliffe Committee's 'interest incentive effect' and its 'general liquidity effect': (1) A rise in interest rates may jack up the terms of finance on every tranche of capital required, including the marginal tranche. (2) A more limited availability of finance may reduce the size of each tranche, so that additional tranches (and therefore more onerous ones) have to be taken to meet the total capital cost of the project.[17]

Professor Tew's description inevitably leads to the conclusion that the "availability" effect of monetary policy, as much as the "incentive" effect, operates on the desire to spend. The only difference appears to be that in the one case spenders are deterred by more onerous terms of finance arising from a rise in "the market rate of interest" (interpreted as a rise in some weighted average of market rates for loans of different maturities and consistent with unchanged risk premia payable by individual borrowers) while in the other case the rise in marginal (and average) "costs" reflects mainly higher (borrower's and lender's) risk premia. Successive tranches become more "costly" because of increasing borrower's risk through loss of control (equity issues), high gearing (debenture issues) or prestige costs of turning to "Shylock".[18] "Shylock" charges higher interest than a bank to cover his greater lender's risk because he knows less about the client's credit standing and/or because he demands less security.

Professor Tew's description of what happens when a restrictive monetary policy impinges on the sort of capital market we know has a plausible ring about it. But it is still, I think, only part of the story. In the first place, it does not adequately describe

14 *Radcliffe Report*, para. 387.

15 Rowan, p. 427.

16 B. Tew, "A Case for Financial Controls?", *The Banker*, January 1960.

17 *Ibid*., p. 30.

18 Cf. Rowan, p. 429.

the situation where credit rationing in some sectors of the capital market operates side by side with a broadly free market in other sectors. To take the simplest case, assume a capital market consisting of (a) banks which ration credit to eligible customers at a fixed advance rate and (b) non-bank financial intermediaries (NFI) which are prepared to lend to anybody and which equate supply and demand by flexible rates. In such a market, the rates charged by NFI will be higher than the bank advance rate, even in the absence of excess demand for bank credit by eligible bank customers, the difference reflecting risk premia. If now the banks tighten credit, demand for NFI credit and NFI rates will rise. This further rise in NFI rates does not reflect risk premia but is simply a rise in free market rates.[19]

Secondly, Professor Tew's description appears consistent with equilibrium between supply and demand for funds at the rates charged in each sub-market. Professor Rowan, on the contrary, emphasises disequilibrium (*excess* demand at ruling rates charged) as the crucial feature of credit rationing and therefore of the "availability" effect. "In the short-run, the operation of monetary policy cannot be analysed by a simple macro-static model of equilibrium."[20] A tightening of rationing in some sub-market, e.g. the banks, implies "an increase in the degree of imperfection in the market for bank loans."[21] "While we are always on the supply curve for loanable funds, we are not always on the demand curve."[22] Spending is affected simply because rationing reduces the amount of finance available—on tolerable terms.

The trouble here arises from the afterthought "on tolerable terms". One wonders whether the intending borrower might not, if he tried hard enough, raise some more money somewhere on some terms; and whether, therefore, this case, too, does not in the end resolve into an "incentive effect" on the desire to spend. The answer is that a high proportion of spenders depend, for all practical purposes, on one or two sources of finance, in the sense that only pressure of extreme urgency would induce them to look elsewhere. For practical purposes, if they cannot obtain finance from their normal sources, that is the end of the matter for them.

The logical difficulties with which Professor Rowan and other commentators on RMT have wrestled seem to me to arise from the fact that the real world exhibits features of all three of the above models. Would-be borrowers subjected to tighter credit rationing by the institutions on which they normally depend (e.g. banks) usually have the opportunity of borrowing more elsewhere on more onerous terms, whether the higher "costs" reflect merely higher risk premia (as in Professor Tew's model) or higher market rates of interest. But to many borrowers these opportunities might as well not exist either because they are unaware of them or because the terms demanded are "intolerable". Wherever and to the extent that this (i.e. disequilibrium between

19 The rise in NFI charges in recent booms in Australia was presumably an example mainly of this situation.

20 Rowan, p. 430.

21 Rowan, p. 435.

22 Rowan, p. 430.

supply and demand) is the predominant feature of the situation, we have, as Professor Rowan has rightly emphasised, the "availability" effect of monetary policy.[23]

The "Roosa Effect"

As Professor Rowan points out, the Radcliffe Committee, unhappily persuaded by a flow of witnesses that little could be expected from the "incentive effect" of higher interest rates, plumped for what, after its inventor, has been called the "Roosa effect": rising interest rates can reduce availability by making financial institutions less willing to lend, "some because capital values have fallen and others because their own interest structure is sticky".[24]

There is no dispute that rising long-term rates can, in principle, limit spending by impeding the activation of idle balances through "switching" by financial institutions and other holders from bonds into cash. But there exists considerable doubt on the likely magnitude of the Roosa effect. Financial institutions can be made less willing to lend by "locking in" their investments only if they are otherwise fully loaned up, if they hold inadequate portfolios of early maturing short-term securities, if bond prices fall below their purchase prices,[25] and if they are reluctant to incur realised capital losses and/or feel obliged to offset paper losses by increasing their liquidity in other directions.[26] The last two conditions are likely to be fulfilled by banks, not only because they usually feel unable to recuperate capital losses by raising their own advance rates but also because, for prestige reasons, they are usually anxious to avoid even the appearance of such losses. Non-bank financial intermediaries are much less likely to be inhibited either by stickiness of own rates or by prestige considerations. Even banks might revise past habits—becoming less reluctant to vary advance rates and more reluctant to hold long-term bonds—if "locking in" through variations in long-term rates became a normal weapon in the armoury of monetary policy.[27] Even allowing for the possibility that "locking in" may affect spenders themselves who are holders of long-term securities, one cannot but agree with the opinion that "the weight placed by the Committee on the Roosa effect is not very plausible"[28] and Professor Rowan seems to share this scepticism.[29]

I would add only two further comments, one semantic, the other of some importance for the logic of RMT.

23 No attempt has been made in this section to adapt the wording to the argument of the first section; it is easy to translate the discussion into effects on *expectations* of spenders about *prospective* availability and/or terms of finance.

24 *Radcliffe Report*, para. 393.

25 S. Katz, "Radcliffe Report: Monetary Policy and Debt Management Reconciled", *Quarterly Review*, Banca Nazionale del Lavoro, June 1960, p. 164.

26 Cf. J. Spraos, "Control by the Stickiness of Rates", *The Banker*, November 1959; Rowan, pp. 434–37.

27 Cf. Spraos, *op. cit.*, pp. 675–79.

28 Gaskin, *op. cit.*, p. 283.

29 Rowan, p. 436.

In so far as the Roosa effect makes financial institutions less willing to lend, it undoubtedly reduces the "availability" of finance. But in the case of bondholder-spenders, where there can be no question of diminished willingness to *lend*, the capital loss incurred in "switching" is surely as much an addition to the cost of finance as a rise in the rate on bank advances;[30] I cannot see that in this case it is "straining the ordinary use of language" to regard this as a "cost effect" on the desire to spend.[31]

Professor Rowan summarises RMT's position on the Roosa effect as follows: "Rising rates are a substitute for high rates in the sense that rising rates can, it seems, restrict the supply of funds from financial intermediaries sufficiently to make it unnecessary to raise market rates to levels which would cause postponement of expenditure by borrowers."[32] This fails to bring out a vital step in the argument of RMT: the fact that the rise in interest rates which accompanies the activation of idle balances through financial intermediaries is, in the first instance, a rise in *short-term* rates (partly reflecting higher risk premia) while the "general liquidity effect" is very largely if not entirely[33] dependent on rising long-term rates.[34] It is because of this that the "general liquidity effect" cannot be expected to operate automatically, but demands active "manipulation" of long-term rates by the authorities.

If this is a correct interpretation of RMT, it invites two comments. First, Australian experience during recent years suggests that the rise in short-term rates which accompanies the process of activation of idle balances may be very considerable. If its effects in discouraging spending are small, it is partly because it occurs in boom conditions when "incentive effects" carry little weight against optimistic expectations, partly because, being largely confined to the short end of the interest pattern, it has no "general liquidity effects". Secondly, while even in a free market long-term rates must be expected to be more stable than short-term rates, the almost complete failure of sharply rising short-term rates in recent booms to be transmitted to long-term rates is clearly to be explained largely by official support of the bond market by the authorities. The "manipulation" of interest rates required for the "general liquidity effect" might therefore (at least in a relatively narrow bond market) involve little more than abstention by the authorities from deliberate stabilisation of the long-term rate.

30 Professor Rowan mentions one or two other possible effects of rising long-term rates on spenders. The only one that might be regarded as affecting availability rather than the costs of finance (though not necessarily "cost in the sense of interest forgone") is the possible effect of increased uncertainty in making enterprises feel a greater need for liquidity (*ibid.*).

31 Rowan, p. 437.

32 Rowan, p. 436.

33 Some references to the "general liquidity effect" in the Report, e.g. the reference to Sir Roy Harrod's "diffused difficulty of borrowing" (para. 460), suggest that, in RMT, it has a somewhat broader connotation than the Roosa effect.

34 Cf. Gaskin, *op. cit.*, p. 283.

Manipulation of Interest Rates

Finally, we come to the last four propositions of RMT, as summarised by Professor Rowan: They are: "(a) overall liquidity for institutional reasons depends upon the whole structure of interest rates; (b) the structure of interest rates rather than the money supply is therefore the centrepiece of monetary action; (c) the manipulation of the structure of interest rates can be encompassed by a 'suitable policy'; (d) debt management forms an important part of any 'suitable policy'."[35]

We have seen that the "availability" effect depends on a rise in *long-term* rates. The questions raised by this part of RMT, therefore, are two: first, the doctrinal question whether long-term rates can be raised by the authorities without reducing the money supply; and if not, whether it is the reduction in the money supply or the rise in the long-term rate that is the more important aspect of the operation. Secondly, the practical question, whether deliberate manipulation of the long-term rate for this purpose can be recommended to the authorities as a "suitable policy".

Let us first grant that the authorities, in certain circumstances, can raise the long-term rate without reducing the money supply. They can do this by exerting "influence...on the expectations of asset holders"[36] and by funding. In the special conditions of the United Kingdom, a rise in bank rate may , through its role as a "signal", induce a rise in the whole pattern of market rates, even without being made "effective" by pressure on bank liquidity. In less degree, the authorities can probably produce similar effects anywhere simply by creating uncertainty about the future of the long-term rate. Funding can raise the long-term relative to the short-term rate.

Professor Rowan, in his anxiety to defend the logical consistency of RMT in rejecting the money supply as the centrepiece, places heavy emphasis on the references by RMT to manipulation of the "structure of interest rates", interpreting this to mean the *relative* rate pattern.[37] This suggests that RMT, when it speaks of official manipulation of interest rates, is thinking primarily of funding. Careful reading of the report does not, in my view, support this interpretation. The report frequently uses the phrase "the whole structure of interest rates", but on each occasion it seems it seems to mean no more by this than "the whole complex of rates", in the sense in which Professor Rowan himself refers to official intervention which, from the short end, is "extended throughout the rate curve".[38]

If what RMT has in mind is simply action to raise the "whole complex of interest rates", it is at once open to Sir Roy Harrod's complaint that it has "abandoned the foundation stone of British monetary theory"[39] in suggesting that such action does not

35 Rowan, p. 421.

36 Rowan, p. 439.

37 Cf. his statement (p. 437) that an "appropriate interest policy...means a selective policy." The same interpretation was advanced more explicitly in Rowan, March 1961, p. 60.

38 Rowan, p. 439.

39 Sir Roy Harrod, "Is the Money Supply Important?", *Westminster Bank Review*, November 1959, p. 4.

involve a reduction in the money supply. On Professor Rowan's somewhat charitable interpretation, RMT does not deny that a reduction in money supply is part of the process but would claim that, since the cut in money supply is too easily offset by activation of idle balances, it is the rise in long-term rates which is the significant deflationary feature.

I would agree with Professor Rowan that "the central point here is remarkably simple and much of the controversy surrounding it seems to have been misplaced",[40] but for rather different reasons. In the most obvious case where official pressure on the money supply is being undermined by activation of idle balances but short-term rates rise in the process, official manipulation of the long-term rate need, as we have seen, in the first instance merely take the form of abstention from support of the bond market. In this case, it is surely obvious that official willingness to allow the long-term rate to rise operates as a "package deal": to the extent that credit rationing prevails, it makes the cut in the availability of money effective by impeding activation of idle balances; at the same time, it enlists whatever incentive effects a higher level of rates may have. Deliberate official action to raise long-term rates (e.g. by open market sales of bonds) operates in just the same way: it reduces the money supply; it may block the channels of liquidity; and it may have incentive effects.

Professor Rowan believes that such "official intervention...extended throughout the rate curve...appears to be what the Committee would like to see."[41] On the other hand, "the Radcliffe Committee had strong reservations" about the "quantitative significance of the 'availability effect'", i.e. it doubts whether "a 'worthwhile' reduction in availability can be attained by a 'practicable' increase in rates".[42] One's impression is that the Committee's doubts related much more to the wisdom of a deliberate policy of varying long-term rates than to the efficacy of the availability effect. The Committee was not unimpressed by the Bank of England's insistence on the difficulties of selling bonds on a falling market; while the authorities have demonstrated their power to restrain a rise in bond prices, "it does not follow that the authorities could have...engineered a fall in bond prices with equal success and equal freedom from untoward consequences."[43] It was also fearful as to what an unstable bond market would do to the strength of Britain's "intricate and highly developed network of financial institutions".[44] For these reasons it declared any policy involving "much larger swings than hitherto in long-term rates of interest...as probably impracticable and certainly so disadvantageous as to warrant ruling it out as a general line of policy."[45] Hence its decision to "assign a relatively minor role to monetary measures in the short-run control of aggregate demand".[46]

40 Rowan, p. 438.

41 Rowan, p. 439.

42 Rowan, p. 436, n. 34.

43 *Radcliffe Report*, para. 576; but see the opposite emphasis in para. 563.

44 *Ibid.*, para. 491.

45 *Ibid.*, paras. 489–90.

46 Rowan, p. 439.

Conclusions

Professor Rowan concludes his analysis by saying that "at a theoretical level it is difficult to quarrel with RMT" but "to assert that short-term RMT is both logically consistent and familiar is not to say that it is correct".[47] RMT is a theory designed, as has been said, to "tell us something about the structure and operation of the monetary system".[48] Can such a theory be useful—even as a theory—if it is not correct? My own view is that the Radcliffe Committee has made a valuable contribution by emphasizing the importance—for a correct understanding of the operation of our type of monetary system and for policy—of certain features of the system which have been unduly neglected in received theory. In its anxiety to shift the emphasis the Committee allowed itself at many points to overstate its case—not least in its playing down of the money supply and its over-emphasis on the Roosa effect. But even its ambiguities, contradictions and errors of emphasis have served a useful purpose in making all of us think more carefully in a field of economics which might have been thought well worked over.

47 Rowan, p. 440.

48 Gaskin, *op. cit.*, p. 293.

Part II

POLICY

6

The Role of Monetary Policy

Invited to give three lectures at Istanbul University in 1954, I used the occasion to survey the changing views about the role of monetary policy, from the neo-classical objective of price stability to Keynes's downgrading of monetary, as contrasted with fiscal, policy as an instrument of demand management in the 1930s and the renewed emphasis on monetary, and especially interest, policy to counter inflation in the 1950s.

Originally published in *Revue de la Faculté des Sciences Economiques de l'Université d'Istanbul*, Vol. XIII - No. 1-4, Istanbul, 1954.

Mr Chairman, I am greatly honoured to be permitted to speak to fellow economists at this ancient University. When you, Mr Chairman, were good enough to invite me to give a number of lectures in your Faculty, and suggested the broad field of money and credit, I found myself in an uncomfortable dilemma between my conviction that theory needs to be closely related to the institutional setting of a country and my regrettable, but profound, ignorance of the institutional framework of your monetary system. I decided to escape this dilemma by selecting the most general policy problem I could find in this field—the role of monetary policy itself. But I am conscious that, even on this level, much that I have to say may not be directly relevant or appropriate to your national problems. In that case, I ask your indulgence in the hope that it may be of interest to my audience to hear how an economist from Australia views the role of monetary policy in his country and others in the English-speaking world. One or two of these have, after all, a not negligible influence on economic events in the rest of the world.

I propose to give three lectures and to divide my subject as follows: In this, the first, lecture, I shall give a brief survey of the changing role of monetary policy—and of economists' views on that role—in the English-speaking countries up to 1945, the end of World War II. In the second lecture, I shall deal with the revival of monetary policy which has taken place, in the USA, Britain and elsewhere, in the last few years and the circumstances which led to it. Finally, in the third lecture, I shall attempt to summarise my own tentative views on the subject. Throughout these lectures, I shall mean, by "monetary policy", deliberate efforts by the monetary authorities to influence economic conditions by control of the money supply, directly or via interest rates; although budget or fiscal policy may, in some respects, be considered as falling within this definition, I shall use the term as excluding measures of budget or fiscal policy.

I. Developments Before 1945

Throughout the nineteenth century, and indeed until about 1930, monetary policy can be said to have had one simple objective: to control the value or purchasing power of money. In classical and neo-classical thought, control of the value of money was all that monetary policy needed to aim at, and it was all that monetary policy could hope to accomplish.

Control of the value of money comprised all necessary objectives of monetary policy, because the two major economic policy problems confronting a nation, domestic stability and external balance, were conceived as revolving around control of the value of money. Economic fluctuations, and the trade cycle in particular, which we now view primarily as fluctuations in the level of economic activity, output and employment, appeared in the 19th century primarily as fluctuations in the general level of prices; the problem here appeared to be to iron out these erratic fluctuations, while at the same time standing constantly on guard against the danger of inflation. The problem of external balance, or balance of payments equilibrium, equally seemed to hinge on control of the value of money; for, as Ricardian theory demonstrated, a pure gold specie standard would maintain international equilibrium automatically by appropriate changes in the domestic money supply and cost-price levels, and a more complex monetary system could achieve the same result by an appropriate central bank policy. If the two objectives, domestic stability and external balance, should come into conflict, the classical prescription gave unquestioned priority to the need for external balance; but this subordination of domestic monetary policy to an international discipline did not seem unduly harsh, so long as domestic instability was thought to involve nothing much worse than instability, by controlled adjustments, in the purchasing power of money.

Control of the value of money, moreover, was all that monetary policy could hope to achieve. This followed from the quantity theory of money with implicit acceptance of Say's Law of Markets. If the demand for money is a function merely of the money value of (income) transactions (implying a constant Marshallian k) and if short-term changes in the national real income can be ruled out by the impossibility of general over-production, the value of money is the only economic variable on which monetary policy, i.e. changes in the supply of money, can exercise any influence. The rate of interest, on this view, is necessarily outside the sphere of monetary action since it interacts solely with real phenomena, productivity and thrift, the allocation of a given national output between the present and the future.

This conception, that the only possible and only necessary objective of monetary policy was control of the general level of money prices, after dominating economic thought for so long, disintegrated in the inter-war period. The cause of its abandonment must be seen, at bottom, in changes in the real economic world, though economic theory hastened to explain and justify it. The two changes in the real world which revolutionised thinking about monetary policy were the disastrous dimensions assumed, in the inter-war years, by the two problems of domestic economic instability and international disequilibrium. After the post-war depression of 1921–23, and more obviously still with the onset of the Great Depression of 1929–33, it ceased to be possible to think of the trade cycle merely in terms of instability of prices, of the value of money. Clearly, the instability of prices was merely a symptom. The real problem, which monetary policy had to tackle if it was to be worth much, was instability in the level of economic activity and mass unemployment. At the same time, the maladjustments in the world economy which the First World War had left behind, aggravated by cyclical disturbances in balances of payments, confronted the revived international gold standard with a far greater task than the pre-war gold standard ever faced. The balance of payments problems of the early 1930s proved altogether too big for the fairweather mechanism of adjustment by changes in domestic money supply and cost-price levels. Whatever chance there might have been of dealing with either of these problems, unemployment and balance of payments difficulties, by the classical remedy of domestic monetary policy aiming at price-cost adjustments, was virtually eliminated by the rigidity in the domestic structure of wages and prices which had developed in the preceding decades with the growth of trade unions and monopolistic elements in business organisation.

Two implications for the role of monetary policy immediately followed: First, domestic monetary policy could no longer be subservient to the requirements of external balance. If the gold standard demanded of deficit countries deliberate monetary deflation, and if monetary deflation reduced output and employment, rather than merely costs and prices, so much the worse for the gold standard. Monetary policy was henceforth to serve the needs of domestic economic stability. National monetary autonomy was to be reconciled with external balance by flexible exchange rates (or direct controls of foreign trade and payments). Second, the prime task of domestic monetary policy came to be domestic stabilisation, not merely of prices, but of output and employment, or, as we should now put it, full employment without inflation.

When the problem for monetary policy was, for the first time, clearly posed in this way in the early 1930s, it was approached with considerable optimism. There was, about 1930, a widespread belief, that monetary policy represented the most promising weapon for economic recovery from depression, and for the maintenance of economic stability generally. Theoretical grounds for this optimism about monetary policy were found partly in such monetary theories of the trade cycle as Hawtrey's which, looking back to English 19th century experience, conceived of it primarily in terms of fluctuations in inventory investment sensitive to changes in the availability of bank credit and short-term interest rates. More important and influential was the new approach to monetary and interest theory for which the foundation had been laid by Wicksell and which had been further developed by D. H. Robertson and Keynes. Wicksell had made the decisive departure from 19th century thinking by showing that monetary factors could influence, not merely monetary phenomena such as the general level of money prices, but also real phenomena such as the rate of real investment. In Wicksell's terminology, the "natural" rate of interest might be determined by real forces, productivity and thrift, but the "market" rate of interest was a monetary phenomenon; and since the rate of investment was a function of the relationship between the "natural" and the "market" rate of interest, monetary policy, acting upon and through the "market" rate, could exercise a powerful influence on the rate of investment and thus on the level of economic activity and employment. A flexible monetary policy, easy credit and cheap money in times of underemployment and depression, and tight credit and high interest rates in times of boom or inflation, seemed to offer the most promising approach to the problem of economic stability.

This confidence in the efficacy of monetary policy, which in England reached its high-water mark in the *Macmillan Report* and Keynes's *Treatise on Money,* was soon followed by disillusionment. The reason was undoubtedly the failure of expansionary monetary policies to overcome the Great Depression. In almost every country, interest rates were greatly reduced, but, with the possible exception of the English building boom, "cheap money" registered no significant successes in terms of economic recovery. Easy money merely increased the liquidity of the banks without contributing noticeably to an expansion of private investment and employment.

The first reaction of academic economics to this failure can be seen in Keynes's *General Theory.* When Keynes began to write his new work, interest and money still occupied a major role in his thinking about income and employment, as the title—*The General Theory of Employment, Interest and Money*—shows. But in the development of his argument, the rate of interest was gradually relegated to a subsidiary role as a determinant of the rate of investment. Keynes's chief reason for becoming increasingly sceptical about the efficacy of monetary policy was his theory of speculation, his fear that "the market" would defeat the efforts of monetary authorities to reduce the long-term rate significantly below what it regarded as its normal and natural level. This fear was not borne out by events of the 1930s. As we have seen, the monetary authorities of most advanced countries had little difficulty in reducing interest rates quite substantially. A more important cause of the failure of monetary policy was brought out by the famous Oxford Inquiry of the late 1930s.

You will recall that a group of Oxford economists attempted to test the generally accepted theoretical assumption that the rate of interest is an important determinant of investment decisions by asking businessmen about it. The answers they received suggested that, by and large, interest rates play a very minor, if any, part in investment decisions in the manufacturing industries covered by the Inquiry. While the results of this empirical inquiry did not remain unchallenged, theoretical reconsideration tended to confirm the conclusion that, with the exception of a few types of very long term and relatively riskless private investment, such as in housing, general purpose construction and public utilities, real investment is likely to be very inelastic with respect to changes in interest rates.

If this was true, little reliance could be placed in a flexible interest policy for economic stabilisation. Cuts in interest rates would do little to stimulate investment in the face of a serious decline in the marginal efficiency of capital; and though very high rates would no doubt sooner or later throttle off investment, they would operate as a very crude instrument, acting too drastically or not at all, and discriminating between different fields of investment in a manner not necessarily desirable on social or economic grounds. At the same time, Keynesian interpretations of the Great

Depression in terms of a tendency towards stagnation or chronic underemployment in the most mature economies seemed to provide a (fallacious but widely accepted) economic case for permanently cheap money. By the end of the 30s, therefore, faith in the usefulness of a flexible interest policy had largely disappeared. Since changes in interest rates could achieve little in ironing out cyclical fluctuations, interest rates might as well be kept as low as possible.

This conclusion did, of course, not imply that there was nothing to be gained by a flexible monetary policy. While investment in many fields might not be responsive to changes in the *price* of credit, it could not but be influenced by changes in the *availability* of credit. Tight money, operating through credit rationing by the banking system and other institutions of the capital market, could certainly be expected the exercise a restrictive influence; and easy money could at least pave the way for expansion. But, under Keynesian influence, the emphasis in ideas on trade cycle control shifted during the 30s from monetary to compensatory budget policy, or fiscal policy, as Hansen called it in America. In any case, before the distinction between a flexible interest policy and a flexible monetary policy operating through credit rationing was clearly worked out, World War II intervened and, for a time, further diminished the prestige of monetary policy.

During the war, "money did not matter". The reason was not, of course, that an economic allocation of resources and avoidance of inflation had suddenly become a matter of indifference. The reason was rather that the chief weight in carrying out these functions of economic policy was thrown on direct administrative controls. Global monetary controls were not discarded, but they were, for the time being, assigned the secondary role of minimising pressure on the system of direct controls and of minimising the financial aftermath of war, where this was possible without detriment to the immediate economic war effort.

This, then, was the situation at the end of World War II. On general theoretical grounds, as well as in the light of the experience of the 30s, there was little faith in a flexible monetary policy to control short-term economic fluctuations, least of all as a defence against underemployment which was widely regarded as the chief danger threatening the Western economies after a probably brief post-war restocking boom. In so far as the danger of post-war inflation was taken seriously, it tended to be assumed that the war-time system of direct controls, which would be maintained for as long as necessary for this purpose, would provide adequate protection, to be supplemented by budgetary (fiscal) policy measures. There would, therefore, be little need for vigorous monetary policy measures which were, in any event, unlikely to cope with problem. Since there was little to be gained by a flexible interest rate policy, full advantage should be taken of the benefits, to treasuries and private investors, of maintaining the extraordinarily low level of interest achieved during the war.

I must warn you again that I have been generalising rather wildly about the situation in a limited group of countries, chiefly the USA, Britain and Australia. But while a more careful analysis would, of course, reveal divergent trends and cross-currents of opinion, I do not think the picture I have drawn seriously distorts the dominant climate of opinion on this subject which prevailed in these, and I believe other, English-speaking countries at the end of World War II. In the second lecture, I shall try to describe the trouble which these ideas encountered in the post-war period.

II. The Post-War Revival

We saw in the last lecture that, at the end of World War II, there was a widespread tendency in the English-speaking countries to discount the role which monetary policy could or should play in the future. We also saw that there were three main reasons for this attitude. First, it was generally believed that the chief post-war problem would again be underemployment, against which monetary weapons had proved notoriously ineffective during the inter-war period. Second, in so far as inflation should continue to be a serious problem for a period, the maintenance of the war-time system of direct controls, which had been so successful during the war, seemed the obvious defence. Third, supplementing or replacing direct controls for economic stability, a compensatory budget policy, aiming at deficits in conditions of underemployment and at surpluses in conditions of inflation, promised in any case to be more effective than a flexible monetary policy operating through control of the money supply and changes in interest rates. Since there was little to be gained by high interest rates, informed public opinion supported rather than opposed the strong demands for maintenance of cheap money made by treasuries concerned with their greatly enlarged national debts.

In the eight years that have passed since the end of the war, there has been a further change of outlook. The sharp controversy over monetary policy that has taken place among central bankers, treasuries, economists and publicists has certainly not resulted in anything like unanimity, but there can be no question that there has, on balance, been a significant revival in the prestige of monetary policy from the nadir of 1945. The abandonment of cheap money in the USA, Great Britain, Australia and elsewhere in 1950/51, and the adoption of the "New Monetary Policy" in the UK, and of somewhat similar policies elsewhere, present the most eloquent testimony to this revival.

The explanation of this course of events is simple. In a nutshell, it is that each of the three major assumptions on which the dismissal of monetary policy had been based proved mistaken. First, instead of depression and underemployment, the post-war years have witnessed a continuous struggle with inflation. Secondly, the system of direct controls, which had so successfully repressed inflation for the duration of the war, was either dismantled under pressure of public opinion or proved much more difficult to administer effectively in peace-time. Finally, disinflationary budget policy encountered far greater obstacles, chiefly of a political character, than had been anticipated. Inevitably, governments were forced to fall back upon monetary policy. Both to make monetary policy effective and because, in these circumstances, it had become a menace in itself, cheap money had to be surrendered.

There is little need for me to enlarge on the first point. It is still difficult to be sure why the post-World War I experience of a brief restocking boom followed by a severe depression and unemployment has not repeated itself. Perhaps more skilful handling of economic policy in the USA had something to do with it. More likely the explanation must be seen in a combination of circumstances. The far greater degree of economic disruption and destruction caused by World War II in Western Europe meant that productive capacity in Europe took longer to revive and that demand for reconstruction and replacement of capital equipment remained at a high level for much longer. Demand for foodstuffs by rapidly growing populations enjoying high and more evenly distributed incomes tended to run ahead of world food supplies, greatly increasing food prices and farm incomes. In Western Europe and the Sterling Area, national economic policies, less inhibited than after World War I by balance of payments considerations along gold standard rules, permitted a high level of effective demand, financed by liquid funds accumulated during the war and by further post-war credit expansion, to spill over into import surpluses which, in turn, maintained some degree of inflationary pressure on the American economy. When, in 1949, there were signs of an incipient slump in the USA, it was nipped in the bud by a vast expansion of defence expenditure which has only recently begun to slacken off. Whether these factors fully explain the course of events or not, the fact remains that the post-war problem so far has been almost continuous inflationary pressure, not underemployment as had been so generally feared.

During World War II, in marked contrast to World War I, monetary and financial policy did not have to bear the brunt of coping with the problem of war inflation. Direct allocation, rationing and price controls assured governments of adequate resources for the war sector and prevented private consumption and investment demand from bidding away resources or bidding up prices. Governments were able to resort freely to credit expansion to finance whatever portion of war expenditure could not be covered by tolerable taxation and loan issues to the public. Direct controls of private investment enabled the monetary authorities to satisfy the public's demand for liquidity and thus keep down long and short-term interest rates. The supply of money increased enormously, but while the war lasted, direct controls on spending, reinforced by patriotic restraint on the part of the public, ensured that demand for money (liquidity-preference) increased more or less correspondingly.

Whether it was reasonable or not to expect that this system could be maintained in the Western countries into the peace, the fact is that it was either dismantled almost immediately, as in the USA, or, where it was largely maintained, as in the UK, ceased to operate as effectively as during the war. The public became increasingly intolerant of direct controls over consumer or business spending. If the authorities reacted to this by removing controls on "unessential" goods or activities, the remaining controls tended to divert resources from controlled essential to uncontrolled unessential production. At the same time, with the restoration of peace, less and less reliance could be placed upon self-restraint in spending by the private sector; effective demand, financed by accumulated liquid funds in the hands of the public and new credit expansion, kept well ahead of the increased flow of goods and services which became available as economic demobilisation proceeded.

On Keynesian principles, it should have been possible to keep inflation in check, even without an extensive system of direct controls, by a compensatory budget policy. Various attempts were made to keep down excess demand by budgeting for surpluses, most strenuously and systematically in the UK. These attempts were not completely unsuccessful, but they proved quite inadequate to cope with the problem unaided. The basic difficulty proved to be the political impossibility of raising taxation to levels sufficient to yield adequate surpluses over and above high and increasing government expenditure. Although taxation continued to absorb some 25–30 per cent of national income in the USA and Australia, and about 40 per cent in the UK, this left little if any genuine surplus above government expenditures which were maintained at similar levels by extraordinary claims on top of the requirements of greatly expanded ordinary government services—military commitments and welfare services including food subsidies in the UK, foreign aid in the USA, capital expenditure for migration and development in Australia. Whether it is true, as is claimed by some, that such rates of taxation actually contributed to inflation by weakening incentives to produce and save—and I confess I remain sceptical about this argument—it certainly proved politically impossible to raise taxation still further, or, for that matter, to secure the required surpluses by cutting down government expenditure. Any government that tried to do so was liable to be thrown out of office at the next elections.

It was, at bottom, this failure of direct controls or budget policy to stem inflation which forced the authorities to look with increasing favour upon the neglected third weapon in their armoury, monetary policy. It would, of course, be quite wrong to suggest that monetary policy had no advocates in the early post-war years. The fight for an active monetary policy in the USA was taken up by the US Federal Reserve against the US Treasury even before the end of the war, and there were economists of the older school in all these countries, to say nothing of bankers, who never tired of warning against the consequences of neglecting orthodox monetary discipline and shook their heads in dismay over the recklessness of cheap money in times of inflation. But it can hardly be denied that, until 1950 or thereabouts, these voices remained in the wilderness; their advocacy of tight money and high interest rates as the cure for inflation never carried the day.

What is more important for my purpose, the substantial victory of this school in 1950/51 was not, I think, gained primarily by intellectual conviction of their opponents that dear money was the answer to inflation. It is true that the authorities in all the three countries I have mentioned placed increasing weight on inflation control by credit restrictions. But a disinflationary monetary policy was conceived in terms of measures to restrict bank liquidity (and thus bank advances) and selective quantitative credit controls rather than in terms of higher interest rates.

If the first and most spectacular step in the revival of monetary policy was, nonetheless, the abandonment of cheap money, the reason was not so much any general belief that higher interest rates would in themselves have powerful disinflationary effects, as the conviction that cheap money was no longer reconcilable with any monetary control of the economy whatever.

As I mentioned in the first lecture, cheap money, with long term rates around 3 per cent and Treasury bill rates at or below 1 per cent, emerged from the war as a firm principle of government policy in all the three countries to which I specially refer. Treasuries insisted on it to keep down the taxation burden of national debt service and the informed public generally favoured it on social and economic grounds. The fact that governments had, during the war, virtually promised to maintain war-time rates as an inducement to the public to buy bonds— "Bonds Are Safe" — seemed to place something of a moral obligation upon them to protect the savings of bondholders against capital loss. In the USA, a belief that even small book losses on the vast bondholdings of banks might have a serious unsettling effect on financial and business conditions was regarded as a further strong argument against permitting any fall in bond prices "below par". Nor did the maintenance of cheap money present any technical problem. All that was required was for the monetary authorities to stand ready to take any excess supply of bonds of the market.

This policy of cheap money, rigidly maintained by official support of the market, might have caused difficulty even had inflation been effectively prevented by direct controls or fiscal policy, or a combination of both. For the monetary authorities, in effect, to guarantee bondholders against any risk of capital loss was to court the risk of what the Americans have called "*monetisation of the debt*", that is to say, of bonds becoming as good as cash and being increasingly treated by the public as a perfectly liquid asset on which 2.5 or 3 per cent was gratuitously available for the asking. Bonds would lose their prime function as an illiquid asset in the hands of the public, and the authorities would lose a useful instrument of control of private spending in so far as spending was influenced by liquid asset holdings.

In the inflationary conditions which actually developed in the post-war years, what would otherwise have remained a hypothetical risk became a very real danger. In boom conditions, many holders would in any case have been tempted to switch from bonds into shares or other assets offering a better yield. The steady decline in the value of money in the years 1948–51 provided a further and much more powerful incentive to desert bonds (or other assets fixed in money terms) for shares or real assets. For while the prices of shares and real assets were rising at least as fast as the general price level, a constantly declining value of money reduced the return on bonds, in real terms, to a negative figure. In normal conditions, the risk of capital losses on sales of bonds would have acted as a powerful deterrent to such wholesale switching of assets; this risk, however, was completely eliminated so long as official bond market support prevented any decline in bond prices. All that happened was that the monetary authorities bought up any excess supplies of bonds thrown on the market, and in the process pumped an equivalent amount of cash into the economy. Moreover, any tendency of the authorities to weaken under selling pressure, or any suspicion by the market that the authorities might consider the risks of monetary expansion too great a price to pay for the maintenance of cheap money, was liable to make matters worse by calling forth a large wave of bear speculation: holders of bonds selling out for fear of capital loss.

An early demonstration of the power of the market to defeat the authorities was provided, in rather exceptional circumstances, by the Dalton experiment of 1947/48. The British Labour Chancellor's attempt to drive bond rate down still further, from about 2⅞ per cent to 2½ per cent, was made in the teeth of what the market regarded as reasonable and sound. The market prevailed, and the experiment was abandoned after it had cost the monetary authorities an injection into the economy of cash to the value of £900 million—a curious vindication of Keynes's theory of speculation, in circumstances rather different from those which he had in mind. It is possible that, in this instance, and again when bear speculation developed in 1950 and 1951, a determined stand by the authorities could have defeated the market.[1] It is even arguable that no immediate harm would have come from giving the public all the cash they were demanding in exchange for bonds, particularly since the support policy in any case made bonds almost as good as cash to the individual holder. What finally forced the authorities to surrender cheap money was the realisation that it made any effective disinflationary monetary policy virtually impossible.

By 1950, it became increasingly clear that neither direct controls (which where retained, to any extent, only in the UK) nor budget policy could adequately restrain inflation. For the first time since the war, governments prepared to tackle the problem by severe credit restrictions.[2] So long, however, as the bond market support policy was maintained, credit restrictions were of little avail. So long as bonds could freely be sold for cash at par, any attempts by the monetary authorities to restrict the liquidity of the banks or the public by open market operations, secondary reserve requirements, or qualitative credit controls could easily be frustrated by bond sales which forced the central bank to hand over whatever amounts of cash the banks or the public demanded. This fact was appreciated as clearly by the market as by the monetary authorities. In consequence, the first signs of a new policy of tight credit were interpreted as inevitably heralding the beginning of the end of official bond market support; and what the market firmly expected it soon helped to bring about. Throughout 1950 and 1951, the belief that the authorities were wavering in their determination to maintain cheap money reinforced selling pressure motivated by the other factors which I have mentioned, and gradually the authorities gave way. In the USA, the Reserve System forced a rise in short rates, in defiance of the Treasury, in September 1950, and in March 1951 par support of the key 2½ per cent bonds was removed. In the UK, bond prices were gradually allowed to slip back during 1951, and by the time the "New Monetary Policy" was inaugurated with a flourish in March 1952, bond yields had

1 Compare Joan Robinson's statement in her recent essay on "The Rate of Interest": "If the authorities' nerves are shaken by the ferocious growls with which the bears have been deafening them all this time, and once allow bond prices to relapse, the growling of the bears turns to joyous yelps of 'I told you so' and the expected future bond rate is so much the higher for ever after." But if the authorities "persist resolutely, a moment will come when the bears are convinced that the new low rate has come to stay." *The Rate of Interest and Other Essays*, Macmillan 1952, p. 30.

2 The fact that in Britain and Australia conservative governments succeeded Labour governments in 1949 no doubt helps to explain the relatively sudden change of emphasis in these two countries, as compared with the USA where the revival of monetary policy began earlier and was more gradual.

been allowed to "find their level" around 4¼ per cent. In Australia, too, support was withdrawn during 1951, allowing bond rate to rise from 3⅛ per cent to 4½ per cent.

The surrender of cheap money cleared the way for tight money policies. Upward adjustments to a higher bond rated made, or followed automatically, in other portions of the interest structure, most spectacularly in Great Britain with the resuscitation of an active bank rate policy, the first since 1932 (except for a brief flutter in 1939). Qualitative credit controls by capital issues control, directives on bank advance policy or other measures, such as restrictions on consumer credit, were tightened in all three countries and steps were taken to reduce bank liquidity. How far these measures deserve the credit for the degree of stabilisation that has undoubtedly occurred since 1951 in all these countries, it is as yet difficult to assess. In Australia, the country with which I am most familiar, tight credit undoubtedly helped to arrest the inflation, although the development of a severe balance of payments deficit in 1951/52, in consequence of a sharp fall in wool prices and a flood of imports, certainly played the major role.

Those of you who are familiar with the complexity of the post-war developments I have tried to analyse in this lecture will recognise my description as a highly simplified, deliberately stylised account designed to bring out what seem to me to have been the crucial factors. But I must add at least one further word by way of qualification and explanation.

Consistent advocates of monetary policy of the older school are likely to accuse me of bias and distortion in the account I have given you. They are likely to interpret the developments of these post-war years as a clear-cut victory of sound over unsound policies and to claim that the abandonment of cheap money owed far more to a long overdue realisation of the need for dear money, high interest rates, as the proper answer to inflation than I have admitted. No doubt, there were voices, among those who influenced policy, who all along condemned cheap money as inherently unsound and who welcomed the higher interest rates of the last two years, for their own sake, as powerful weapons for the restoration of economic stability. Similarly, in the lively academic and popular controversy over monetary policy that has accompanied these developments,[3] the Right Wing has consistently argued for tight and dear money, not as a weapon of last resort but as the obvious and most effective, though austere, cure for our ills. But I am inclined to believe, nonetheless, that the recent revival of monetary policy is more correctly described, as I have tried to do, as a reluctant and none-too-hopeful resort to a *pis aller* than as a confident unsheathing of a well-tried weapon. In saying this, I am, of course, guided to some extent by my own views about the merits and deficiencies of monetary policy in present-day conditions. These views I shall try to elaborate, by way of conclusion, in the third and last lecture.

3 I should like to refer you to two excellent symposia: an American one, in the *Review of Economics and Statistics*, August 1951; and a British one in the *Bulletin of the Oxford Institute of Statistics*, March/April and August 1952.

III. Today and Tomorrow

In the first two lectures, I attempted to survey the shifts and changes in the role of monetary policy which have occurred in the Englishspeaking countries over the decades. In this final lecture I propose to put before you my own present state of mind on the part which monetary policy can and should play in the advanced Western economies of which I have spoken.

Two years ago, I gave my inaugural lecture at the Canberra University College on "The Unimportance of Money". The title, of course, was meant to be facetious, but not entirely undescriptive of the point of view I put forward. The emphasis was on the decline in the prestige of monetary policy that had occurred since the early 30s and the increasingly subsidiary role which money was destined to play. I have somewhat changed my opinion since then, at least in emphasis. In summing up today, I will start, on the contrary, by stressing the continuing importance of monetary controls.

I am now prepared to concede that we went too far in the late 30s and war years in our dismissal of monetary policy. True, the extent to which it is necessary to rely on monetary policy depends a great deal on the powers of direct control over the economy available to governments. The more effective and far-reaching the government's direct controls over the use and allocation of resources, the less is the need for an active monetary policy. Conversely, the more difficult, for political or administrative reasons, it is to enforce an effective system of direct controls, and the more vigorously direct controls are rejected as involving undue interference with individual liberty and free enterprise, the greater the weight that needs to be placed on indirect global controls through budget and monetary policy. That, of course, accounts for the strong ideological element in the recent controversies over monetary policy. The sponsors of an active monetary policy have come mainly from strong believers in economic liberalism, while the tendency to discount the importance of monetary measures has been strongest among those, on the Left, who have been more prepared to let governments interfere with market forces. But, however far-reaching, these are still differences of degree. Money does matter in any reasonably advanced economy, even one which is completely centrally planned and controlled. A convincing illustration of this fact was provided by the drastic monetary reform which became necessary in the Soviet Union in 1948. The problem which it was designed to solve was essentially part of the same problem as worried the Western countries, the problem of excessive money supply remaining as the aftermath of war finance. The Soviet government, like the governments of some of the continental countries, Belgium, Western Germany and Czechoslovakia, among others, tackled it by a pretty ruthless surgical operation. It is possible that, even in a centrally planned and controlled economy of the Soviet type, there may be scope for more refined forms of monetary management.

If monetary management has its part to play even in centrally controlled economies, its role is obviously very much more prominent in the predominantly private enterprise economies of the West which, for the present at any rate, are not willing to give their governments extensive powers of direct control in time of peace.

In recent discussions, disputants have sometimes argued about the relative merits of budget policy and monetary policy as if it was necessary to choose between them. Clearly, economic policy will need to employ both instruments. But there is some point in considering the points of relative strength and weakness of each, in the light of which the emphasis may be on one or the other at different times and for different purposes.

Experience has shown, I think, that, broadly speaking, monetary policy is much more likely to be effective in restriction than expansion, while, for quite different reasons, a compensatory fiscal policy for expansion is much easier than one aiming at restriction. There are no serious technical obstacles to restriction of bank liquidity by central banks equipped with adequate powers; nor can there be any doubt that a tight money policy can be made effective in curtailing private investment, provided the public does not already hold too large a volume of liquid assets and non-banking institutions of the capital market do not represent too large loopholes. There are far more serious limitations upon monetary policy as an instrument for stimulating economic activity. Relaxation of credit rationing can act as a stimulus only when there is a "fringe of unsatisfied (eligible) borrowers". This condition may be satisfied when small adjustments are desired in relatively prosperous conditions e.g. "letting up" lest disinflation should go too far. But it is unlikely to be satisfied in periods of slump or depression. The 30s have, I think, proved fairly conclusively that, in such conditions, neither mere monetary expansion nor even all practicable cuts in interest rates are likely to do more than remove financial obstacles to recovery.

The reverse seems to hold of a compensatory budget policy. Increases in government expenditure, which make direct claims on resources, and suitably directed cuts in taxation, which stimulate private spending almost equally effectively, can exercise a positive influence in stimulating economic activity in a manner which cannot be expected of any monetary measures. As an instrument for the control of inflation, on the other hand, budget policy has proved politically very difficult to handle effectively, as I showed before. To some extent, the contrast between budgetary and monetary action for disinflation probably reflects the more direct control exercised over the former by politicians sensitive to public opinion and pressure groups. Credit restrictions can be very nearly as unpopular as correspondingly disinflationary budget surpluses. But central banks, even when they are publicly owned and under ultimate control of the government of the day, do not require prior parliamentary approval for their actions as do treasuries for their expenditure and taxation proposals. This is not to suggest that inflation can be effectively controlled by monetary policy alone without reinforcement by politically courageous budget policies. In particular, since monetary action exercises its restraining effect only on the private sector (including perhaps local authorities) and since there are undoubtedly limits to the proportion of national income that can be absorbed by taxation in a predominantly private enterprise economy, inflation can hardly be avoided if governments themselves claim too large a share of the nation's resources. But we can claim at least that, for the control of booms and inflation, monetary policy remains an indispensable, and perhaps even the most reliable and effective, instrument, in the absence of a comprehensive system of direct controls.[4]

One other claim can be made for monetary over budget policy. Largely again because of the institutional fact of parliamentary control over budget policy, monetary action undoubtedly represents a more flexible instrument. The fact that budget policy can usually be revised only once a year, with further lags of several months before some of the taxation and expenditure decisions can become economically effective, constitutes a severe limitation upon the usefulness of budget policy as an instrument of control of business conditions where timing may often be the essence of the problem. Suggestions that governments might be given power to vary tax or expenditure rates in between budgets, at their discretion or in automatic response to movements in some indicator of economic activity, stand little chance of acceptance by parliaments jealous of their prerogatives. By contrast, central banks can operate at virtually a moment's notice, unobtrusively or with a flourish, as they choose. Their advantage is to some extent offset by difficulty in estimating in advance the magnitude and speed of response of business activity to their operations; but the advantage in flexibility is nonetheless real and important.

We may agree, then, that monetary policy is indispensable for restrictive control of business activity and enjoys the special advantage of flexibility. But it is hardly enough to talk of monetary policy in general; and as soon as we attempt to differentiate between different types of monetary action, we raise a host of further controversial questions. The two most important are, first, how far monetary policy should concentrate on mere regulation, via bank liquidity, of the aggregate volume of credit to be made available to the public, leaving the distribution of the total among individual borrowers and fields of investment to the banks, or whether the monetary authorities should concern themselves with distribution through qualitative controls; and secondly, how far monetary policy should make use of deliberate changes in interest rates as an instrument of control. Both questions have been hotly debated in recent years. Into both the ideological issue of controls versus freedom (and the price mechanism) once again intrudes, economic liberals inevitably preferring overall qualitative controls and reliance on the price mechanism (in the form of interest rates) to credit rationing. My own view is that, here again, no sane policy can come down hard on one side or the other. What is required is the most judicious use of a combination of all these measures.

The extreme liberal argument for complete retreat from all qualitative credit controls and a return to mere regulation of the aggregate money supply is not convincing and is unlikely to be practical politics in our time and day. If credit is to be rationed in any case, instead of being supplied to the highest bidder, there is little reason to assume that such rationing will yield a greater measure of welfare to the community if left to private banks than if it is carried out according to the policy of the monetary authorities; there is certainly a strong case for qualitative controls discriminating between broad fields of investment, leaving selection of individual borrowers to the expertise of bank managers. Indeed, there is reason to believe that

4 The wheel seems to have come full circle: I am almost echoing what, in the first lecture, I described as the 19th century view, i.e. that the objective of monetary policy is to control the value of money.

banks themselves find it useful to take shelter behind central bank directives on advance policy when illiquidity obliges them to turn away customers. On the other hand, there is no question that qualitative controls of bank or any other credit are difficult to enforce if lending institutions are under no incentive, through illiquidity, to restrict credit. This is the basic case for using control of bank liquidity, that is to say, of the aggregate money supply, to supplement and reinforce qualitative controls.

Staunch economic liberals may agree that, if credit rationing is to be used at all, there is little reason for insisting that all the rationing should be left to private financial institutions without any broad directives or intervention by the monetary authorities. But they will argue that rationing in any form is undesirable in normal circumstances; that here, as in other aspects of economic policy, the best regulator is the price mechanism. In the field of monetary policy, this means active use of interest rates as a means of controlling aggregate demand for, and distribution of, credit. On this issue, I confess, I remain an almost unrepentant sceptic.

There has been endless theoretical discussion of the *modus operandi* of changes in interest rates. I cannot possibly cover the whole ground and must confine myself to a few rather dogmatic pronouncements. Since I have already argued that monetary action is less effective in the direction of expansion than restriction, I shall limit my observations to the case for increases in interest rates for disinflation; they apply, *a fortiori,* to the case for reduction in interest rates for expansion. To start with, we must rule out any significant restrictive effects of increases in interest rates on consumption spending out of current income. Economists know little about the interest elasticity of saving; but since there are reasons for thinking that saving may have either positive or negative interest elasticity, it is safe to assume no significant net effects in the short run. The possibility that an increase in interest rates may have a deterrent effect on business spending can, of course, not be so summarily dismissed. I am doubtful whether changes in overdrafts, bill or bond rates of the magnitude which are at all likely to occur will ever arrest a really lively inflationary boom. So long as business firms expect prices to rise by 5–10 per cent per annum, fractional changes in interest rates are unlikely to deter them from borrowing for investment in stocks or any but the most long-lived fixed capital. There are, it is true, some fields of investment which are likely to be fairly sensitive to changes in long-term rates; I mentioned in my first lecture housing, general purpose construction and private public utility investment as the chief examples. But once this discriminatory effect of interest rates is admitted, it may itself be advanced as an objection. It is true that, on purely short-term considerations, there may be a case, in conditions of inflation, for postponing the longest-term investments which will take longest to bear fruit in terms of additions to effective productive capacity. But on every other ground, it may be thoroughly undesirable to deter basic investment of this character and allow a free rein to quick-profit investment in booming luxury consumer industries. There are other more indirect ways in which higher interest rates may exercise a wholesome damping effect. A higher bank rate was the traditional method used by the Bank of England as a signal to commercial banks to tighten credit. A rise in long-term rates is likely to have a depressive effect on all sections of the capital market, including share prices, and may sometimes be more effective in keeping new issues off the market than any capital issues control.

I do not deny that, in these ways, an all-round rise in interest rates can be a significant aid to disinflation. As against this, however, I would urge, on social rather than economic grounds, that high interest rates are undesirable, that cheap money is "a good thing". Many of the economic arguments advanced in recent years by the defenders of cheap money have, I believe, been weak or fallacious. The treasury case for cheap money, as a protection of taxpayers against a high interest burden on the national debt is weak if dear money is an effective counter to inflation; for taxpayers will certainly suffer more if inflation gets out of control and will pay more if disinflation has to be carried out by budget surpluses based on high taxation. The stagnationist argument for permanently cheap money is fallacious, for what would be needed to counteract stagnation by encouragement to investment is not a permanently low rate of interest but a steadily declining rate; and for such a policy, if it were needed, a high rather than a low rate clearly provides the more promising starting point. Nor can we be over-impressed by the complaint that an increase in the rate of interest inflicts capital losses on bondholders. Bondholders cannot expect interest *and* immunity against capital loss, though some of them had legitimate grounds for complaint in recent years that governments had misled them, by overzealous war savings propaganda and repeated affirmation of cheap money policy, into believing that "Bonds Are Safe". The remedy for bondholders is, of course, not to invest funds in bonds which they are likely to require in cash before maturity. To my mind, the case for cheap money rests on social rather than economic grounds: the grievous effect of a high interest burden on farmers and small businessmen in times of low prices, and more generally, the undesirable redistribution of income through larger transfers from debtors to creditors, a redistribution which is still, on balance, from the less to the more well-to-do and from the active and productive to the relatively inactive rentier sections of the community. The strength of this argument depends, of course, in part on whether one believes an increase in interest rates to be readily reversible or not. Keynes's fear that it is much easier to raise interest rates than to reduce them has not, on the face of it, been borne out by the events of the past twenty years. But on a longer view, his judgment here, as in so many other matters, may have been sounder than it looks today. My conclusion on this controversial question, therefore, is that I am neither sufficiently confident of the efficacy of increases in interest rates nor sufficiently indifferent to the merits of cheap money to feel any enthusiasm for a forthright policy of high interest rates as an instrument of monetary control of inflation.

But, and this is my final point, I have been persuaded by the events of the post-war years to qualify this conclusion in one important respect. I have become convinced that a policy of rigid official support for a specified low bond rate is intolerable. Once the authorities commit themselves to support a given level of bond prices *à outrance,* they not only deprive bonds and bond interest of their economic function by "monetisation of the debt"; they also lose all control of monetary policy. However desirable cheap money may be, it must not take the form of a permanent guarantee that bond rate will never rise.

In the last resort, this dilemma is probably insoluble. But I do not think it needs to present itself ever again in quite so stark a form as it did in the post-war years. Earlier use of active restraint on credit expansion and more courageous use of a compensatory budget policy should, in similar circumstances, succeed in greatly reducing the rate of inflation and thus the degree of pressure on the bond market. Greater restraint by the authorities in public commitments to permanently cheap money, the development of techniques of permitting slight variations in bond rate while keeping one jump ahead of the market, and possibly also further experiments with non-marketable securities (or wider facilities for investment in longer-term fixed deposits) which will induce the public to pay more careful regard to maturities in their investments and avoid panic sales, these and other measures may help to resolve the dilemma. It presents both a lesson and a challenge to the art of monetary management.

7

Overdrafts and Monetary Policy

In the 1960s concern was expressed that the British (and Australian) overdraft system of bank lending, under which customers were given the right to overdraw their accounts up to an agreed limit, weakened central bank control of money supply, then still the centrepiece of monetary policy. The unused part of the customers' limits is an addition to their liquidity as good as cash but free of charge. The article (here reprinted without the lengthy statistical section) proposed a commitment fee to limit undue accumulation of unused limits.

Originally published in the Banca Nazionale del Lavoro *Quarterly Review*, No. 70, September 1964.

It has been known for some time that the overdraft system of bank lending can hamper monetary policy.[1] In both the 1955 and 1960 booms in Australia, advances continued to rise while the trading banks, under central bank direction, were cutting back new lending. In 1961 and 1962, while the authorities were effectively encouraging the banks to pursue freer lending policies, advances first continued to decline and then stagnated; by February 1964, advances, though much above recession level and continuing to rise, accounted for little more than one-half of total overdraft limits, a situation which gave rise to fears of an uncontrollable "explosion of advances" in a new boom.

So erratic has been the behaviour of the system in recent years in Australia that there have been suggestions for its abandonment or at least for reform.[2] To decide whether anything needs to be done, and what can or should be done, has not been easy because of our ignorance of the working of the system. "Nobody has made a study of the nature and habits of the animal".[3] To remedy this omission is the object of this article.[4]

1 Cf. H. C. Coombs, *The Development of Monetary Policy in Australia*, E. S. & A. Bank Research Lecture 1954, University of Queensland Press, 1955, p. 15; H.W. Arndt, *The Australian Trading Banks*, 1st edition, Cheshire, 1957, pp. 62f., 194f. A fairly extensive search of the literature of money and banking outside Australia and New Zealand has uncovered more than passing references to the subject of this article only in Lavington's *The English Capital Market* (Methuen, 1921, p. 136), Keynes's *Treatise on Money* (Macmillan, 1930, vol. I, pp. 41f., 236, vol. II, p. 35), and in the *Report* of the Irish Commission of Inquiry into Banking, Currency and Credit (Dublin, 1938, p. 59).

2 H.W. Arndt, *loc. cit.*; Financial Editor, *Sydney Morning Herald*, 15 January 1961; *Australian Financial Review*, 17 January 1964, 2 March 1964.

3 *Sydney Morning Herald*, 12 November 1960.

4 I should like to thank several colleagues, including especially Dr. A. R. Hall, Mr. C. P. Harris and Professors Brian Tew, R. S. Sayfers and B. H. Beckhart, for helpful comments on an earlier draft of this paper. None of these has any responsibility for opinions expressed or for any remaining errors of fact.

The overdraft is a Scottish invention.[5] In the countries of the British Commonwealth (except Canada) it has for long been the main form of bank lending, in contrast to the fixed loan which is normal in North America and predominates in most other parts of the world.[6] The main differences between the two methods are familiar.

In the case of the fixed loan, the customer applies for, and the bank grants, a loan of a fixed amount which is at once credited to the customer's current account and debited to his loan account, and on which interest is due from that moment. Whether the loan is repayable over an agreed period or not, once repaid the loan (or any part of it) dies and cannot be revived without new approval by the bank. With the overdraft method, the customer in the first instance merely seeks the bank's approval to overdraw his account, usually subject to an agreed "limit". Actual borrowing takes place only as the customer draws against the approved limit, and interest is payable only on the daily debit balance, the "advance outstanding".

The overdraft has obvious advantages to the customer. One is its flexibility. So long as the limit is not exceeded the debit balance can be varied up and down without the need for renewed approval. Although the bank will normally require security and carefully investigate the applicant's credit-worthiness, the overdraft method lends itself to more informal arrangements—from a nod to a closed eye.

The other advantage is that in the unused part of his limit the customer obtains an addition to his liquidity which is as good as cash but which is free of charge. This of course does not mean that bank credit is necessarily cheaper under the overdraft method; the average cost depends on the rate of interest and other terms and charges.[7]

5 Cf. Adam Smith's account: "The commerce of Scotland, which at present is not very great, was still more inconsiderable when the two first banking companies were established; and those companies would have had but little trade, had they confined their business to the discounting of bills of exchange. They invented, therefore, another method of issuing promissory notes; by granting, what they called, cash accounts, that is by giving credit to the extent of a certain sum (two or three thousand pounds, for example), to any individual who could procure two persons of undoubted credit and good landed estate to become surety for him, that whatever money should be advanced to him, within the sum for which the credit had been given, should be repaid upon demand, together with the legal interest " *(Wealth of Nations,* ed. E. Cannan, book II, ch.II). See also, W. T. C. King, *History of the London Discount Market,* London, 1936; T. Balogh, *Studies in Financial Organization,* CUP, 1947, p. 74.

6 In the American banking system, a number of variants of the overdraft are in use, including revolving credits subject to a commitment fee and confirmed lines of credit but their share in total bank credit is insignificant (cf. B. H. Beckhart (ed.), *Banking Systems,* Columbia University Press, 1954, p. 871, and *Business Loans of Commercial Banks,* Ronald Press, 1959). In some western European countries overdrafts are used under a variety of names but, except in the Netherlands and in Italy, they account for a small or negligible part of bank lending (cf. R. S. Sayers (ed.), *Banking in Western Europe,* Oxford, 1962, pp. 18, 206, 276, 327, 366, 390).

7 The customer under the fixed-loan system can reduce the net interest cost of the loan by placing on time deposit or reinvesting in the money market any temporary surplus funds. In Australia the banks usually compensate customers who have to borrow by fixed loan (such as some local authorities) or by the somewhat similar overdraft "subject to reduction arrangement" by granting an interest setoff, at or somewhat below overdraft rate, on the customer's daily credit balance on current account, up to the debit balance on loan account. In the United States, on the other hand, it is still general practice for banks to require borrowers to keep on deposit with the lending bank a sum equal usually to not less than 20 per cent of the loan. The effective cost of borrowing is thereby raised above the nominal rate of interest.

Most of the Australian trading banks, moreover, some years ago introduced two types of charge related to the overdraft limit: an "establishment fee" and an "overdraft management (or service) charge".[8] But these were specifically designed merely to reimburse the bank in part for the administrative costs of an overdraft limit, the costs of investigation and valuation on establishment in the case of the former charge, the costs of running a loan account in the case of the latter. The charges are a small fraction of the overdraft rate of interest and moreover graduated so as to be negligible for large accounts. The fact remains, therefore, that while the full rate of interest is payable on the used part of an overdraft, the unused part is almost a free good.

From the point of view of the economy as a whole, and for the purposes of monetary policy, three features characterise a banking system which uses the overdraft, as contrasted with the fixed loan, method of lending. First, a different significance attaches to "money supply" as an indicator of liquidity. Secondly, a different significance attaches to bank advances as an indicator of the volume of bank credit and of its effects on the level of spending. Finally, and most important, the monetary authorities face an additional difficulty in their efforts to keep the economy on an even keel. We will examine each of these features in turn.

Money Supply and Liquidity

The difference here is that, under the fixed-loan method, an increase in bank credit granted is at once fully reflected in an equal increase in money supply in the form of bank deposits, while under the overdraft method bank deposits come into existence only as and when customers draw against their limits. Since a customer to whom his bank has granted an overdraft limit is just as free to draw a cheque whether his account happens to be in credit or (up to his limit) in debit, unused overdrafts are clearly ready spending power no less than deposits.[9] It has therefore often been suggested that countries which use the overdraft method should include the volume of unused overdrafts in their statistics of money supply.

The New Zealand Royal Commission of 1956 forthrightly defined the money supply in this way:

8 See Commercial Banking Company of Sydney, *Annual Report* 1962; also *Australian Financial Review*, 11 May 1961. The ANZ Bank's service charge was in 1961 reported to range from £2 p.a. on limits up to £500 to a maximum of £10 p.a. on limits above £50,000 (*Melbourne Herald*, 14 April 1961). No official information on these charges has ever been published in Australia. In New Zealand, the overdraft service fee, introduced in November 1961, "is based on the limit or the highest actual advance recorded (whichever is the higher) during the year ended 31 October and it rises in steps from £1 for limits up to £100, to £50 for limits over £50,000 " (*Money and Banking in New Zealand*, Reserve Bank of New Zealand, Wellington, 1963, p. 5).

9 "Thus it is not in the least essential to the efficient working of the cheque-money system that any of those who have cheque books should also have deposits" (J. M. Keynes, *op cit.* vol. I, p. 41).

> Money is anything which is immediately available and generally acceptable in payment for goods and services or in settlement of a debt. In New Zealand, there are three things which appear to us to satisfy these criteria of immediate availability and general acceptability:
> (a) The coin and notes in circulation;
> (b) The deposits on current account standing to the credit of the customers of the trading banks...;
> (c) The unexercised portion of overdraft authorities granted to customers by the trading banks.[10]

One practical reason why this definition has nowhere been officially adopted is that, until recently, statistics of unused overdrafts have not been available. But even in New Zealand, where such statistics have been collected and published for many years, the Reserve Bank has hitherto resisted the advice of the Royal Commission. It explained in its evidence to the Royal Commission: "Unexercised overdraft authorities are not included in the volume of money for several reasons. They are not freely transferable from one person to another; some of them are merely nominal and may never be used; and finally many bank customers could obtain unexercised overdraft authorities if they desired, but this fact is not recorded in the statistics".[11]

These may not be entirely convincing arguments for excluding unused overdrafts from the money supply. But they draw attention to a point which has since then been much more emphatically stressed by the Radcliffe Committee: that money supply, however defined, is an inadequate measure of the liquidity of the public. The liquidity of the public is important as a determinant of the current and prospective level of aggregate effective demand. From this point of view, what matters is not merely the money supply in the public's hands but all factors affecting its "general liquidity position", including its holdings of highly liquid and near-money assets, and its current and expected borrowing facilities. Whether unused overdrafts are included in the money supply, or taken into account among the no less important other aspects of the public's general liquidity position, does not therefore matter very much.

For those, however, who continue to attach special importance to changes in the money supply, the case for including unused overdrafts remains powerful. It is worth noting in this connection that the familiar "money formation table"—like its more sophisticated cousin, the flow-of-funds account—inevitably neglects unused overdrafts because they do not appear as liabilities in the accounts of the trading banks. Paradoxically, the Australian trading banks meticulously record their "contingent liabilities" under confirmed letters of credit, guarantees, etc.,[12] but never so much as mention their much larger and very real demand liabilities in the form of unused overdraft limits. Nor do these *de facto* liabilities ever seem to have been brought into the reckoning in the rules of thumb of British deposit banking, all of which have traditionally run in terms of ratios of cash or liquid assets to *deposits*, rather than to deposits-plus-

10 Royal Commission on Monetary, Banking, and Credit Systems, *Report*, Government Printer, Wellington, 1956, para.151; cf. also para 160.

11 *Monetary and Fiscal Policy in New Zealand*, Reserve Bank of New Zealand, Wellington, 1955, p. 32.

12 Cf. H.W. Arndt, *The Australian Trading Banks*, Cheshire, 1961, p. 113.

unused-limits.[13] The explanation no doubt is that overdraft limits are nominally revocable at will. No doubt also the trading banks, in the practical management of their affairs, pay due regard to their commitments under unused limits.[14]

Limits and Advances

More important than the difference in the significance of money supply under the two systems of bank lending is the difference in the significance of bank advances.

Where bank advances take the form of fixed loans of the American type, a rise in "advances outstanding" over a period reflects the excess of new loan approvals over repayments of old loans. This is not so under the overdraft system. Here we have two distinct series, each reflecting the net balance of two opposing forces: (a) *limits* (outstanding), a rise in which reflects an excess of new overdraft *approvals* over *reductions* or cancellations of existing limits; and (b) *advances* (outstanding), a rise in which reflects an excess of *drawings* (normally against existing limits) over *repayments* of old loans. (In the rest of this article we shall use the italicised words for brevity as here defined.)

"The relationship between loan approvals and drawings against them"—and therefore between limits and advances—"is complex and varies with circumstances".[15] The complexity of possible relationships, the obverse of the overdraft's flexibility, is best illustrated by listing the main types of overdraft transaction.

Type I *The customer secures an overdraft limit which may remain unchanged from year to year and against which he draws from time to time.* The customer

13 A notable exception, as so often, is Lavington who observed in 1921: "The English banks make their advances partly by way of loan, partly by way of overdraft. A simple statement of the ratio between their reserves and their lodgments, therefore, will give an accurate idea of their ability to meet contingencies only if it is supplemented by information as to the extent to which they have lent in one way or the other" *(The English Capital Market,* Methuen, 1921, p. 136). The Irish Commission of Inquiry of 1938 put it more bluntly "Where the overdraft system prevails...the quick assets of the banking system should be contrasted, not merely with the current volume of liabilities revealed by the balance sheet, but with the total volume of liabilities really outstanding so long as the existing overdraft facilities are maintained" *(op. cit.,* p. 159). Keynes noted the point but then proceeded to ignore it throughout his subsequent analysis, on the thin excuse that he was also ignoring "the fixed minimum deposits retained by customers by agreement with their banks to remunerate the latter" (a practice common in the United States but surely not in the countries which use overdrafts) and that "perhaps these two sources of error may be regarded as roughly cancelling one another out" *(op. cit.*, vol. II, p. 35). Another excuse sometimes advanced for ignoring unused limits among the liabilities of trading banks, that it is "highly unlikely that the whole would be used at one and the same time" (Mr McKenna in evidence before the Macmillan Committee, quoted T. Balogh, *op. cit.,* p. 75), is no more convincing since it would, after all, apply equally to deposits.

14 The ANZ Bank went further and took the view in 1962 that the large volume of unused limits also imposed an obligation on the monetary authorities "to ensure that the trading banks are provided with sufficient resources to meet their commitments legitimately entered into in accordance with official policy" *(Annual Report 1962,* p. 18).

15 Reserve Bank of Australia, *Annual Report 1962*, p. 19.

"operates on an overdraft". All his cheque payments represent borrowing and increase the volume of bank advances, all his receipts represent repayments and reduce the volume of advances (except in periods when his account is in credit). This type of overdraft is particularly convenient for primary producers and others with seasonal credit requirements. But it is also commonly used by importers and others to finance fluctuating holdings of stocks. If all overdrafts were of this kind, limits would change little, rising secularly with gradual growth in the number of customers, and perhaps in their average limits. Short-term changes would be confined to advances.

Type II *The customer secures an overdraft limit "subject to reduction arrangement"*, that is to say, subject to repayment (usually coupled with corresponding reduction in the limit) in regular instalments. This type of overdraft, normal for housing loans but used also for other purposes, often involves drawing of the full amount of the loan in one lump sum, probably with little if any lag behind the establishment of the limit. Sometimes, for instance where there is a series of progress payments, the lag will be longer and distributed over a period. On average, there is likely to be a fairly short and fairly stable lag of drawings behind approvals. The other characteristic feature of this type of overdraft, which makes it most like the fixed loan, is that the limit, in effect, dies away with each repayment instalment, not to be revived; reductions coincide with repayments or follow them more or less closely.

Type III *The customer secures a new or increased overdraft limit linked to some specific planned expenditure.* Here again the object may be the traditional use of bank credit to finance investment in working capital (stocks). But the expenditure may also be of a seasonal nature (e.g. a primary producer's shortfall of receipts in the off-season); or it may be the purchase of a car or the payment of doctors' bills; or a major business investment in fixed capital, such as the purchase of equipment or the construction of a building. The new or increased limit may be for the whole or part of the planned expenditure. Approval will usually (though not necessarily) be secured before the decision is taken to go ahead with the spending plan. Drawings will usually lag behind approvals, the lag depending partly on the interval between the granting of the overdraft and the placing of the order or orders (or letting of the contract), but primarily on the interval between the placing of the order and the presentation of the bill or account for payment. In this case, the limit is not necessarily reduced *pari passu* with repayments. Frequently, however, such overdrafts are subject to a more or less formal understanding that they will be repaid over a period and that no substantial new drawings are made without renewed approval by the bank. Reductions, therefore, will tend to be closely related to repayments. On the other hand, there is here in the nature of the case scope for great variety as regards the period for which such advances are outstanding, i.e. the interval between drawings and repayments.

Type IV *The customer secures an overdraft limit without any firm or immediate intention to use it.* Whether or not banks knowingly grant such overdrafts is not clear. But it is generally believed to be common practice for firms to secure limits, as a kind of nest egg of liquidity, especially when credit is temporarily easy after a squeeze and "the going is good" or in anticipation of a squeeze. To the extent that overdrafts are of this type, approvals and limits may rise, with drawings and advances following only much later if at all.

Type V *Customers may secure overdraft limits solely as security against trade credit.* This is commonly done in Australia by importers, in connection with documentary letters of credit. The overdraft limit here serves much the same purpose as a bank acceptance of a trade bill.[16]

Type Va A variant of the preceding type became common practice in Australia in 1963 in connection with so-called "inter-company lending". Company A would borrow short-term funds from company B at a rate of interest substantially below bank overdraft rate, using an unused overdraft limit as backing. In this case, unlike the preceding one, the individual transactions occurred without the knowledge of the banks concerned, and against existing rather than specially established limits.[17]

Type VI *The customer secures no formal limit,* knowing that he can rely on the bank to allow him to overdraw his account, within reason, as and when required. This appears to be very common in the case of the large company whose custom is so valuable that the bank cannot easily afford to say No. Here limits are, in effect, zero; all changes are in advances.

Type VII *The customer overdraws his account without an approved limit, or in excess of his limit.* Here, as in the preceding type, advances are quite independent of limits, but this case which probably involves a great mass of small accounts is much less important. At any time, some part of total advances outstanding will be of this type, but the amount will not fluctuate greatly (although it may have a tendency to rise when credit is tight).[18]

16 In Australia, it is common for woolbuyers, in anticipation of credits from their overseas principals which may arrive through any one of several banks, to establish temporary overdraft limits with all these banks. These multiple limits have little significance and are excluded from the Australian statistics for limits (but the temporary wool advances arc included in the statistics for advances).

17 For information about this inter-company lending, see *Australian Financial Review,* 3 October 1963, 17 January 1964, 2 March 1964; also Bank of New South Wales, *Annual Report 1963,* pp. 19f.

18 In New Zealand, the published statistics for total credit limits are compiled by adding statistics for unused limits to total advances; they therefore include advances of this and the preceding type. In Australia, the banks are requested to include only formal limits in their returns of new approvals and limits outstanding; overdrawn current accounts and advances in excess of limits will therefore generally be excluded. The difference is quite significant. It means, for example, that the New Zealand statistics for limits reflect the substantial seasonal drawings without or in excess of formal limits for tax payments, while the corresponding Australian statistics would not generally do so.

Finally, we must take account of two ways in which limits or advances may change at the initiative of the bank rather than the customer:

Type VIII *Advances will be increased* whenever banks debit interest to accounts. If half the banks (accounting for one-half of advances) do so annually in a given month, and overdraft rate is 6 per cent, this can bring about a 3 per cent rise in advances in that month quite independent of drawings and repayments.[19]

Type IX *Banks may reduce limits* and even recall advances at their own initiative. It is customary for banks in Australia to review most customers' limits once a year. Such review may lead to a request to the customer to reduce his limit. In addition, the central bank has once or twice in recent years directed the trading banks to take steps to reduce limits, and banks have undoubtedly done so. Whether banks ever nowadays call in advances (i.e. demand repayment) on any significant scale is more doubtful, though it is said that they did so in Australia in the weeks following the November 1960 emergency measures.[20]

When one surveys this list, and allows for the fact that the relative importance of the various types of overdraft may change from time to time, one is tempted to conclude that no valid generalisations about the relations between limits and advances under the overdraft system are possible, that anything can happen. As we shall see later, the position is probably not quite so bad in practice. Meanwhile, it may help to pursue taxonomy a little further.

In the first place, we can summarise the likely main influences on the four determinants of net changes in *limits* and *advances.* Changes in *approvals* will reflect mainly changes in the public's spending plans and liquidity, but may also reflect changes in the degree of severity of credit rationing by the banks. Changes in the rate of *reductions* of limits will mainly reflect repayments, but may also be influenced by bank policy. Changes in the rate of *drawings* will reflect chiefly payments by customers which, in turn, will be related in various ways to their spending plans. Finally, changes in *repayments* will partly reflect changes in current cash receipts by customers (which in turn will vary not only with their incomes, but also with their rate of borrowing from other sources, such as overseas capital inflow or company railings in the capital market); in part also they will echo past rates of approval to the extent that advances are subject to more or less regular repayment arrangements.

Secondly, while it is true that "changes in policy operate in the first instance upon the rate at which new loans are being approved and tend to be in the opposite direction to the current pressures of bank borrowing as manifested in movements in advances",[21] one cannot identify limits as reflecting influences from the supply side and advances as reflecting influences from the demand side in the market for bank credit. The banks, as suppliers, can refuse to increase and perhaps marginally even reduce limits; to the

19 Cf. Financial Editor, *Sydney Morning Herald,* 15 November 1960.

20 *Ibid.*, 21 December 1960.

21 Reserve Bank of Australia, *Annual Report 1962*, p. 19.

extent to which there is excess demand for overdrafts, they can stimulate an increase in limits by relaxing credit rationing; in theory, though hardly in practice, they can recall advances. But what happens to advances and even to limits is much more dependent on demand than on supply. For, as is well known, banks "can take the horse to the water but cannot make it drink" and, in practice, they find it difficult to resist strong pressures of demand for credit.[22]

Thirdly, the ratio of advances to limits (i.e. the proportion of limits used) will fluctuate with advances where overdrafts are of types I, VI, VII and VIII distinguished above. It will fluctuate with limits where overdrafts are of types IV, V and IX. In the case of type II, the advances/limits ratio will tend to stay close to 100 per cent. In the case of type III, the ratio may fluctuate widely with changes in both limits and advances. It may therefore be possible to discover something about the relative prevalence of the various types of overdraft by examining the behaviour of the advances/limits ratio.

But, fourthly, care is needed in interpreting movements in the advances/limits ratio. Even in the simple case where advances follow quite regular fluctuations in limits with a stable three months' lag the movement in the ratio is by no means simple. In particular, even in the months in which advances and limits are rising or falling by the same amount, the ratio changes for obvious arithmetic reasons.

Limits, Advances and Spending

So far we have discussed the relationships between limits and advances under the overdraft system without enquiring in which of the two series we are more interested and why.

Until a few years ago, this question would have sounded odd. It was taken for granted that changes in bank credit—actual lending by banks and actual borrowing by customers—are properly measured by statistics of advances outstanding; and that, if we are interested in what is happening to (bank-financed) spending, it is again to the trend in advances that we must look. This view still prevails in countries like the United Kingdom where it has not yet been thought worthwhile to publish statistics of overdraft limits.

In Australia and New Zealand, statistics of limits have in recent years been collected and published. But even here, except to the extent that limits (and approvals) have been treated as indicators of trading bank *policy*, changes in limits have been thought interesting only because they precede changes in advances and may therefore be useful for short-term forecasting if—but only if—it is safe to assume a fairly stable lag of advances behind limits.

In the light of recent developments in monetary theory, these assumptions need to be reconsidered.

Presumably we are interested in what is happening to the level of (bank-financed) spending because, in the short run, it is the level of spending or effective demand that

22 Cf. H. W. Arndt, *The Australian Trading Banks*, 1961, p. 62.

determines the level of economic activity, production and employment. But, as the Radcliffe Report has stressed, what matters for the level of effective demand is not the volume of money paid out in a period, but the volume of orders placed; "decisions to spend", not "acts of spending".[23] The events that will cause more labour to be employed and more output to be produced are the decisions to place an order for goods or to let a tender for a construction project, not the acts of writing out cheques when the bills finally come in.

If this view is accepted it ceases to be obvious whether advances or limits are the more significant indicator of trends in (bank financed) effective demand. The answer now depends largely on which types of overdraft predominate.

If all overdrafts were of types II or III, where the bank's loan approval normally triggers the decision to spend, the series for limits would certainly be the decisive indicator of trends in effective demand; the subsequent change in advances would reflect merely the economically relatively uninteresting rate at which drawings were made to pay bills. In the case of overdrafts of types I, VI and VII, on the other hand, where the change is only in advances (whether because limits remain unchanged or because they are dispensed with), it is obviously the series for advances that measures trends in spending in both senses.

It seems likely that in Australia types II and III—overdrafts of the housing-loan type and overdrafts granted to finance some specific planned expenditure—account for a considerable part of total bank credit, and for an even larger part of the cyclical changes in bank credit in which we are most interested. But the other three major categories—spending by primary producers and others operating on an overdraft with a virtually unchanging limit, by large companies operating without a formal limit, and in some circumstances by customers overdrawing their accounts without or in excess of limits—are by no means negligible.

To this division into two broad classes of overdrafts secured at the initiative of customers corresponds a parallel division of cases where banks take the initiative in tightening or relaxing credit rationing. Although banks can directly influence only approvals, not drawings (and therefore limits, not advances), it may be the rate of approvals which matters most for their customers' decisions to spend (as contrasted with their acts of spending). "Notwithstanding the time lags between the approval of loans and their drawing, a stimulus can be given to the economy when approvals are high and rising by providing assurances of financial accommodation; when approvals are low or falling, expenditure can be dampened by the lack of such assurances."[24]

The picture is further complicated by the fact that, as we saw, both limits and advances may be influenced by factors which have nothing to do with the current level of spending (in either sense), such as the two types of overdraft limit IV and V which are not intended to lead to drawings, and the factors listed under VIII and IX above (reductions of limits and debiting of interest by the banks).

23 Cf. H. W. Arndt, "Radcliffe Monetary Theory", *Economic Record,* September 1962, pp. 341ff.

24 Reserve Bank of Australia, *Annual Report 1962,* pp. 19f; cf. also A. G. Hart, *Money Debt and Economic Activity,* Prentice Hall, 1948, p. 75.

In all the circumstances it is clearly impossible to say *a priori* which of the two series, limits or advances, is the more significant indicator of trends in (bank-financed) spending. But there can be little doubt that limits are important in their own right, not merely as heralds of advances.

Statistical Evidence

For the first time in the long history of the overdraft system we now have, for two countries, some statistical evidence of the working of the system. The Reserve Bank of New Zealand has for some years published monthly statistics of unused or total overdraft limits and in recent years also a classification of limits by classes of borrowers.[25] In Australia, the Reserve Bank has, since February 1962, published two new series of statistics.[26] One is a monthly series of "new and increased lending commitments" (approvals);[27] the other a series (monthly from September 1961) for "overdraft limits" (limits). Both series relate to the major trading banks and both exclude temporary advances to wool buyers and term loans.[28]

Graph I shows the series for limits, together with two series for advances (one excluding temporary advances to woolbuyers and term loans but seasonally unadjusted, the other seasonally adjusted but including the two components) for the period July 1961 to March 1964.[29] It also shows the two corresponding series for the advances/limits ratio. Unfortunately, the monthly series for limits does not go back far enough to indicate what might have been a normal cyclical relationship between advances and limits before 1961; and since 1961 conditions in Australia have been highly abnormal. But until more time has elapsed, we must make do with what evidence we have.

There is a suggestion that limits turned down before (seasonally adjusted) advances late in 1960.[30] Limits declined faster than advances in the early months of 1961,[31] but

25 Reserve Bank of New Zealand, *Bulletin.* See also footnote 18 above.

26 Reserve Bank of Australia, *Statistical Bulletin;* for both series up to July 1963, see Financial Supplement, September 1963.

27 The Reserve Bank has been collecting statistics of approvals since the mid-50s; the first reference to these data appears in its *Annual Report 1957*, p. 13.

28 See also footnotes 6 and 8; the Reserve Bank also publishes term loan approvals and a series for total approvals including term loans; but there is no comparable series for limits.

29 No seasonally adjusted series for advances excluding temporary advances to woolbuyers and term loans is as yet available.

30 The position is not entirely clear. A note in the *Statistical Bulletin,* February 1962 (p. 103) says that approvals "dropped sharply in the second half of that year" (1960). The *Annual Report 1961* at one point (p. 20) implies that approvals began to fall between August and October 1960, at another (p. 21) says merely that "before the end of 1960 the rate of new lending by banks began to fall".

31 Between October 1960 and April 1961 limits fell by 7.3 per cent, advances (seasonally adjusted) by 4.6 per cent. It has been suggested that the rapid decline in limits is partly accounted for by the fact that "a considerable number of weekly new approvals are thought to be specifically for terms of three months or less", in effect "tiding-over arrangements" (Financial Editor, *Sydney Morning Herald,* 15, March 1962).

in the second half of the year rose rapidly while advances continued to decline or stagnate. Encouraged by the central bank, the trading banks had no difficulty in finding customers willing to take up new loan approvals, but advances failed to respond, partly because business confidence for long remained sluggish, partly because a combination of influences—expansionary monetary and budget policies, running down of accumulated stocks, and sustained capital inflow—added to the liquidity of the public, and thereby both increased the rate of repayments and kept down demand for bank credit.[32]

In 1963 all these factors were unexpectedly but very greatly reinforced by an export boom which, between January 1963 and February 1964, added nearly £250 million to international reserves. By March 1962, the (unadjusted) advances/limits ratio had already fallen to 55 per cent. In the next two years limits rose by another £200 million, and the ratio fell to 51 per cent in February 1964. Unused limits reached the record total £912 million. Obviously, this could not be explained in terms of any normal lags of drawings behind approvals. A considerable part of the new or increased limits granted in those years must have been overdrafts of type IV—aimed at a "nest-egg of liquidity"—and meanwhile used in part as in type Va, as backing for inter-company credit. To that extent, it is arguable, undrawn limits were not really unused, but inter-company credit took the place of bank advances.

In any case the February 1964 figure is somewhat misleading since it was a seasonal low.[33] A turning point may have been reached two months earlier. In relation to seasonally adjusted advances, the ratio reached its lowest point in December 1963. In the following months, under moderate central bank restraint, the rise in limits appeared to slow down while (seasonally adjusted) advances looked like staging the long-feared "explosion".

The corresponding data for New Zealand where monetary conditions have not been so abnormal yield rather more evidence about the relations between limits and advances (Graph II). There is a clear tendency for advances to lag behind limits. A deseasonalised series for limits would probably show a lag of about 3 months at the mid-1961 peak, but rather longer lags of 6–9 months in the two troughs of 1959–60 and 1962–63. This may well be a normal feature, reflecting the greater ability of banks to restrict than to expand advances. In New Zealand, as in Australia though to a much less degree, the advances/limits ratio has declined in the last three years, possibly here also reflecting a tendency to secure limits against a rainy day while credit conditions were relatively easy.

As the Reserve Bank of Australia points out in its *Statistical Bulletin,* it is possible, by deducting the monthly net increase in limits from the monthly rate of approvals, to

32 For another account of this episode, see *The Australian Economy 1963,* Government Printer, Canberra, p. 14.

33 It should also be noted that the ratio as here defined excludes term loans which had risen to £50 million by March 1964. As Graph II shows, the shift towards term loans partly accounts for the relative stagnation of other advances and therefore for the abnormally low advance/limits ratio.

Table I Limits and advances, Australia (major trading banks)

Second Wednesday in		1. Limits	Advances		Ratio of advances to limits	
			2. Actual[a]	3. Seasonally adjusted[b]		
		£m	£m	£m	2/1%	3/1%
1960	July	1,682	1,030	1,041	61.1	62.0
	Aug		1,046	1,056		
	Sept		1,053	1,068		
	Oct	1,688	1,060	1,076	62.8	63.6
	Nov		1,052	1,078		
	Dec	1,682		1,040	1,076	
1961	Jan	1,624	1,025	1,072	63.0	66.0
	Feb		996	1,056		
	Mar		970	1,042		
	Apr	1,565	977	1,027	62.3	65.8
	May		975	1,008		
	June		981	1,014		
	July	1,572	999	1,016	63.6	64.6
	Aug		993	1,005		
	Sept	1,587	971	992	61.0	62.3
	Oct	1,606	966	992	60.0	61.8
	Nov	1,620	951	986	58.8	60.7
	Dec	1,647	943	988	57.1	60.0
1962	Jan	1,651	939	990	57.0	60.0
	Feb	1,665	924	990	55.5	59.2
	Mar	1,683	928	1,002	55.0	59.2
	April	1,701	964	1,019	56.7	59.9
	May	1,714	984	1,020	57.2	59.6
	June	1,722	994	1,025	57.8	59.6
	July	1,733	1,026	1,042	59.1	60.0
	Aug	1,744	1,025	1,042	58.6	59.8
	Sept	1,752	1,013	1,037	58.3	59.1
	Oct	1,753	1,007	1,036	57.7	59.1
	Nov	1,767	1,001	1,040	56.7	58.8
	Dec	1,771	996	1,048	56.1	59.2
1963	Jan	1,763	990	1,058	56.0	59.9
	Feb	1,767	975	1,067	55.0	60.3
	Mar	1,783	976	1,080	54.6	60.4
	April	1,794	1,007	1,090	56.2	61.0
	May	1,798	1,024	1,089	57.0	60.6
	June	1,812	1,034	1,094	56.9	60.5
	July	1,824	1,043	1,088	57.1	59.7
	Aug	1,836	1,048	1,093	57.2	59.5
	Sept	1,846	1,022	1,078	55.2	58.2
	Oct	1,862	1,015	1,084	54.4	58.2
	Nov	1,874	1,004	1,090	53.6	58.2
	Dec	1,884	986	1,094	52.1	57.9
1964	Jan	1,865	973	1,085	52.1	58.1
	Feb	1,870	958	1,096	51.1	58.6
	Mar	1,879	969	1,123	51.6	60.0
	April	1,883	1,010	1,138	53.6	60.1
	May	1,897	1,034	1,150	54.5	60.6
	June	1,907	1,049	1,160	55.0	60.7

Notes: [a] Excluding temporary advances to woolbuyers and term loans.
[b] Including temporary advances to woolbuyers and term loans.

Source: Reserve Bank of Australia, *Statistical Bulletin*; seasonally adjusted advances: *Australian Financial Review*.

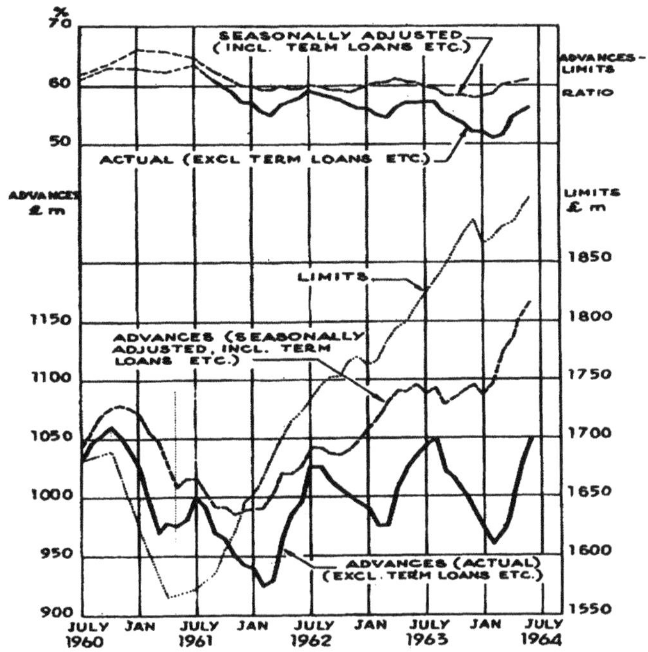

Graph I Limits and advances, Australia

calculate approximately the reductions (or cancellations) of limits during the month.[34] By making the further, obviously somewhat heroic, assumption that reductions of limits occur in the main *pari passu* with repayments of advances, we can calculate also apparent drawings (Table III). Graph III shows approvals (monthly rate) together with apparent reductions and apparent drawings as thus calculated.

The first surprising fact brought out by Table III is the high mortality of overdraft limits. For every £10 million of new approvals per month, about £7.5 million are offset by reductions or cancellations of old limits, yielding a net increase in limits of only £2.5 million. One commentator, writing early in 1962, found this high rate of reductions so surprising that he took it to be an abnormal feature of that year.[35] In fact, as the graph shows, the monthly rate of reductions has continued to rise since 1962, following the rise in limits.[36]

Hardly less intriguing is the relation between approvals and drawings revealed by Graph III. Two points deserve attention. In the first place, it will have been noticed in

34 Financial Supplement, September 1963, p. 14. For this calculation, it is necessary to multiply the published weekly rate of approvals by 4 or 5 depending on the number of weeks between the second Wednesdays of the preceding and the current month.

35 Financial Editor, *Sydney Morning Herald,* 15 March 1962, 11 January 1963.

36 The monthly average of apparent reductions was £30.6 million in 1961–62 (October–June), £35.0 million in 1962–63, and £37.7 million in 1963–64 (July–March).

Table II Limits and advances, New Zealand

Last balance day in		1. Limits	Advances		Ratio of advances to limits
			2. Actual	3. Seasonally adjusted	2/1%
		£m	£m	£m	
1959	July	285.1	167.3		58.5
	Aug	286.1	164.6		57.5
	Sept	286.8	165.7		57.6
	Oct	288.2	163.4		56.8
	Nov	287.1	160.9		56.0
	Dec	291.6	161.5		55.2
1960	Jan	291.3	162.7	170.8	55.9
	Feb	293.1	160.5	170.6	54.9
	Mar	304.5	182.1	169.3	60.0
	Apr	304.1	177.1	170.6	58.3
	May	303.0	173.8	173.0	57.3
	June	304.5	173.5	175.6	57.0
	July	307.9	173.7	177.1	56.5
	Aug	307.8	174.1	176.0	56.7
	Sept	312.5	178.8	181.8	57.2
	Oct	314.7	183.2	187.5	58.1
	Nov	319.1	185.1	190.7	58.0
	Dec	324.8	187.0	193.2	57.9
1961	Jan	324.3	190.3	199.6	59.0
	Feb	334.3	196.8	206.6	59.0
	Mar	349.0	233.3	212.5	66.8
	April	347.0	228.5	219.0	65.9
	May	344.3	223.5	221.9	65.0
	June	341.6	217.3	221.3	63.5
	July	340.5	218.8	223.7	64.0
	Aug	338.2	217.3	224.2	64.5
	Sept	336.1	217.8	224.2	65.0
	Oct	335.1	213.8	223.2	63.6
	Nov	332.5	208.4	217.3	62.7
	Dec	327.8	205.0	213.9	62.6
1962	Jan	326.7	197.9	209.4	60.5
	Feb	323.8	187.2	202.1	58.0
	Mar	334.4	217.2	205.3	65.0
	April	332.2	213.7	205.2	64.0
	May	327.7	203.5	201.3	62.0
	June	326.6	195.1	199.7	59.7
	July	323.6	189.9	198.0	58.8
	Aug	325.8	189.6	196.1	58.1
	Sept	328.0	192.7	198.0	58.9
	Oct	329.6	192.0	196.8	58.2
	Nov	331.1	186.9	195.0	56.4
	Dec	333.9	195.1	197.5	58.6
1963	Jan	333.7	187.0	195.2	57.9
	Feb	331.9	179.4	193.0	54.0
	Mar	337.1	205.2	196.4	61.0
	Apr	337.5	204.3	196.0	58.9
	May	337.2	199.2	197.6	59.0
	June	337.0	196.2	200.7	58.1
	July	340.2	199.2	202.9	58.5
	Aug	339.9	195.2	202.0	57.2
	Sept	342.3	197.4	204.2	57.5
	Oct	(346.7)	205.0	207.9	(59.0)

Table II Limits and advances, New Zealand (continued)

Last balance day in		1. Limits	Advances		Ratio of advances to limits
			2. Actual	3. Seasonally adjusted	2/1%
		£m	£m	£m	
	Nov	(348.6)	199.6	209.4	(57.2)
	Dec	(352.3)	199.2	206.2	(56.5)
1964	Jan	(350.8)	202.0	212.3	(57.5)
	Feb	(352.1)	197.7	211.5	(56.0)
	Mar	(362.0)		218.1	

Note: An amount of £19.2 million, added to the published figures for limits from October 1963 in order to bring the figures for one bank into conformity with the standard definition, has here been deducted to retain comparability within the series.

Source: Reserve Bank of New Zealand, *Bulletin*; seasonally adjusted advances: ibid., April 1964, p. 44.

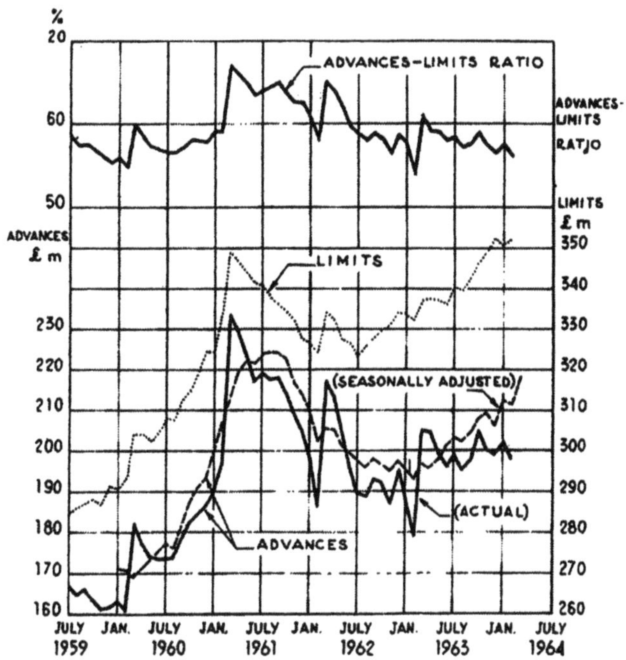

Graph II Limits and advances, New Zealand

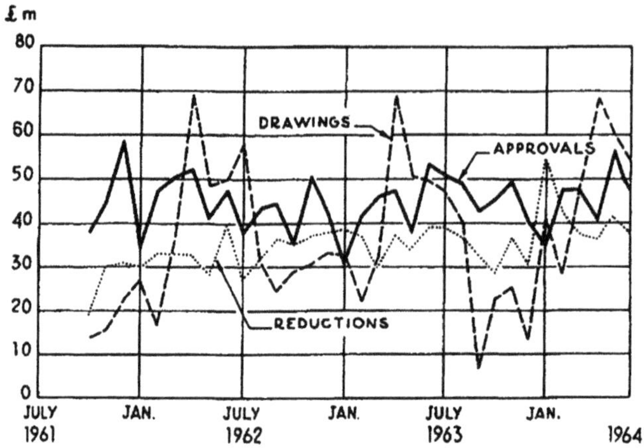

Graph III Approvals, reduction and drawings, Australia

comparing Graphs I and II that limits in New Zealand show a pronounced seasonal pattern (with the same March peak as advances), while at first sight limits in Australia show no such pattern (except for a sharp dip each January).[37] Graph III suggests faintly that in Australia, too, approvals (and therefore limits)[38] vary seasonally broadly in step with advances. This is interesting because it implies that not all seasonal bank credit is of type I, i.e. seasonal drawings against a permanent limit. Some considerable part appears to be of type III, a limit being established (or increased) for a few months and reduced with repayment of the seasonal advance.

Secondly, Graph III tells us something about the relation between month-to-month changes in approvals and drawings. In about half the months during the three-year period covered by the graph, drawings appear to have followed approvals with a lag of one month; in the other half (most of which consists of the period May–December 1963) approvals and drawings seem to have moved together. With monthly data, one cannot infer more from this than that there appears to be a lag of some weeks. But the evidence confirms the impression that, of those overdrafts which account for month-to-month changes in advances, a considerable portion consists of type III, approval being sought not long before the actual drawing.

One disadvantage of all these statistics is that they are too highly aggregated. It seems likely that a good deal more light could be thrown on the behaviour of overdrafts if separate data on approvals and limits of various categories of borrowers were

37 In the case of New Zealand, the March peak reflects payments of provisional and company tax in the last month of the financial year; a substantial part of these consist of drawings in excess of or without formal limit. The January dip in Australia appears to reflect the fall in approvals that occurs with the holiday shutdown of industry in that month and the practice of some banks in including in their returns to the central bank each January and July all reductions in overdrafts subject to monthly reduction of limits. (Cf. *Australian Financial Review*, 31 July 1964, p. 4.)

38 The seasonal movement in limits is most clearly seen in the month-to-month changes in column 2 of Table III.

Table III Approvals, reductions and drawings, Australia (£ million)

		1. Approvals (monthly rate)	2. Limits (net monthly change)	3. Apparent reductions (1-2)	4. Advances [a] (net monthly change) (3+4)	5. Apparent drawings
1961	Oct	37.6	18.8	18.8	-5.3	13.5
	Nov	44.4	14.5	29.9	-14.7	15.2
	Dec	57.5	26.8	30.7	-8.9	21.8
1962	Jan	34.4	4.4	30.0	-3.4	26.6
	Feb	47.0	13.8	33.2	-14.8	16.4
	Mar	50.0	17.3	32.7	3.6	36.3
	Apr	51.6	18.6	33.0	35.7	68.7
	May	40.8	12.6	28.2	20.1	48.3
	June	47.5	8.2	39.3	10.7	50.0
	July	37.6	10.9	26.7	31.3	58.0
	Aug	43.2	11.5	31.7	-0.5	31.2
	Sept	44.5	7.8	36.7	-12.6	24.1
	Oct	35.6	0.8	34.8	-5.6	29.2
	Nov	50.5	13.6	36.9	-6.5	30.4
	Dec	42.4	4.4	38.0	-4.6	33.4
1963	Jan	30.8	-8.2	38.2	-6.0	32.2
	Feb	41.5	4.6	36.9	-15.2	21.7
	Mar	45.6	15.9	29.7	1.1	30.8
	Apr	47.6	10.4	37.2	31.4	68.6
	May	38.4	4.4	34.0	16.4	50.4
	June	53.0	14.2	38.8	10.7	49.5
	July	50.4	11.6	38.8	8.4	47.2
	Aug	49.0	12.3	36.7	3.6	40.3
	Sept	42.4	10.1	32.3	-26.2	6.1
	Oct	45.2	15.9	29.3	-6.7	22.6
	Nov	49.5	12.3	37.2	-11.7	25.5
	Dec	40.4	9.3	31.1	-17.8	13.3
1964	Jan	35.2	-19.1	54.3	-13.1	41.2
	Feb	47.5	4.9	42.6	-14.5	28.1
	Mar	47.6	9.8	37.8	10.9	48.7
	Apr	40.8	4.0	36.8	40.9	77.7
	May	56.0	14.4	41.6	24.3	65.9
	June	46.8	10.7	36.1	14.3	50.4

Note: [a] Actual, excluding term loans, etc.
Source: Reserve Bank of Australia, *Statistical Bulletin*.

available. No such data are published for Australia (although the Reserve Bank obtains a classification of limits for its own use). For New Zealand, a classification of limits, corresponding to that for advances, has been published at six-monthly intervals for the last three years (Table IV). Graph IV shows movements in the advances/limits ratio for some of the main classes of borrowers. The information is in many ways surprising.

Contrary to what one might expect, farmers made very intensive use of their limits, their advances/limits ratio being exceeded only by that for personal loans. (The fact that the ratio was somewhat lower for sheep farmers suggests that the average ratio for primary producers may be a little lower in Australia.) It is urban business, manufacturing and commerce (especially finance) that has the low ratios, or in other

Table IV Advances/limits ratios by classes of borrowers, New Zealand

Classes	1961 Jan %	1961 July %	1962 Jan %	1962 July %	1963 Jan %	1963 July %	1964[a] Jan %
1 Farming etc	73.3	75.1	78.6	79.0	77.1	75.3	(71.5)
1 (b) mainly sheep	73.6	73.1	77.6	75.4	76.1	70.3	(66.5)
3 Manufacturing	51.0	61.4	57.8	55.2	51.0	56.6	(50.3)
7 Commerce	55.0	60.0	58.0	53.5	48.5	51.5	(51.0)
7(a) mainly importers	64.6	69.6	58.0	64.8	56.0	61.7	(59.5)
7(f, g) finance	48.7	59.1	51.5	41.4	42.3	42.4	(42.6)
10. Personal	74.2	78.1	78.1	78.3	77.2	78.1	(76.0)
Total	*58.4*	*65.2*	*62.9*	*60.1*	*57.2*	*59.9*	*(56.0)*

Note: [a]Not strictly comparable since limits include £19 million on new definition of overdrafts.
Source: Reserve Bank of New Zealand, *Bulletin*.

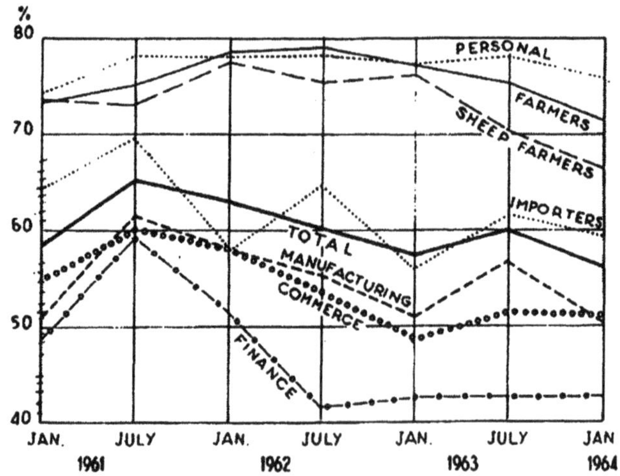

Graph IV Advances/limits ratios by classes of borrowers, New Zealand

words, holds the bulk of the unused overdrafts. (New Zealand importers, however, still subject to fairly tight selective control of advances, have a higher ratio in New Zealand than the rest of commerce.)

The graph brings out a number of interesting points. The movement in the overall ratio (rising to a peak with advances in July 1961 falling until January 1963, followed by a smaller rise to July 1963) reflects the movement of the ratios for manufacturing and commerce. The ratio for farmers continued to rise for another year after the 1961 credit squeeze. The finance group appears to have felt the squeeze in 1961 but has since then been able to hold on to a large volume of unused limits. The oddest feature of the graph is an apparent seasonal movement—high in July and low in January—which is most marked for importers but also shows itself in the personal and manufacturing categories. It is clearly unrelated to the seasonal pattern of all advances which is dominated by the March peak for tax payments.[39]

One important aspect on which none of the available statistics throws any light is the extent to which changes in limits, advances and the advances/limits ratio are influenced by firms of different size. Some banks in Australia have found that the relation between advances and limits is much more stable if the large accounts are eliminated from the statistics. Similarly, in England quite large slices of total bank advances are thought to be due to a few giant firms who use overdrafts as stop-gaps in their capital development programmes. A size analysis of the statistics of limits and advances would be useful to test this point.

The Problem of Unused Limits

At various points in the preceding discussion reference has been made to the problem which unused limits present to the central bank in its efforts to maintain the economy in internal balance. We must now look at this aspect more closely. What precisely are the disadvantages for monetary policy of the overdraft, as compared with the fixed-loan, method of bank lending?

It is worth emphasising that some of the main obstacles to the effective use of monetary and banking policy for economic stabilisation have nothing to do with the difference between the two methods. The difficulties that central banks sometimes have in controlling the lending policies of commercial banks—in the sense of the rate at which banks are prepared to grant loan approvals—are clearly independent of the method of lending. Nor are the difficulties in controlling the current level of spending through expansion and contraction (or restraint upon expansion) of bank credit necessarily any different under the two methods.

The difficulties in using banking policy to stimulate spending in a recession are no worse under the overdraft than under the fixed-loan system. In so far as a rise in the level of (bank-financed) spending depends on a rise in the level of "actual borrowing" from banks, the real trouble is the sluggishness of response of *advances* to an easier lending policy by the banks, and there is no reason to suppose that this is any greater under the overdraft system. In so far as spending decisions are stimulated by the "assurance of financial accommodation"[40] provided by an easier lending policy, the effect is probably much the same whether customers, under the overdraft system, are induced actually to apply for new or increased limits, or whether, under the

39 The explanation in the case of advances to importers appears to be that in June, the last month of the import-licensing year, importers tend to hold large stocks of imported goods and therefore use their limits more fully than in January after the Christmas spending period. In the case of manufacturing and personal advances the apparent seasonal pattern is probably spurious.

40 See p. 77 above.

fixed-loan system, they are merely made more confident that they will be able to secure bank accommodation when the need arises.

The difficulties banks experience in a boom in resisting pressures of demand for credit are also unlikely to be affected by the method of lending. Neither refusal of additional accommodation nor recall of outstanding advances is any easier under the fixed loan system.

In fact, the special problems of the overdraft method arise entirely from the existence of unused limits. Unused limits constitute a reservoir of liquidity, additional to deposits, which does not exist where all bank credit takes the form of fixed loans. An increase in unused limits presents a problem for monetary policy because it constitutes an increase in the liquidity of the private sector. In turn, "the importance of the growth of liquidity in the private sector lies in the scope it gives to the community to change its behaviour quickly should its attitudes and expectations change—to spend more freely and to move into less liquid assets, increasing the capacity of others to spend more freely".[41]

Even in its effects on the liquidity of the public, the overdraft system makes less difference than might appear at first sight. In the interval between the approval of a bank loan and its use for cheque payments, the borrower's liquidity is increased to exactly the same extent whether the increase takes the form of a larger credit balance on current account or an equivalent unused limit.[42] The special features of the overdraft system, in fact, reduce to two points, both of which we have noted before.

First, the liquidity of the public is liable to be under-estimated if unused overdraft limits are ignored, and it is in any case difficult to assess so long as the only available statistics relate to deposits and advances. Once statistics of limits are collected and published, this point loses most of its significance. Both Australia and New Zealand have now gone a long way in this direction, though the Australian Reserve Bank might follow the New Zealand example by publishing a classification of limits, and the New Zealand Reserve Bank the Australian example by publishing statistics of approvals.

Secondly, unused limits under the overdraft system cost nothing,[43] while on their equivalent under the fixed-loan system—the unused part of a bank loan—the customer has to pay the same rate of interest as on the used part.[44] Under the fixed-loan system customers have a strong incentive to economise in the holding of borrowed deposits. So long as an unused limit is virtually a free good, the total volume of unused limits held on average by the public will be larger, and unpredictable substantial increases in advances more likely, than would be the case for their equivalents under the fixed-loan system.

41 Reserve Bank of Australia, *Annual Report 1963*, p. 16.

42 In the case of the fixed-loan system the increase (in terms of the Fisher equation) raises M, in the case of the overdraft system it raises V in the first round; there is of course no difference in subsequent rounds.

43 Subject to the qualifications noted on p. 69 above.

44 Subject to the qualification noted in footnote 7 above.

To distinguish this defect of the overdraft system from other problems of monetary control common to all forms of bank lending is not to play down its importance. It is a serious defect which, as we have seen, has on two earlier occasions aggravated the difficulties of monetary policy in Australia and may yet prove even more troublesome. What can and should be done to remedy it?

The Case for a Commitment Fee

Nothing as drastic as sudden complete abolition of the overdraft system and its replacement by the American-type fixed-loan method is likely to commend itself in countries in which the overdraft has been part of their way of life. The overdraft has advantages to the customer which will not be lightly given up.

An approach towards more gradual diminution of the role of the overdraft and its disadvantages may emerge in Australia from the recent introduction of the term loan. As term loans increasingly replace traditional overdrafts for longer-term requirements, especially for the acquisition of fixed assets, overdrafts will represent a declining part of bank credit.

For the rest, the main practical question is whether something should be done to discourage the retention of unused limits by a commitment charge. When I proposed this in 1957,[45] the suggestion met with two main objections in trading bank quarters.

First, it was claimed that overdraft limits were in many cases so informal that no precise volume of limits could be determined. The successful collection of statistics of limits has disposed of this point. Secondly, it was argued that the trading banks could not impose a charge for granting a limit without abandoning the fundamental principle that the limit was revocable at any time at their discretion. Here again the proof of the pudding has been in the eating: the banks seem to have had no difficulty in reconciling their right to cancel limits at will—a somewhat tenuous right in practice—with the establishment fees and overdraft management fees which most of them have adopted in recent years.

There remain two more substantial difficulties. One is that a commitment fee would fall severely on primary producers and others who retain a limit from year to year for purely seasonal use during a few months of the year. Since fairly stable unused limits during the off-season months present no problem for monetary policy, there is a case for meeting this difficulty by the banks granting a partial or complete rebate of the fee for any part of his limit which the customer agrees in advance to use only during three or four specified months of the year.

The other difficulty arises from the fact mentioned before that a powerful and valuable customer does not need a formal limit since his bank can hardly refuse credit as and when he wants it. A commitment charge would simply lead all the larger and weightier customers to rely on this fact and do without a formal limit. This might be a real difficulty for an individual bank. But it is hard to believe that all trading banks

45 *The Australian Trading Banks,* 1st edition, Cheshire, 1957, p. 194.

acting together, as they tend to do in these matters, could not enforce the practice of insisting henceforth on a formal limit for all customers.

It has been reported that early in 1964 the Australian trading banks themselves submitted to the Reserve Bank proposals for a commitment fee.[46] The immediate occasion was reported to be the development of inter-company lending on the security of unused bank overdrafts. A commitment fee of 1½ per cent would bridge the gap between the then minimum bank overdraft rate of 5½ per cent and the current market rate of short-term inter-company loans of about 4 per cent and could thus be expected to shepherd the borrowers back to the trading banks and the lenders to fixed deposits or the official short-term money market.[47] For companies that chose to continue to use an unused limit as security for inter-company borrowing, the fee would, in effect, serve as an acceptance commission.

The newspaper reporting the proposal was doubtful whether the Reserve Bank or the Federal Government would agree to "such a sweeping change as an across-the-board commitment fee—which could be of great significance to bank profits".[48] The additional revenue which such a fee would yield to the banks can easily be exaggerated. It is true that on the April 1964 level of overdraft limits of £1,880 million an across-the-board fee of 1½ per cent would yield over £28 million a year. But if the fee is applied to unused limits only (by being absorbed in overdraft interest on debit balances), if it also replaces the present establishment and management fees, if it is wholly or partially rebated for limits confined to seasonal overdrafts, if it serves to stimulate further resort to term loans, and, above all, if it succeeds in its main object of encouraging customers to keep unused limits to a minimum, then the extra revenue from such a fee might turn out to be relatively small.[49]

Perhaps Australia's experience in 1961–64 was altogether exceptional and the New Zealand Reserve Bank right when it said, as recently as 1963, that "allowing for very short-term deviations there is on the whole a fairly stable relationship between limits and actual advances".[50] But if, as I am inclined to think, this is too complacent a view, then a commitment fee circumscribed in the manner suggested is probably the best approach to the problem.

46 *Australian Financial Review,* 17 January 1964; also 2 March 1964.

47 The case of inter-company lending suggests an alternative formulation of the problem of unused limits. Banks normally act to a considerable extent as lenders of last resort for trade credit. Hence the commonly observed phenomenon of rising advances in a liquidity crisis. The widespread resort to inter-company lending in Australia during the 1963–64 boom, apart from doing the banks out of business, involved the risk that a tightening of credit conditions would lead to wholesale substitution of bank credit for inter-company trade credit. But this is merely another way of describing the risk of wholesale use of the unused limits which served as security for inter-company lending.

48 *Australian Financial Review*, 17 January 1964.

49 One commentator (Financial Editor, *Sydney Morning Herald,* 12 November 1960) has adumbrated the idea of variable commitment fees as a technique of monetary control; it is hard to see that any useful purpose would be served by influencing unused limits through a varying commitment fee (rather than used limits through a varying advance rate).

50 *Money and Banking in New Zealand,* Reserve Bank of New Zealand, Wellington, 1963, p. 6.

8

Two Kinds of Credit Rationing

Banks ration credit. The amount of credit granted varies with the perceived riskiness of the borrower. But at any given level of interest rates, there is, as Keynes put it, "an unsatisfied fringe of borrowers the size of which can be expanded or contracted, so that banks can influence the volume of investment...without any change in the level of bank rate". Governments ration credit through changes in interested rates and sometimes through provisions for concessional credit. This article discussed the implications of the two kinds of credit rationing.

Originally published in the Banca Nazionale del Lavoro *Quarterly Review*, December 1982.

There is wide agreement among economists that government control of interest rates is undesirable. Two arguments against legal ceilings on interest rates are that they discourage mobilisation of savings and encourage capital intensity. Another is that the resultant excess demand requires credit rationing which is liable to discriminate among borrowers in socially undesirable ways. To quote one recent statement of this latter argument, if

> an administratively determined institutional nominal interest rate...holds the real rate...below its equilibrium level...nonprice rationing of investible funds must occur. This typically takes place on the basis of quality of collateral, political pressures, 'name', loan size, and covert benefits to responsible loan officers. These criteria can be counted on to discriminate inefficiently between investment opportunities. Indeed there will be a preference for traditional, low-yielding investments because these appear safest and simplest to finance. Interest rate ceilings discourage risk-taking by the financial institutions; risk premia cannot be charged when ceilings are binding. This itself rations out a large proportion of potential investors.[1]

An obvious objection to this argument against legal ceilings on interest rates is the well-known fact that banks ration credit even in the absence of any legal control of interest rates. Indeed, discrimination between borrowers on the basis of collateral and credit rating is a characteristic feature of credit rationing by banks, while some forms of government control of interest rates, such as concessional credit for priority borrowers, can, at least in principle, discriminate among borrowers in a socially more desirable way.

1 M. J. Fry, "Money and Capital or Financial Deepening in Economic Development?", *Journal of Money, Credit, and Banking*, (1978), reprinted in W. L. Coats, Jr., and D. R. Khatkhate (eds, *Money and Monetary Policy in Less Developed Countries*, Pergamon Press, Oxford, 1980. The author pleads guilty to having made similar statements; see footnote 18 below.

The object of this article is to clear up the confusion by distinguishing more clearly between these two kinds of credit rationing, between what, for brevity, might be called "bank rationing" and "government rationing" of credit.[2]

Bank Rationing

The facts about bank rationing are not in dispute. "In the loan market...sellers (i.e. lenders) classify their customers according to the risk of losing the principal and interest payments, and no single interest rate moves so as to equate the quantities offered and demanded".[3] Or, as Keynes put it in a famous passage, "so far...as banks are concerned, lending does not—in Great Britain at least—take place according to the principles of a perfect market. There is apt to be an unsatisfied fringe of borrowers, the size of which can be expanded or contracted, so that banks can influence the volume of investment by expanding or contracting the volume of their loans, without there being necessarily any change in the level of bank-rate".[4]

This is not to say that banks charge precisely the same interest rate to all borrowers. Rates on advances "vary according to the nature of the advance, the estimation of risk, and the value of other business brought to the bank by the customer. There are generally, however, ruling rates for advances which are similar for all trading banks and apply to most advances".[5] Similarly, the size of the fringe of unsatisfied borrowers is expanded or contracted, not in general by changes in the ruling average loan rate but "through changes in the degree of stringency with which credit is rationed".[6] "When they wished to foster an expansion of credit, bankers became more tolerant about raising overdraft limits and more ready to grant accommodation to new borrowers".[7]

Why do banks ration credit? More precisely, why do banks supply credit at a rate of interest below the rate which would equate supply and demand, so that credit has to be rationed? There is now an extensive theoretical literature on this subject. Most of the explanations follow Stigler in emphasising information costs. "The lender cannot afford to acquire the information to subclassify a given borrower into a more homogeneous risk class, and so this borrower is grouped with a higher-risk man... Information costs are the costs of transportation from ignorance to omniscience, and

2 Thanks for helpful comments on an earlier draft, coupled with the usual disclaimers of responsibility, are due to B. Bolnick, G. Dorrance, M. Dowling, W. E. James and V. Joshi.

3 R. N. McKean, "Liquidity and the National Balance Sheet" in American Economic Association, *Readings in Monetary Theory*, Blakiston, New York, 1951, p. 69.

4 J. M. Keynes, *A Treatise on Money*, Macmillan, London, 1935, Vol. I, p. 212.

5 Royal Commission on the Monetary and Banking System of Australia, *Report*, Government Printer, Canberra, 1937, para. 568.

6 H. W. Arndt, *The Australian Trading Banks*, 1st ed., Cheshire, Melbourne, 1957, p. 64. British bankers of the old school were reluctant to admit that this could happen. "That could only be done, however, by lowering the banks' standards of security and credit-worthiness" (W. Manning Dacey, *The British Banking Mechanism*, Hutchinson, London, 1951, p. 92).

7 C. G. F. Simkin, "Banking in New Zealand" in R. S. Sayers (ed.), *Banking in the British Commonwealth*, Clarendon Press Oxford, 1952, p. 330.

seldom can a trader afford to take the entire trip".[8] Unable, beyond a point, to differentiate the riskiness of different borrowers, or finding it uneconomic to try to do so, banks are deterred from raising the loan rate by two considerations which have been called the adverse selection effect and the incentive effect.[9] The former refers to the fact that those who are willing to pay higher interest rates are likely to be higher-risk borrowers, so that, as interest rates rise, the average riskiness of those who borrow increases, possibly reducing the bank's profits. The latter refers to the fact that higher interest rates which reduce the return on projects which succeed, are likely to induce firms to undertake projects with lower probability of success but higher payoffs when successful.[10] For either reason, or both, the interest rate which maximises banks' profits will be below the highest rate they could charge, i.e. the rate which would equate supply and demand. Another explanation which used to be popular among bank managers though it does not seem to figure in the theoretical literature is that, if an aspiring borrower's project appears to the bank unlikely to yield an adequate return to cover debt service at the ruling loan rate, it is even less likely to do so at a higher rate.

The trouble with all these explanations of credit rationing is that they focus on banks and ignore the rest of the capital market. Take this statement by McKean:

> If customers fell into discrete compartments or risk-categories, this would simply mean that several loan markets and interest rates existed. But even within a single broad risk-category, each borrower presents a different degree of risk; and a loan to one customer is a different commodity from a loan to another...Some rationing is inevitable.[11]

The fact, however, is that, in all countries, the capital market is segmented; several loan markets and interest rates do exist. In less developed countries, besides banks, there is an informal sector of money lenders from whom borrowers excluded by bank rationing can obtain credit at higher rates; and in developed countries, there is a spectrum of non-bank financial intermediaries at the far end of which are fringe institutions which offer credit at high rates to virtually anyone, no questions asked. As the Radcliffe Committee reported,

> there was also general agreement among witnesses, from trade organisations and from banks, that firms denied the bank credit they wanted resorted to finance companies (from whom they could borrow either by straight loan or by hire purchase agreements), the accepting houses, and even the discount houses. Such alternative credit was more costly, sometimes much more so.[12]

In other words, while it may be true that banks are as a rule unwilling to supply credit to borrowers of varying degree of perceived riskiness at varying interest rates sufficient to

8 G. J. Stigler, "Imperfections in the Capital Market", *Journal of Political Economy*, June 1967, p. 291.

9 J. E. Stiglitz and A. Weiss, "Credit Rationing in Markets with Imperfect Information", *American Economic Review*, June 1981, pp. 393f.

10 *Ibid.* Keynes took the opposite view. "If a venture is a risky one, the borrower will require a wider margin between his expectation of yield and the rate of interest at which he will think it worth his while to borrow" (J. M. Keynes, *The General Theory of Employment, Interest and Money*, Macmillan, London, 1936, p. 145).

11 R. N. McKean, *op. cit.*, p. 69.

12 Committee on the Working of the Monetary System, *Report*, HMSO, London, 1963, para. 457.

cover the extra risk in each case, this is not true of the capital markets as a whole, or not to nearly the same degree. A special explanation is needed to account for the difference of behaviour between banks and less conservative financial intermediaries.

Two explanations suggest themselves. One is the need of deposit banks to maintain the confidence of holders of demand deposits. "For deposit banks are, of all concerns, the least adapted to the bearing of serious risks".[13] If a deposit bank showed itself willing to lend to any borrowers, however risky, provided they were willing to pay a rate of interest high enough to cover the bank's lender's risk, its depositors might take these very interest rates as worrying evidence that the bank was taking more risks in its lending policy than was prudent for a deposit bank. Another possible explanation is that deposit banks are more susceptible to the moral pressure exerted by public anti-usury sentiment which is widely prevalent in most countries. Respectable banks do not want to appear as "loan sharks".

So much for the positive economics of bank rationing. What about its welfare effects? Economists seem agreed that credit rationing by banks is unlikely to lead to the most desirable allocation of credit. "It is not at all sure that [banks] have an incentive to behave in a socially optimum way".[14] This has not always been the conventional wisdom. Adam Smith favoured usury legislation precisely because a ceiling on interest rates would exclude high-risk borrowers. "If the legal ratewas fixed so high as 8–10 per cent, the greater part of the money which was to be lent, would be lent to prodigals and projectors, who alone would be willing to give this high rate".[15] By "prodigals" Smith probably meant both spendthrifts liable to squander money on frivolous consumption and borrowers who had little if any intention to repay. By "projectors" he probably meant optimists who had unwarranted confidence in the economic prospects of their projects. These are clearly two categories of high-risk borrowers whom any bank would hope to avoid, and if bank rationing normally excluded only these two categories it would be difficult to object to it on welfare grounds.

In practice, however, bank rationing is generally believed to operate as a socially inefficient allocative mechanism. "Restrictive credit rationing almost certainly discriminates in favour of the bank's existing customers against newcomers and probably also in favour of valuable (and that almost certainly means large) customers of the bank".[16] "Banks may look at the creditworthiness of their customers primarily in terms of their net worth, which might not be correlated with the productivity of their investments".[17] "The easiest criteria available to bank managers for rationing credit, the quality of collateral the borrower can offer and his credit standing both tend to

13 W. Manning Dacey, *op. cit.*, p. 91.

14 V. Galbis, "Financial Intermediation and Economic Growth in Less Developed Countries: A Theoretical Approach", *Journal of Development Studies*, January 1977, reprinted in W. L. Coats and D. R. Khatkhate, *op. cit.*, p. 82.

15 Adam Smith, *Wealth of Nations*, Modern Library, New York, 1973, p. 339.

16 H. W. Arndt, *op. cit.*, p. 65.

17 V. Galbis, *op. cit.*, p. 82.

favour the well-to-do".[18] Particularly in less developed countries, the typical criteria for nonprice rationing, as Fry has put it rather strongly, "can be counted on to discriminate inefficiently between investment opportunities".[19] In other words, bank rationing which seeks to eliminate high-risk borrowers by allocating credit on the basis of collateral and credit standing is liable to discriminate against smaller, poorer, newer and more enterprising borrowers among whom there may be many who would make good use of credit, able and willing to service debt at higher than ruling bank loan rates (but below those of fringe institutions and money lenders which usually include an element of monopoly profit and have to cover high transaction costs).

Government Rationing

In order to assess the economic significance of credit rationing which arises from government control of interest rates, it is necessary to distinguish between two quite distinct forms of control. The first consists of overall legal ceilings on interest rates which may be confined to bank (loan and/or deposit) rates or may extend to all interest rates. The second takes the form of concessional credit for defined target groups of borrowers.

Legal ceilings on interest rates are sometimes justified on questionable economic grounds—high interest rates add to costs and are therefore "inflationary"—or on vaguely distributional grounds, to safeguard borrowers against "exploitation" by banks. (Anti-usury sentiment, reflected in outright condemnation of interest on moral grounds by the Catholic Church in medieval Europe and by adherents of strict versions of Islam, such as the Khomeini regime in Iran, presumably rests largely on such distributional grounds.) Adam Smith, as we saw, approved of interest ceilings to avoid squandering of scarce capital by "prodigals" and "projectors".

For our purposes, it is enough to note that overall legal ceilings on bank lending rates which leave the allocation of credit to the banks may be assumed to result in discrimination between borrowers on broadly the same criteria as bank rationing without controls. The effect of the offer of credit at lower interest rates is to swell the fringe of unsatisfied borrowers and thus to require more stringent rationing by the banks. The effect is the same as that of more stringent rationing necessitated by a decline in bank liquidity, except that in the case of interest control the customers most likely to be rationed out are the new ones attracted by lower rates, while in the case of reduced bank liquidity the axe has to fall on some of the bank's regular customers.

Interest ceilings can also have other undesirable effects. Attempts to limit interest rates through "cheap money" policies inhibit adequate control of money supply. In less developed countries, legal ceilings on lending rates, which are often reinforced by legal ceilings on deposit rates (and in any case motivate banks to keep down deposit rates), discourage the mobilisation of savings if either the public's saving rate or its

18 H. W. Arndt, "Monetary Policy Instruments in Indonesia", *Bulletin of Indonesian Economic Studies*, November 1979, p. 119.

19 M. J. Fry, *loc. cit.*

currency–deposit ratio is at all interest elastic; they constitute "financial repression".[20] Legal ceilings on lending rates are also liable to encourage inappropriately capital-intensive techniques and patterns of industry. Legal ceilings on bank deposit rates alone, leaving lending rates uncontrolled, allow scope for oligopolistic behaviour by banks, increasing bank profits through a widening of spreads.[21] Again, if legal ceilings on deposit and lending rates are confined to banks, they have the effect of diverting funds to other uncontrolled sectors of the capital market. But none of these other effects detracts from the similarity between this form of government rationing and bank rationing as regards the allocation of credit among borrowers.

There is no such similarity between bank rationing and the other form of government rationing, that implied in the provision of credit on concessional terms to categories of borrowers who, it is believed, cannot afford or for other reasons should not be made to pay market rates of interest.[22] In developed countries, target groups for concessional credit usually include applicants for housing loans, but also often such categories as war veterans, age pensioners and other disadvantaged groups. In developing countries, the most important categories of "priority" borrowers are usually farmers and small-scale firms. The objective may merely be to correct the socially undesirable discrimination, which is believed to result from bank rationing on the assumption, which may or may not be warranted, that the authorities are better able to make a socially optimal selection. In this case, all that is needed is to earmark specified amounts of credit for target groups but at the ruling lending rates. Beyond this, credit on concessional terms, i.e. below ruling bank lending rates, could be justified on any of the usual welfare-economic grounds for intervention in the market—externalities, protection and distributional considerations.

If widespread home ownership is believed to be in the national interest, the case for government intervention could be based on the external economies of concessional credit to home buyers; similarly, if in developing countries it is thought important to encourage farmers to buy fertiliser to expand food production. The case for concessional credit to small-scale industry could be based on the argument for infant industry protection, to help such firms on their feet. (Imperfections of the capital market, after all, can serve to justify infant industry protection even where economies of scale accrue internally to the firm.) The same argument might also be applied to farmers, for example, if there are grounds for believing that, once they recognise the beneficial effects of fertiliser application on their yields, and once their incomes begin to rise in consequence, they can do without concessional credit. With respect to pensioners in developed countries, but also to low-income farmers in developing countries, concessional credit might be justified on straight welfare grounds, as the most administratively practicable and effective method of income redistribution.

20 R. I. McKinnon, *Money and Capital in Economic Development*, Brookings, Washington, 1973; E. S. Shaw, *Financial Deepening in Economic Development*, OUP, New York, 1973.

21 V. Galbis, *op. cit.*, pp. 72, 83.

22 Cf., e.g., C. H. Hanumantha Rao, "Farm Size and Credit Policy", *Economic and Political Weekly*, December 1970, reprinted in W. L. Coats and D. R. Khatkhate, *op. cit.*,; B. Bolnick, "Concessional Credit for Small-Scale Enterprise", *Bulletin of Indonesian Economic Studies*, July 1982.

All these, it should be emphasised, are only *prima facie* justifications for concessional credit. The benefits of such credit may be outweighed by social costs and may in any case not go to those for whom they are intended.

Much depends on the manner in which concessional credit is financed. If concessional loan rates are financed by controlled deposit rates (in effect, by a tax on depositors), they have all the adverse effects of financial repression. It was this situation that Shaw had in mind when he declared the subsided loan rate to represent "repression at its worst".[23] Concessional credit subsidised, overtly or covertly, by the central bank, e.g. by central bank refinance of commercial bank credit on concessional terms, as is the practice in Indonesia, may be hardly less undesirable if it operates as an inflation tax.[24] On the other hand, one can conceive of concessional credit schemes subsidised from the government budget which, provided they do not add too greatly to the overall tax burden, would, at least in principle, not be open to these objections.

In practice, loopholes and the operations of the political market are liable to distort the allocation of credit in greater or less degree. If the intended beneficiaries of concessional credit on-lend at commercial rates to other who can make more profitable use of it, at least the distributional, though not the allocative, purpose of the scheme may be served. But very often the actual beneficiaries turn out to be not the poor but those with political clout—relatively affluent aspirants for housing loans, farmers or industrial pressure groups in developed countries and village élites or politically influential urban interests in developing countries. Nevertheless, while bank rationing in its nature favours the better-off, government rationing in the form of concessional credit for target groups can in principle benefit low-income borrowers; how far it will do so in practice depends on the integrity and efficiency of the bureaucracy and on the working of the political process.

Conclusion

Advocates of financial development, following the lead given by Shaw and McKinnon, have made a powerful case against government control of interest rates. Our quarrel is not with the policy conclusion but with one frequently used argument. Statements which rest the case on the discriminatory effects of credit rationing have confused the issues by attributing to government controls the consequences which normally flow from credit rationing by banks even in the absence of government control. As Drake has recently pointed out, even complete abolition of government control of bank interest rates may not achieve the objectives hoped for by advocates of financial development if banks act collectively as a cartel and refrain from raising deposit rates and if they, in conformity with normal banking practice, discriminate in lending against the less creditworthy borrowers, which may in practice mean "against

23 E. S. Shaw, *op. cit.*, p. 86.
24 H. W. Arndt, *op. cit.*, (BIES).

small-scale producers, peasant farmers, certain ethnic groups, females, the uneducated and so forth".[25]

Credit rationing involved in concessional credit to priority categories of borrowers can in principle alleviate some of the adverse effects of credit rationing by banks. Whether it always, or usually, does so in practice is much more doubtful. There is room for legitimate differences of opinion, here as in many other areas of economic policy, about the relative likelihood and seriousness of market failure and government failure.

25 P. J. Drake, *Money, Finance and Development*, Robertson, Oxford, 1981, p. 225.

One cannot help asking oneself whether this is enough. The political constraints on fiscal policy have in the 1980s saddled monetary policy with most of the burden both of short-term stabilisation and of medium-term winding down of inflation. Once again, as sixty years ago, the evidence casts doubt on the capacity of monetary policy alone, operating through the cash rate supplemented only by "jawboning", to rein in booms or lift the economy out of recessions. No wonder there is "a preference on the part of the Bank for relatively more of the burden of adjustment to be borne by fiscal policy". But is there really nothing that can usefully be done to restore to the central bank a more effective role in the maintenance of internal balance?

And what about external balance? To someone of my generation of economists, brought up to believe that the two main objectives of macroeconomic policy are internal and external balance and the two instruments demand management and the real exchange rate, nothing in the Governor's paper is more striking than the absence of any reference to the balance of payments. Mr Fraser has made it clear in other public statements that he does not hold with those who think Australia's current account deficit and external debt do not matter. But implicitly he treats this as a problem virtually beyond the purview of monetary policy. Except to the extent that pursuit of low inflation helps, the central bank has no influence on the real effective exchange rate. Australia's international competitiveness has to be tackled through microeconomic reform. The nominal exchange rate, except for occasional smoothing out, must be left to market forces. In fact, monetary policy for internal balance impacts perversely on external balance, high interest rates to restrain the boom causing appreciation and vice versa. Perhaps this new impotence of central banks is irremediable. But one would have liked Mr Fraser to address the question.

10

Full Employment in Historical Perspective

A historical account of the "full employment" objective, from Say's law to the Keynesian revolution, the post-World War II "full employment" target, stagflation and the remaining problem of structural unemployment in western countries.

Originally published as Working Paper No. 3/94, September 1994, The Full Employment Project, the University of Melbourne.

In the first (1890) edition of Marshall's *Principles of Economics,* the leading pre-1914 textbook, there is just one passing reference to unemployment, to the effect of "irregularity of employment" on wages in particular occupations (Marshall 1890, p. 583). Half a century later, full employment had become a prime objective of economic policy in western countries. "Governments seemed justified in the eyes of their public opinion in giving the abolition of unemployment precedence over all other economic objectives" (Arndt 1944, p. 251). How did this elevation of the "full employment" objective come about?

This essay gives an account of its emergence during the first half of this century. An epilogue speculates more briefly about the reasons why confidence about full employment has evaporated in the past two decades.

Say's Law

The 1890s and early years of this century were years of depression and quite severe unemployment in Britain and elsewhere. In 1895 a House of Commons Committee reported on "Distress from Want of Employment" (Hutchison 1953, p. 412) and in 1905 Joseph Chamberlain went so far as to say that "the question of unemployment, believe me, has now become the most important question of our time" (Hutchison 1981, p. 140). But for the most part, unemployment was seen as part of the social problem of poverty which the 1905 Royal Commission on the Poor Law (of which Beatrice Webb was a member) was set up to address.

In 1909, Beveridge, aged 30, published the first major book on the subject: *Unemployment: A Problem of Industry.* He called it a problem of industry because he thought of unemployment as primarily due to "disorganisation of the labour market"—immobility of labour as between occupations and locations—and therefore concluded that employment exchanges had become "an indispensable part of the State's machinery for dealing with unemployment" (Beveridge 1909, 2nd ed. 1930, p. 352). "The problem of unemployment—and this is a point that cannot be too strongly emphasised—is insoluble by any mere expenditure of public money" (*ibid.*, p. xv).

This was in line with the prevailing view of mainstream economists. They still adhered to the notion that general unemployment was impossible because of Say's Law that supply creates its own demand. As J. S. Mill had explained: "The person who saves his income is no less a consumer then he who spends it… [Through saving] he supplies food and clothing...to be used by productive labourers" (quoted Hutchison 1953, p. 349). This orthodoxy had been challenged from time to time by various heretics, from Karl Marx to J. A. Hobson. But their under-consumptionist arguments failed to overcome the logic of Say's Law. The decades 1870–1914 were in economics what Hicks called "the static epoch" (Hicks 1966) when attention was concentrated on optimum allocation of resources in a fully employed economy. While economists began to write about business cycles (Aftalion 1908, Hawtrey 1913, Mitchell 1913, Robertson 1915), they lacked the tools of economic analysis to tackle the problem of general unemployment.

World War I was followed by a severe post-war depression. The great mass of the unemployed in the USA led President Harding to call a Conference on Unemployment (Mitchell 1944, p. 43) and Britain remained severely underemployed even during the "great prosperity" years of the 1920s. But Britain's problems were generally attributed by economists to structural changes, the decline in the traditional export industries in the "depressed areas" of Wales and the North brought about by the war and greatly aggravated by overvaluation of sterling with restoration of the pre-war parity in 1925—"the economic consequences of Mr Churchill", as Keynes put it. Another strand in mainstream thinking, associated especially with the name of Pigou, was that, in Beveridge's words (1930, p. xiv) "the question of unemployment [is] a question of wages". Since the wage is the price of labour, so the argument ran, it stands to reason that to increase the demand for labour it is necessary to reduce its price.

The Keynesian Revolution

During the 1920s, however, economists began to make inroads into the logic of Say's Law. Marshall and his school had answered Malthus's question "what happens if part of income is saved, not spent?" by pointing to the rate of interest (the price of capital) as the regulator which keeps saving (the supply of capital) in balance with investment (the demand for capital). Even before 1900 the Swedish economist, Knut Wicksell, had questioned this, saying that the rate of interest in the money market may not always equal the "natural" rate which would maintain saving and investment in balance at full employment. Robertson and Keynes now followed up this line of reasoning. But until well into the 1930s they thought of the problem in terms of fluctuations in the price level and focused on monetary policy as the appropriate instrument, and this was still the centre of Keynes's attention in the great opus *The Treatise on Money* on which he worked during the years of the Great Depression (1929–33).

As unemployment rose to 15 per cent in Britain, to 25 per cent in the USA and to 30 per cent in Germany, the capitalist world seemed overcome by what Keynes, in a 1931 lecture at Chicago University, called "the greatest economic catastrophe of the modern world" (Keynes 1931, p. 3). In moving words, he spoke of "the devastating effects that unemployment is bound to produce for the individual workers. The moral effects of enforced inactivity lasting week after week, or even month after month... Dull resignation to an uncontrollable fate and desperate rebellion against the injustice of an economic system that can afford no work to a man who is able and willing to do it...; it is almost a miracle that this situation has not led to grave social disturbance in many European countries" (*ibid.*, p. 47).

In the British public policy debate, Keynes supported Lloyd George's call for counter-cyclical public works and (briefly) tariff protection. Meanwhile, in the USA, Roosevelt fought the Depression with an array of measures, from increases in the price of gold (ostensibly to counter the decline in the price level) to public works as part of his New Deal, uninformed by any clear understanding of the economic problem, while Hitler in Germany got rid of unemployment through rearmament.

The analytical breakthrough came with Keynes's *General Theory* (1936). The emphasis shifted from fluctuations in money and prices to fluctuations in income and employment (a shift only partially reflected in the title in which money and prices still figured with employment). A capitalist economy, Keynes now argued, cannot be assumed to be in stable full employment equilibrium because (planned) saving may exceed (planned) investment. The rate of interest may not function as an effective equilibrating mechanism (and a cut in the general level of wages does not help because wages are income as well as cost). Underemployment is due to deficiency of aggregate demand (spending), and the appropriate remedy is for the government to maintain aggregate spending at full employment level by a counter-cyclical fiscal policy.

The full employment objective stands at the centre of the *General Theory*. It appears in the first few (rather esoteric) pages when Keynes refers to "inexactness of adjustment which stands in the way of continuous full employment" (1936, p. 7). A few pages later follows Keynes's definition: "The absence of 'involuntary' unemployment. This state of affairs we shall describe as 'full' employment, both 'frictional' and 'voluntary' unemployment being consistent with 'full' employment thus defined", (p. 15). A little further on, an alternative definition (the full import of which became apparent only much later) is provided: "A situation in which aggregate employment is inelastic in response to an increase in effective demand for its output" (p. 26).

Diligent search has turned up, as the first appearance of the term "full employment" in the English (or American) literature, nothing earlier than a brief note by Keynes in the *American Economic Review* for December 1933 (p. 316). The Oxford English Dictionary, blissfully unaware of the extensive discussion in and around the *General Theory*, gives priority to Crowther's *Outline of Money* (1940).

In fact, the term "full employment", like the term "economic development" (Arndt 1981), appears to have occurred first in Australia. The Australian economist E. R. Walker in his book *Australia in the World Depression*, based on his Cambridge PhD thesis and completed early in 1933, referred several times to "full employment of available resources" (Walker 1933, p. 188ff). But the context was entirely theoretical, a discussion of the turning point in the trade cycle. Even in his 1936 book on *Unemployment Policy* there is no mention of full employment as a policy objective; the discussion of policy measures is concerned only with "the diminution of unemployment" (Walker 1936, p. 79), and this applies to the Australian economic literature throughout the 1930s. In the special issue of the *Annals* of the American Academy of Political and Social Science of November 1931, *An Economic Survey of Australia,* edited by D. B. Copland, there is an article on "Unemployment and its Amelioration" (Copland 1931, p. 176); Giblin in his Inaugural Lecture (in which he developed a version of the multiplier before R. F. Kahn) was concerned only to assess the effect on national income of a fall in exports of £50 million (Giblin 1930, p. 10); and Theodore, Treasurer in the Scullin Labor government of 1929–32, advocated an expansionary monetary policy "which would stimulate production, reduce unemployment and restore prices to their 1929 level" (Schedvin 1970, p. 226). Full employment as a policy objective does not seem to have been put forward until World War II.

In the latter 1930s, while the Keynesian analysis was assimilated by the economic profession, the British and American economies experienced halting recovery from the Depression. In 1937, with unemployment in Britain still at almost 12 per cent, Keynes came to be concerned that the boom was approaching the danger point of inflationary pressures: "We are approaching, or have reached, the point where there is not much advantage in applying a further general stimulus at the centre We are in more need today of a rightly distributed demand than of a greater aggregate demand" (Keynes 1937). In the USA, A. H. Hansen, the chief expositor of Keynesian thinking, was even more concerned about the danger of secular stagnation to which Keynes had given some attention in the *General Theory* (e.g., Hansen 1939).

All these concerns were pushed into the background by the outbreak of World War II in September 1939. The demands and controls of war restored full employment in Britain, and within a few months after Pearl Harbor, in the USA. But it was the experience of wartime full employment and wartime thinking about the post-war world that conferred on the "full employment" objective the imprimatur of popular and official orthodoxy.

Planning for Post-war Full Employment

"Next to war, unemployment has been the most widespread, most insidious and most corroding malady of our generation: it is the specific social disease of western countries in our time" (*The Times,* 23 January 1943). So deeply and widely was this felt that Paul Samuelson was merely voicing a general consensus when he said, in a volume on *Post-war Economic Problems* that "the most important of [these] problems is that of providing for *continuing full employment*" (Harris 1943, p. 27). The post-war problem loomed as both a short-term and a long-term one. With post-World War I experience in mind, a severe post-war depression was widely expected; Samuelson predicted immediate post-war unemployment in the USA of 5 million; other predictions ran as high as 19 millions (Lekachman 1967, p. 136). Hansen feared a long-term problem: "This is the essence of secular stagnation: recoveries...leave a hard and seemingly immovable core of unemployment" (Hansen 1939, p. 370).

Full employment figures prominently among the plans for a better post-war world which engaged much of British and American public opinion, in a wave of idealism amidst the horrors of war. They poured forth in a torrent of articles, pamphlets and studies and were discussed in countless public meetings and in adult and army education classes. Official thinking about full employment after the war began in England as early as February 1941 when John Jewkes, Director of the Economic Section of the War Cabinet Secretariat, invited James Meade to examine the means by which a high and stable level of employment could be maintained beyond the end of the war (Cornish 1981, p. 1). In 1943, Sir William Beveridge published his report on *Social Security*, the blueprint for Britain's post-war welfare state. Meade wrote to Keynes: "The great public support which the Beveridge Report has received has suggested to me that there ought to be a similar publication on the subject of post-war unemployment" (which would incidentally provide an opportunity to explain to the public that the immediate post-war problem may be inflation rather than unemployment, though after two years, he added, we may be back in the 1930s). "What we really require is a Keynes Report to follow up the Beveridge Report" (Letter to Keynes, 8 January 1943, in Keynes 1980, p. 14f.). Keynes was unenthusiastic, but Meade pushed on. A Steering Committee on Post-War Employment was appointed in July 1943 to oversee the preparation of a White Paper. Meanwhile, Beveridge was preparing his unofficial report on *Full Employment in a Free Society* (Beveridge 1944). Both appeared almost simultaneously in 1944, the White Paper under the sober title *Employment Policy* (White Paper 1944).

The British White Paper stimulated similar work in other countries, including the USA and Australia. In the USA, Senator Murray's Full Employment Bill finally passed Congress in the much attenuated form of the Employment Act of 1946 which aimed merely at "conditions under which there will be afforded useful employment for those able, willing and seeking work, and to promote maximum employment, production and purchasing power" (Lekachman 1967, p. 140). In Australia, Prime Minister Curtin, on his return from London in July 1944, authorised the preparation of a document comparable to the British White Paper. The basis for this was a document drafted by Dr H. C. Coombs in 1942. Where the British White Paper had defined the objective with studied moderation as "a high and stable" level of employment, the Australian White Paper aimed forthrightly at "Full Employment in Australia" (Commonwealth of Australia 1944). Coombs defined this as a state in which "there will be a few more jobs available than men and women to fill them, that there will be a slight but persistent shortage of labour" (Coombs 1944, cited Cornish 1981, p. 23). It was strenuous lobbying by the Australian delegation to the San Francisco conference of 1945 which secured the inclusion in the United Nations Charter of a pledge by all member countries to promote full employment (Articles 5–56) (Crisp 1965).

When World War II ended in 1945, the "full employment" objective had come to be accepted by governments and public opinion in all Western countries. Few would have dissented from the view expressed by one of the British government's most senior advisers: "No Government of the future can hope to stay for long in power if it lets large-scale unemployment destroy the physical and spiritual condition of life among the people" (Franks, 1947, p. 21).

The 'Full Employment' Target

The contrast between the British (and American) words "high and stable level of employment" and the Australian "full employment" reflected widespread uncertainty and intensive debate about the proper target. Beveridge said in his report that "full employment means...having always more vacant jobs than unemployed men" (Beveridge 1944, p. 18). He thought that, allowing for "frictional unemployment" (workers moving between jobs, etc.), this would imply "a reduction of unemployment to not more than 3 per cent" (*ibid.*, p.21). Keynes was sceptical: "No harm in aiming at 3 per cent unemployed, but I shall be surprised if we succeed" (Keynes 1980, p. 381). In 1937, as we saw, he had doubted whether, with unemployment still at 11–12 per cent, aggregate demand could safely be further stimulated. During the war, when unemployment was down to 0.5 per cent, he suggested 4.5 per cent as an equilibrium level of unemployment for peacetime (Hutchison 1981, p. 118). Joan Robinson, in a 1946 paper, took the view that 5 per cent should be manageable but attempts to reduce the unemployment rate to 2 per cent "would involve great sacrifices of liberty" (Robinson 1951, p. 106). The Oxford economists who did much of the spadework for Beveridge explained that there was a statistical minimum of "frictional and seasonal unemployment" and that this, depending on "mutable institutional factors" could vary between 5 and 2 per cent (Oxford Institute 1944, p. iii). Pigou thought "a moderate inflationary tendency if it enables unemployment to be kept at a low level would be well worth enduring" (Pigou 1944, p. 72). But Meade feared that unemployment might need to be as high as 10 per cent to secure wage inflation of no more than 2 per cent (Meade 1948, p. 71).

At issue in this debate was "full-employment income" defined as the point at which further expansion of aggregate demand (whether private or government spending) would run into production bottlenecks, rising costs and aggressive wage demands (Hansen, quoted Lekachman 1967, p. 116). This was the issue which was later expressed in the Phillips curve trade-off between wage inflation and unemployment, in Friedman's "natural" rate of unemployment and more recently in NAIRU (the non-accelerating-inflation rate of unemployment).

To everyone's surprise, the fear that there would be a severe post-war depression, as after World War I, proved unfounded. The unwinding of the war economy was accomplished fairly smoothly and quickly, as private investment and consumption expanded using wartime forced savings to make up for wartime shortages. Within a few years, the Western countries began to enjoy a sustained period of virtually full employment without serious inflation, and before long the meaning of full employment was progressively, and more and more ambitiously, redefined. In England, Joan Robinson came to think any target above 2 per cent "cold-blooded and out-of-the-question"; R. F. Kahn declared the Beveridge 3 per cent target obsolete; and Harrod claimed that Keynes (who had died in 1946) would have objected to raising the unemployment rate from 1.5 to 2.5 per cent (cited Hutchison 1981, p. 126).

In Australia, by 1960, according to Prime Minister Chifley's biographer, the Australian White Paper's "ideas of the criterion of full employment...proved much too cautious in terms of post-war reality as it later emerged" (Crisp 1961, p. 194). In 1965, the Vernon Report conceived "full employment in terms of a zone, rather than a precise figure" and suggested that "the full-employment zone may be considered as commencing when registered unemployment as a proportion of the work force lies between 1.0 and 1.5 per cent" (Committee of Economic Enquiry 1965, p. 34). In 1970, Professor John Nevile quoted the 1957 Budget Speech which spoke of the "well adjusted situation we now enjoy" when the seasonally adjusted level of unemployment was about 1.5 per cent, but thought we could and should do better: "The present author believes the distress caused by unemployment is of sufficient importance for the Australian community not to be content until unemployment is at least reduced to 1 percent" (Nevile 1970, p. 30).

That very year, 1970, saw the beginning of the end of the post-war golden age. A commodity boom, partly triggered by US deficit expenditure to finance the Vietnam war, raised inflation rates worldwide, reaching its peak in the 1973–74 OPEC doubling of the price of oil and leading to the abandonment of the Bretton Woods regime of stable exchange rates. In Australia the policies of the Whitlam Government contributed to a wage explosion. But, contrary to the conventional wisdom of the Phillips curve, unemployment and inflation *both* got worse. The world encountered the hitherto unheard-of phenomenon of stagflation. In Australia, while the average rate of inflation rose from 3.8 per cent in the 1960s to 13.2 per cent in the 1970s, the unemployment rate also rose from 1.7 to 3.6 per cent. From then on, unemployment continued to rise, with cyclical fluctuations, to 6.7 per cent in 1979 and 9 per cent in 1983. This year (1994) the prime minister, Mr Keating, expressed satisfaction that the unemployment percentage had been brought down from 11 to 10 per cent. The situation, while somewhat better in the USA, is even worse in much of western Europe.

What Went Wrong?

The first point to note is that the present situation is very different from that of the 1930s. During the Great Depression, unemployment rose because production and national income, prices and employment declined catastrophically. Between 1929 and 1933, GNP declined by 30 per cent in the USA and 10 per cent in Australia, industrial production by 45 per cent in the USA and 30 per cent in Australia. US wholesale prices and money supply also fell by one-third. Nothing like this has happened in the past decade. Production has fallen slightly in recession years, but employment has continued to grow and inflation accelerated until 1990 in Australia and most OECD countries. Yet unemployment has remained stubbornly high. Why?

The question has been debated endlessly, and I do not pretend to have the answers. But one can point to less and more likely contributing factors. The contrast between the experience of the 1930s and 1980s suggests that deficiency of aggregate demand which was clearly the main cause in the 1930s has, except to a minor extent in temporary recessions, not played this role in the 1980s. Massive deficit finance therefore is not now an appropriate policy. One is tempted to suggest that, most of the time, the OECD economies are at "full employment level of income" in Hansen's sense of the point at which further expansion of aggregate demand would run into "production bottlenecks, rising costs and aggressive wage demands". Unemployment appears again, as Beveridge thought in 1909, to be a problem of "disorganisation of the labour market". The Keynesian revolution with its emphasis on aggregate demand has, it seems, virtually become irrelevant.

It is frequently suggested that the root of the problem is the decline in the rate of economic growth in OECD countries, from around 5–6 per cent p.a. in the 1950s and 1960s to 2–3 per cent at present. No doubt a higher rate of growth of output would bring a higher rate of growth of employment. But this merely pushes the question further back. Why has growth declined? The hypothesis sometimes advanced that the world is in the downward phase of a long (Kondratiev) cycle, following the upward phase of the 1950s and 1960s, is not very plausible. Investment opportunities, arising from technological change and population growth, are not obviously less than in the 1920s and 1960s. For the same reasons Keynes' and Hansen's spectre of "secular stagnation" does not provide a plausible explanation.

The contrast between slow growth in the OECD countries and rapid growth in the countries of East Asia suggests another broad explanation; economic growth has slowed down in OECD countries because, in the context of their democratic political process, it has increasingly come into conflict with other policy objectives, especially equity and the environment, and also the regulatory constraints these call forth. Governments in the "insulated states" (Haggard 1990) of East Asia have been able to pursue economic growth much less hindered, as yet, by such pressures.

Three or four other developments in OECD economies, some not unrelated to the last point, are widely believed to be contributing to the problem. One is mismatch of skills arising from three ways in which demand for relatively unskilled labour has been declining: technological change, especially the computer revolution, which has displaced labour in offices; microeconomic reform which, for the sake of higher productivity and competitiveness, has involved job-shedding in the public and private sectors; and loss of comparative advantage in labour-intensive industries, such as textiles, to newly industrialising countries. A second is the income support provided by the dole and other welfare services; this has undoubtedly reduced the pressure on people to take any job anywhere. (In Indonesia, there is little open unemployment; only middle class youth with some educational qualifications, able to rely on family support while they look for attractive employment, can afford to be unemployed.)

Whether the great increase in the female participation rate should be added as a third factor is more debatable. In so far as it cannot be accommodated by a corresponding increase in aggregate demand for labour, it should be seen as another source of mismatch of skills or frictional unemployment. The consequent spread of part-time employment certainly further blurs the definition of "full" employment.

A fourth, and perhaps the most fundamental, is the rise since the 1930s in NAIRU—the rate to which unemployment can be reduced before skill shortages and wage pressures push up inflation. One reason for this rise is the greatly increased power of trade unions since the 1930s, only partially offset by a recent opposite trend. Another is the greatly increased elasticity of inflationary expectations, itself the result of decades of life in a full-employment economy. It is the readiness with which firms, trade unions, consumers and speculators respond to any signs of higher inflation with inflationary behaviour, pushing up prices, that makes governments so reluctant to adopt expansionary policies or carry them very far into a cyclical upswing.

Some relate the rise in NAIRU to the breakdown of the Bretton Woods system in the 1970s. The national monetary autonomy afforded by floating exchange rates implied freedom from international pressure for responsible fiscal and monetary policies. International capital mobility virtually rules out a return to the international discipline of pegged exchange rates, and the European Community's difficulties in achieving a single currency point to the need for some flexibility. But this merely underlines the dilemma for macroeconomic policy in the world economy of the 1990s.

Whether or not this diagnosis of the causes of the problem makes it easier to develop effective remedies, it clearly makes it a lot more difficult to define "full employment".

References

Aftalion, A. (1908), "La réalité des surproductions générales", *Revue d'Economie Politique.*

Arndt, H. W. (1944), *The Economic Lessons of the Nineteen-Thirties,* OUP, London.

—— (1981), "Economic Development: A Semantic History", *Economic Development and Cultural Change,* April.

Beveridge, W. H. (1909), *Unemployment: A Problem of Industry,* 2nd ed. 1930, Longmans, London.

—— (1944), *Full Employment in a Free Society,* Allen & Unwin, London.

Committee of Economic Enquiry (1965), (Vernon) *Report,* Vol. 1.

Commonwealth of Australia (1945), *Full Employment in Australia* (White Paper), Parliamentary Papers No 11.

Coombs, H. C. (1944), "A High Employment Economy", Joseph Fisher Memorial Lecture, University of Adelaide.

Copland, D. B. (ed.) (1931), *An Economic Survey of Australia, The Annals,* Philadelphia.

Cornish. S. (1981), *Full Employment in Australia: The Genesis of the White Paper,* Department of Economic History, Faculty of Economics, Australian National University, Canberra.

Crisp, L. F. (1961), "The Australian Full Employment Pledge at San Francisco", *Australian Quarterly,* Vol. 19, No 1.

—— (1965), *Ben Chifley*, Longmans, Melbourne.
Franks, O. (1947), *Central Planning and Control in War and Peace*, London School of Economics, Longman Green & Co, London.
Giblin, L. F. (1930), *Australia 1930*, Melbourne University Press.
Hawtrey, R. G. (1913), *Good and Bad Trade*, Constable, London.
Haggard, S. (1990), *Pathways from the Periphery: The Politics of Growth in the Newly Industrializing Countries*, Cornell University Press, Ithaca.
Hansen, A. H. (1939), "Economic Progress and Declining Population Growth", *American Economic Review*, reprinted in *Readings in Business Cycle Theory*, Blakiston, Philadelphia, 1944.
Harris, S. E. (1943), *Post-war Economic Problems*, McGraw Hill, New York.
Hicks, J. R. (1966), "Growth and Anti-Growth", *Oxford Economic Papers*, November.
Hutchison, T. W. (1953), A *Review of Economic Doctrines, 1870–1929*, Clarendon Press, Oxford.
—— (1969), *Economics and Economic Policy in Britain, 1946–66*, Allen & Unwin, London.
—— (1981), "Keynes versus the Keynesians" (Hobart Paper 1977), in *The Politics and Philosophy of Economics*, Blackwell, Oxford.
Keynes, J. M. (1931), "An Economic Analysis of Unemployment", in Q. Wright (ed.) *Unemployment as a World Problem*, University of Chicago Press 1932.
—— (1933), Letter, *American Economic Review*, December.
—— (1936), *The General Theory of Employment, Interest and Money*, Macmillan, London.
—— (1937), "How to Avoid a Slump", *The Times*, London, 13 January.
—— (1980), *Collected Writings*, Vol. XXVII, Macmillan, London.
Lekachman, R. (1967), *The Age of Keynes*, Allen & Unwin, London.
Marshall, A. (1890), *Principles of Economics*, Macmillan, London.
Meade, J. E. (1948), *Planning and the Price Mechanism*, Allen & Unwin, London.
Mitchell, W. C. (1913), *Business Cycles*, National Bureau of Economic Research, New York.
—— (1923), "Business Cycles", reprinted in *Readings in Business Cycle Theory*, Blakiston, Philadelphia, 1944.
Nevile, J. (1970), *Fiscal Policy in Australia*, Cheshire, Melbourne.
Oxford Institute of Statistics (1944), *The Economics of Full Employment*, Blackwell, Oxford.
Pigou, A. C. (1944), *Lapses from Full Employment*, Macmillan, London.
Robertson, D. H. (1915), A *Study of Industrial Fluctuations*, P. S. King, London.
Robinson, Joan (1945), *Collected Economic Papers*, Vol. 1, 1951, Blackwell, Oxford.
Schedvin, C. B. (1970), *Australia and the Great Depression*, Sydney University Press, Sydney.
The Times, (1943), Editorial, 23 January.
Walker, E. R. (1933), *Australia in the World Depression*, P. S. King, London.
—— (1936), *Unemployment Policy*, Angus & Robertson, Sydney.
White Paper, *Employment Policy*, CMD 6527, HMSO, London.

Part III

NATIONAL ACCOUNTS AND EXTERNAL RELATIONS

11

Public Finance and National Income

This note, an exercise in Keynesian income theory, discussed whether budget operations should be treated as a dependent or independent variable.

Originally published as "Public Finance and the National Income" in the *Economic Record*, December 1948.

Professor Tew, in his Note in the *Economic Record* of June 1948,[1] argues plausibly against the conventional treatment of public loan expenditure as an "independent" component of the national income in multiplier theory; but the matter can hardly be left where he leaves it in his Note.

It has generally been recognised that any hard and fast distinction between "independent" and "dependent" components of the national income such as is implied in the theory of the multiplier is unrealistic. Even the components singled out in Keynes's original highly simplified model, private investment and consumption, were admitted to fit only approximately into the two categories, private investment being itself a function of income and consumption being quite capable of independent variations. In fact, one might say that the theory of the multiplier was originally little more than a striking and illuminating formulation of the hypothesis that the consumption function can, for purposes of broad aggregative analysis, be assumed to be fairly stable, so that consumption can be treated as a function of income and income as a function of investment.

The origin of the multiplier concept as a device for drawing attention to a particularly important functional relationship in a highly simplified model of the economy makes it rather doubtful whether much is gained by trying to press all the variables of a more complex and realistic model into the multiplier framework. Certainly, the division between "independent" and "dependent" factors is bound to be even more arbitrary than in the case of private investment and consumption, and the appropriate classification will largely depend on the institutional framework which is assumed.

In relation to public finance, for instance, a case could be made for treating budget operations as entirely "dependent." This would be appropriate wherever we can assume, as a first approximation, that the budget is balanced annually and that independent changes in the rates of taxation can safely be neglected. On these assumptions, which are not so very remote from Gladstonian finance, public finance could be treated as affecting only the size of the multiplier. In modern conditions,

1 B. Tew, "A Note on the Multiplier," *Economic Record*, June 1948, pp. 109–111.

however, such treatment which makes public finance a completely passive factor is obviously inappropriate.

The conventional procedure since Keynes has been to treat budget operations as affecting the multiplicand by making "loan expenditure," or rather the budget deficit (or surplus), the independent component. This procedure has the great advantage over the first that it emphasises budget policy, side by side with private investment (and the balance of payments) as the main (relatively) independent variables. Like the first, it can never be more than a rough approximation, reasonably realistic wherever we can assume that the levels of public expenditure and taxation are determined primarily with an eye to the size of the budget deficit (positive, negative, or zero). Professor Tew objects to this procedure on the ground that the budget deficit cannot be assumed to be completely uninfluenced by changes in the national income. True, but on so rigid an interpretation of the criterion of independence probably no component of the national income would qualify, certainly not private investment. At least as weighty an objection to the conventional procedure is that it treats the full amount of tax revenue as a negative item which implies the quite unrealistic assumption that taxation falls wholly on private expenditure and none of it on saving.

Professor Tew's proposed alternative, to treat "total public expenditure" as the independent component, is not much better. By his rigorous test of "independence" it does not qualify either, as he himself admits; it is preferable to "loan expenditure" on this score only in so far as tax revenue is, on the whole, more likely to be influenced by changes in the national income than public expenditure. It escapes the second objection only by neglecting taxation policy altogether as a potential determinant of national income. If, as Professor Tew may have had in mind, taxation policy is to be treated as a separate factor influencing the multiplicand, new difficulties arise. If we simply deduct tax revenue from the multiplicand we come up against the objection already mentioned. The alternative procedure of allowing for taxation policy by including in the multiplicand any changes in consumption induced by changes in tax rates breaks down in practice over the impossibility of differentiating between these "independent" and dependent changes in consumption expenditure.

One cannot help suspecting that statistical calculations of the multiplier are in any case bound to be so rough, and the possibilities of using the results of any such calculations for practical purposes so hedged around with qualifications, that it does not matter very much which procedure is used.[2] The real answer would seem to be that for most purposes for which we need to analyse the effects of budget operations on the national income—whether it is in connection with forecasts or with problems

2 Of course, the size of the multiplier which is obtained by the two methods may differ substantially, but for any practical purposes it will have to be interpreted in terms of the method used, and that will usually mean going back to a more detailed analysis. Assume, for instance, that an attempt is made to calculate the multiplier and the data show that, in a given period, national income increased by £100 million, private investment by £25 million, government expenditure and tax revenue both by £25 million (the budget remaining balanced) and consumption by £50 million. In that case, the method favoured by Professor Tew would yield a multiplier of 2, the 'loan expenditure' method a multiplier of 4. But these figures would mean nothing except in relation to the method by which they were obtained.

of budget policy—the technique of multiplier analysis is altogether too crude an instrument.

For such purposes, it is better to follow Lord Beveridge and Mr Kaldor by considering each branch of budget policy separately as it affects total national outlay. Public expenditure is itself a component of income-generating total outlay and indirectly affects private outlay—consumption through the multiplier effect and perhaps also investment through the "acceleration" effect. Taxation affects total national outlay through its effects on private outlay.[3] Finally, account must also be taken of a factor which is usually ignored in this type of analysis, the possible effects on total outlay of different methods of financing the budget deficit, whether via interest rates on private investment or directly on private consumption.[4] Such an analysis can be pursued to any degree of refinement which is considered necessary for the purpose in hand.

3 A variant of this approach which indirectly makes use of the multiplier concept in the form of the consumption function has recently been used both by Mr Kaldor and in the American post-war national income forecasts where the tax structure is included in the parameter. (*Cf.* N. Kaldor, Appendix C to Beveridge, *Full Employment in a Free Society*; also J.R.N. Stone and E.F. Jackson, "Economic Models with Special Reference to Mr Kaldor's System," *Economic Journal*, December 1946.)

4 The most obvious relevance of this aspect is, of course, in a war economy.

12

A Pioneer of National Income Statistics

Sir Timothy Coghlan, Government Statistician of New South Wales, 1886–1905, not only made NSW for a time the country with the best national income statistics in the world, but also made major original contributions to national income accounting, especially the first parallel estimates of national income, output and expenditure. The article drew attention to his contributions.

Originally published as "A Pioneer of National Income Estimates", in the *Economic Journal*, December 1949.

The name of T. A. (later Sir Timothy) Coghlan is probably known to a few outside Australia as that of the author of a monumental social history of Australia.[1] In Australia he is also remembered as the Government Statistician of New South Wales, who, during the years 1886–1905, with great industry and fine judgment, made New South Wales for a time the country with the best official statistics in the world and laid the foundation for the collection and presentation of official statistics for the whole Australian Commonwealth.[2] But it seems to be little known, outside the narrow circle of those who have worked on the national income of Australia,[3] that Coghlan was also a pioneer of national-income estimates. It would seem that his estimates were the first official estimates of national income anywhere; and he also seems to have been the first (if Gregory King be left in a class by himself) to have attempted parallel estimates of national income, output and expenditure on lines at least approaching modern techniques.[4]

1 T. A. Coghlan, *Labour and Industry in Australia*, 4 vols., OUP, 1918.

2 Coghlan was born in Sydney in 1856. He studied engineering and entered the New South Wales public service in 1873 as an engineer. It was by an accident that he turned to statistics when he was appointed, in 1886, to the newly created post of Government Statistician. The trial period of appointment grew into a twenty years' occupancy of the post, during which he greatly developed the statistical services of the colony and made himself a statistician of the front rank. Among his special interests was demography, which figures largely in his numerous semi-official publications. His standing was recognised by his election as Honorary Fellow of the Royal Statistical Society in 1893. According to the author of the obituary notice in the *Journal of the Royal Statistical Society* (1926, p. 785), Coghlan's evidence in favour of graduation and differentiation of income taxation before the British Select Committee on Income Tax in 1905 had some influence on the Committee's recommendations. In 1905 Coghlan retired as Government Statistician to take up the post of New South Wales Agent-General in London, which he filled, with a few short interruptions, until his death in 1926.

3 There are references to Coghlan's estimates in F. C. Benham, *The Prosperity of Australia* (P. S. King, 1930, pp. 26f.) and in C. Clark and J. G. Crawford, *The National Income of Australia* (Sydney 1938, pp. 53–55). But the extensive bibliography of national income in Bowley's *Studies in the National Income* (p. 209) refers only to Coghlan's later estimates of 1897 and 1902 for Australia as a whole.

The year-book of New South Wales which Coghlan initiated in 1887 and which appeared from then until 1901 over his name under the title *The Wealth and Progress of New South Wales*.[5] From 1890 onwards, Coghlan also reprinted these estimates, and later extended them to the other "Australasian" colonies, in a serial publication, *The Seven Colonies of Australasia*,[6] the predecessor of the *Commonwealth Year Book*.

Coghlan, in all his published work, was extremely sparing with references in his sources and explanations of the methods by which he arrived at his estimates.[7] Fortunately, however, the working sheets for a number of his published volumes have been preserved.[8] These contain, in his own hand and in meticulous detail, every step in the calculations for most of his estimates and enable us to trace his sources and methods. In the main, Coghlan relied upon the major official collections of statistics such as censuses, but also on newspapers and journals and personally gathered information. Where other sources failed, he did not hesitate to make guesses—sometimes startlingly daring guesses—in the light of his own very sound judgment and intimate knowledge of the economy of New South Wales.

Income

Coghlan's first estimates of the national income of New South Wales were for the years 1886, 1887 and 1889.[9] In the absence of any income-tax data (income tax was not introduced in New South Wales until 1897) he relied chiefly on census data and output estimates. He therefore presented his estimates divided up according to "sources of income." As he pointed out later, these early estimates were "more a matter of speculation than exact calculation."[10] For the years 1887 and 1889 he also published estimates of wage incomes for each industry group.[11]

4 These claims cannot be fully substantiated without reference to some early works in the literature of national-income estimates which are not accessible to the author of this essay. It would be of some interest to hear whether the claims can be challenged.

5 T. A. Coghlan, *The Wealth and Progress of New South Wales, 1886/7–1900/1*, series of 13 volumes, Government Printer, Sydney, 1887–1902; hereafter quoted as *W & P*.

6 T. A. Coghlan, *A Statistical Account of the Seven Colonies of Australasia, 1890–1901/2*, series of 9 volumes, Government Printer, Sydney, 1890–1902; two further volumes were published in 1904 under the title *A Statistical Account of Australia and New Zealand 1902/3 and 1903/4*.

7 In the case of his official publications, his plea of defence would probably have been reasons of space and the conventional notion of his time that *official* figures required no further authority.

8 Working sheets relating to the issues of *W &P 1886/7, 1887/8, 1888/9, 1890/1, 1892, 1894 and 1900/1*, and a few relating to the issues of the *Seven Colonies* have been preserved. They have kindly been made available to the author by Mr S. R. Carver, New South Wales Government Statistician, Sydney.

9 *W & P 1886/7, p. 420; 1887/8, p. 552; 1889/90, p. 705; 1893*, p. 697. The last of these estimates was published by Coghlan as an estimate for "the years 1892" (*W & P 1893*, p. 697). This, as far as it is now possible to ascertain, seems to have been an error; as the working sheets show, the estimate was based on the occupational structure of the 1891 Census and on official production data (e.g., for mineral production) for 1891.

10 *W & P 1893*, p. 697.

11 *W & P 1887/8*, p. 552, and *1889/90*, p. 705.

Table I Sources of national income of New South Wales (£1,000)

	1886[a]	1887	1889	1891	1894
Pastoral industry	10,500		13,400	13,326	9,292
Dairy farming		17,850	1,400		5,118
Agriculture	3,750		5,650	5,209	
Forestry and fisheries	b			c	410
Mineral production	3,000		4,450	4,554	4,264
Manufacturing	5,750	5,776	5,700	9,840	7,940
House rents[d]	7,000	5,900	6,120	6,883	5,661
Professional	2,500	2,760	2,700		3,129[e]
Civil servants and government employees	2,500	1,405	1,620[g]	5,108[f]	2,978h
Other tradesmen and labourers	8,000	—	—	—	—
Other mechanical and labouring	—	8,409	—	—	—
Personal and household service	1,500	2,018[i]	4,680	4,397	3,574
Food distribution	b				
Trade and commerce, n.e.i.	3,500	—	—	—	—
Commerce, trade, etc.	—	—	8,000	6,338	7,468
Trade and shipping	—	3,168	—	—	—
Other trade and earnings of capital	—	4,278	—	—	—
Shipping	2,500	—	1,800[j]	3,931	3,184
Transport (by land)	—	—			
Construction	—	—	5,870	6,414	5,834
Female wage earnings	—	2,711	—	—	—
Miscellaneous pursuits	—	—	1,560	400	228
Total	*50,500*	*54,275*	*62,950*	*66,400*	*59,080*

Notes:

[a] See comment, page 119.

[b] No allowance for this occupation in 1886 estimate.

[c] Probably included in "miscellaneous pursuits."

[d] In the estimates for 1886, 1887 and 1889 and 1889 this item included rents of business properties outside the primary and secondary industries.

[e] Professional and municipal-service incomes.

[f] Excludes state railway and postal employees' earnings included under specific designations.

[g] Includes earnings of state railway employees.

[h] Earnings of all state employees, other than railway employees.

[i] This item, like all others for specific industries in the 1887 estimate, excludes female earnings.

[j] Excludes wages and profits of state railways.

The working sheets show how Coghlan gradually refined his methods for successive estimates. The first estimate for 1886 was crude indeed. Incomes from primary industry were derived from his own output estimates with some adjustments for costs (such as value of seed in the case of agriculture). Income from trade and commerce was obtained by adding 5 per cent of the sum of exports and imports to the published net profits of banks and financial institutions; income from manufacturing by taking 70 per cent of the sum of the aggregate value of machinery and a figure of £1,000 per factory to represent wages and profits; wage and professional incomes in other industries by assigning figures for average annual earnings (based on wage-rate

Table II Types of national income of New South Wales (£1,000)

	1891	1894	1898
Wage-earners	25,500	23,636	29,679
Persons working on own account	7,326	6,959	8,176
Professional	5,108	5,633	
Civil servants			2,539
Employers with earnings of capital owned in New South Wales	18,533	14,181	19,505
House rents	6,883	5,661	
Absentee incomes	3,050	3,010	4,527
Total	*66,400*	*59,080*	*54,426*

data with allowance for idle days) to broad occupational groups whose sizes were obtained from revised census data of 1881. In the later estimates the latter procedure was greatly refined by applying separate figures of annual earnings to small sub-groups of wage and salary-earners, including some primary and all manufacturing industries. Some industry groups ignored in the first estimates were added, and the estimates of profit incomes improved by using several (still crude) methods as checks upon each other.

The normal decennial census of 1891, coupled with a special Census of Industries held for the first time in the same year, enabled Coghlan to produce a considerably improved estimate for 1891[12] which he considered "a fair approximation to the amount and to the sources of incomes."[13] A new estimate on the same lines was made for 1894.[14] Table I reproduces these five estimates.

The estimates for 1891 and 1894 were also published in the nowadays more familiar form of income accounts by types of income. The introduction of income tax in 1897 enabled Coghlan for the first time to draw on income-tax returns for his estimates of national income.[15] The result was the estimate for 1898. This appeared only in the form of division by types of income.[16]

Table II gives Coghlan's three estimates of income in this form. From 1899 onwards Coghlan published four successive estimates of the national income of Australia and New Zealand which contain totals for national income of New South Wales.[17]

All Coghlan's income estimates were estimates of private income produced. He excluded government property income (e.g., the profits of the state railways and tramways) even though data for this were readily available, but generally included

12 *W & P 1893*, p. 697; see also note 5, p. 617.

13 *Ibid.*

14 *W & P 1894*, p. 749.

15 *W & P 1897/8*, p. 967. Coghlan explains that these estimates "are based upon the statistics of income subject to taxation supplied by the taxation department, and upon the direct statements of pastoralists, manufacturers, and other employers of labour" (*ibid.*). Unfortunately, the working sheets relating to these estimates do not seem to have survived.

16 A slightly revised form of this estimate appeared in *W & P 1898/9*, p. 927.

17 *Seven Colonies 1899/1900*, p. 736; *1901/2*, p. 764; *Australia and N.Z. 1902/3*, p. 322; *1903/4*, p. 530.

incomes accruing to foreign residents.[18] The incomes of banks and other financial institutions were not shown separately but "included with the industries from which they are primarily derived." Thus, in 1891, "the income derived from the pastoral industry is set down as £13,326,000, but a very large portion of this amount consists of the earnings of financial institutions, though, as might naturally be supposed, the exact amount so earned and the amount to be set down as belonging to the nominal owners cannot be determined with any pretension to accuracy."[19] The figures for rent of dwellings included imputed rents of owner-occupiers. Coghlan nowhere discussed the national-income concepts which he adopted. But on most points, the definitions underlying his estimates can be inferred. For instance, in deriving income estimates from output data, he made no allowance for depreciation, so that his estimates must be taken as estimates of *gross* national income or product.[20] Presumably, they represent national income at factor cost,[21] but included the (then very small) item of transfer payments.[22]

Expenditure

Coghlan's first estimate of the national expenditure of New South Wales was for the year 1888.[23] It was actually no more than an estimate of private consumption expenditure, presented under the quaint title "the Cost of Living." Coghlan added the explanation that "while the income amounted to 54 millions,[24] the expenditure amounted to 48.7 millions, the balance of 5.3 millions representing the savings of the people and the earning of absentees."[25]

Coghlan displayed considerable ingenuity in constructing his consumption estimates from very scanty data. The working sheets show that he relied mainly on estimates of average daily or weekly consumption per head or per family, which may have been obtained by more or less formal budget inquiries or from mere personal impressions. But he also drew on a great variety of other data. A pleasing example is his method of estimating annual expenditure on amusements by calculating the gross

18 In the estimates of Australian national income in the last two issues of *Seven Colonies*, however, the incomes of debenture holders in England are excluded on the interesting ground that "these are not in any colony subject to taxation" (*Seven Colonies, 1899/1900*, p. 736.)

19 *W & P 1893*, p. 698.

20 As shown by the attempt in the working sheets to allow for "wear and tear" in accounting for the difference between income and consumption; cf. Table III. The 1898 estimate, however, being based on income-tax returns, may represent *net* national income.

21 This would be the case even where the income estimates were derived from output data; for the latter were ostensibly based on values at the place of production.

22 Even the small portion of public-debt interest which accrued to domestic residents did not represent a transfer payment, since the debt was preponderantly productive. The working sheets, however, show that incomes of "pensioners and annuitants" were included in the national income.

23 *W & P 1888/9*, p. 334.

24 This does not appear to have been a separate estimate for 1888 but based on the 1887 estimate.

25 *W & P 1889/90*, p. 380.

Table III National expenditure of New South Wales (£1,000)

	1888	1890	1894	1897	1898	1900
Consumption						
Food and beverages	15,750	15,873	16,239	18,654	—	18,347
Fermented liquors	4,680	4,774	3,931	4,086	—	4,769
Tobacco	780	1,194	1,208	1,039	—	1,259
Clothing and drapery	7,470	8,392	6,567	7,158	—	8,231
Furniture	900	806	477	716	—	680
Rent (dwelling)	6,000	6,727	5,661	5,761	—	5,511
Locomotion	1,640	1,706	1,600	1,776	—	2,053
Fuel and light	1,780	1,797	1,853	1,960	—	1,760
Domestic service[a]	1,990	1,918	} 1,450	} 2,428	—	} 2,371
Lodgings	—	—				
Medical and nursing	920	1,428	1,432	1,519	—	1,512
Religion, charities and private education	860	716	754	944	—	1,213
Art and amusement	1,050	996	998	1,111	—	1,290
Books and newspapers	600	765	758	804	—	765
Direct taxes not falling on trade	—	—	—	734	—	519
State services, postage, succession dues	730	743	579	288[b]	—	398[b]
Other household expenses	1,550	2,815	1,950	2,013	—	1,866
Miscellaneous expenses	2,000	1,482	1,199	1,272	—	1,275
Total	*48,700*	*52,132*	*46,656*	*52,263*	*52,563*	*53,819*
Savings, etc.						
Local rates	—	—	506	—	793	—
Losses by fire[c]	—	—	—	—	(400)[c]	—
Calls by banks	—	—	750	—	—	—
Conditional purchase (of land from the Crown)	—	—	1,052	—	1,105	—
Life insurance premia	—	—	910	—	910	—
"Savings" (at least)	—	—	3,300	—	4,000	—
Absentee incomes	—	—	3,010	—	5,505[d]	—
Wear and tear[c]	—	—	—	—	—	—
(Balance)	—	—	(2,896)	—	(250)[e]	—
National (private gross) income	—	—	*59,080*	—	*64,426*	—

Notes:

[a] Includes other forms of "personal attendance."

[b] "Not incidential to earning incomes"; postage and telegrams only.

[c] Not published; taken from working sheets.

[d] The difference between this figure and the corresponding figure in Table II is due to the fact that the figure in Table II related to 1897, the 1898 estimate not having been available when the estimate of national income for 1898 was prepared.

[e] Clearly, this balance is too small to allow for depreciation and suggests that the figure of £4 million for (net) "Savings" was an overestimate.

takings of theatres, music halls, race courses and other places of entertainment on the basis of number of establishments, seating capacity, prices of tickets and number of performances per year.

New estimates of private consumption were later published for 1890, 1894, 1897 and 1900,[26] while somewhat peculiar partial revisions of the estimate for 1890 appeared as "estimates" for 1892 and 1893.[27] For two of the later years, Coghlan also attempted to bridge the gap between income and consumption by analysing the various forms of saving; but he had to content himself with the publication of estimates for a few of the component items.[28] These have been added to his estimates of consumption in Table III. Neither his publications nor his surviving working sheets show evidence of any attempts at independent estimates of private investment. When income tax was introduced, Coghlan was careful to add "direct taxes not falling on trade" as a new item in the Cost of Living. From 1900 onwards Coghlan published corresponding estimates of consumption for the whole of "Australasia."[29] Table III gives his five independent estimates of the national expenditure of New South Wales.

Output

In one sense, Coghlan's estimates of national income "by sources of income" really represent what would nowadays be called estimates of national output; and, as has been pointed out, they were at least partially obtained by the output method. But Coghlan also presented separate estimates of "general production" which were, in effect, the "value added" by the primary and secondary industries.[30] These were probably among his most careful and reliable estimates, although even here he frequently found it necessary to publish later revised estimates for individual items as better data came to hand.

For some of the major-industry groups, e.g., mineral production, official output estimates had been collected and published for many years back. Coghlan also had at his disposal crop returns for agriculture and had begun to obtain from manufacturing

26 *W & P 1890/1*, p. 743; *1894*, p. 308; *1897/8*, p. 1053; *1900/1*, p. 775.

27 *W & P 1892* (p. 849) presented the 1890 estimate, with revised figures only for food and drink, fermented liquor and tobacco, as "an estimate for 1892." *W & P 1893* (p. 781) gave a "revised" estimate for 1892 which merely added £2 million to the total, allocating £1.4 million for "lodging" to the item "personal attendance and service" and £0.6 million to the item "art and amusement"; these additions, which were hardly based on any very scientific calculation, disappeared again from the 1894 estimate. The slim extra volume of the series which was published during the depression while the 1894 volume of Wealth and Progress was delayed (T. A. Coghlan, *A Statistical Survey of New South Wales 1893/4*, p. 235) gives yet another version of the original 1890 estimate, with new estimates only for food and drink, fermented liquors and rent, as an "estimate for 1893." These are not the only occasions where Coghlan resorted to rather high-handed procedure, though they probably enhanced rather than diminished the practical usefulness of his volumes to his contemporaries and do not, as such, detract from the scientific quality of those of his estimates which were specifically prepared.

28 *W & P 1894*, p. 751; *1898/9*, p. 928.

29 *Seven Colonies 1901/2*, p. 367; *Australia and N.Z. 1902/3*, p. 536; *1903/4*, p. 901.

30 Value of output *minus* cost of raw materials and fuel. In aggregating the value of output of the various industry groups, Coghlan, from 1894 onwards, made further deductions for "raw materials twice included" (e.g., feeding-stuffs already included in agricultural output) *(W & P 1894*, p. 569). The figures for mineral production, however, seem to have been taken straight from the estimates of the Department of Mines without any deduction for the substantial value of fuel and other raw materials used.

Table IV Value of production of New South Wales (£1,000)

	1888	1890	1891	1894
Agriculture	4,150	4,131	3,584	3,396
Pastoral industry	13,059	13,360	14,725	11,168
Dairy farming		2,888	2,736	2,548
Forestry and fisheries	786	1,343	1,502	689
Mining	3,800	5,004	6,396	4,858
Manufacturing	5,770	(7,615)[a]	7,798	7,627
	—	—	—	*30,286*
Less: Raw materials twice included	—	—	—	185
Total primary production	—	*26,726*	—	—
"Value of production"	*27,564*	*(34,341)[a]*	*36,741*	*30,101*

Note: [a] Not included in original estimate; estimate for manufacturing from *W & P 1893*, p. 472.

firms annual returns of value of output and raw materials. Coghlan's first published estimate of "total production" was for 1888, as part of a corresponding estimate for all the "Australasian" colonies.[31] This was followed by new estimates for each subsequent year, and by two estimates, first published in 1894, for the two earlier census years, 1871 and 1881.[32] Table IV reproduces the estimates.[33]

Each of these estimates is reproduced here as it was first published. Almost every component estimate was later revised. Thus, the three earlier estimates of pastoral production were later brought into line with the 1894 estimate, which was the first to be based on a more careful attempt to value output at the place of production; the 1888 figure for agricultural production relates to the crop year 1887–8, the other three to the crop years ending in March of the following year; the mining estimates were later revised upward chiefly to allow for previously unrecorded production of iron; the estimates for dairy farming and manufactures were frequently adapted to changed classifications of subdivisions of the industries (undertaken largely in order to secure some uniformity with the official statistics of the other Australian colonies); and so forth. The apparent violent fluctuations in the output of forestry and fisheries must also be ascribed to revision of estimates which had to be made on exceedingly scanty data.

Coghlan was aware that the "valued added" by the various industries exceeded their contribution to the net national product,[34] and he appears to have made an attempt

31 *Seven Colonies 1890*, pp. 137 f.

32 *Seven Colonies 1894*, p. 269.

33 The estimates for 1888, 1890 and 1891 are from *Seven Colonies* (*1890*, pp. 137 f.; *1892*, p. 196; *1894*, p. 269); that for 1894 from *Wealth and Progress* (*1894*, p. 569). The estimate which is here presented as an estimate for 1891 was, like the corresponding national income estimate, published as an estimate for 1892; cf. note 5, p. 617.

34 He explained (*Seven Colonies 1901/2*, p. 689) that, after deducting wages from the value added in the process of manufacture, "rent, insurance, depreciation, etc." still had to be allowed for before one could state "the profits on the business." A more detailed list of the items composing the difference between value added and income produced was given by Coghlan's successor in the first issue of the *Official Yearbook of New South Wales 1904/5*, p. 238 : "A considerable margin must be allowed for such items as renewal of, and depreciation in, plant and machinery, etc., insurance, rent (when the buildings are not owned by the manufacturers) advertising rates taxes other than duty or income tax."

to ascertain the true income produced by the manufacturing industries but found the results too unsatisfactory for publication.[35]

The deficiency of his production data precluded Coghlan from presenting his income, output and expenditure estimates in the modern form, as parallel and alternative statements of the same magnitude. Neither could it be claimed that he fully appreciated the value of this procedure as a means of checking the reliability of each set of accounts. In other respects, however, Coghlan made bold use of his statistical data to reveal economically significant trends and relationships. Thus he calculated, and speculated on the significance of, the ratios of national income to (primary and secondary) "production" in each of the "Australasian" colonies;[36] the ratio of national (private) income to national (private) capital;[37] national income per head of working population;[38] the distribution of income between different income groups;[39] trends of real income (value of output at constant prices);[40] and international comparisons for several of these relationships.[41]

Yearbook of New South Wales 1904/5, p. 238 : "A considerable margin must be allowed for such items as renewal of, and depreciation in, plant and machinery, etc., insurance, rent (when the buildings are not owned by the manufacturers) advertising rates taxes other than duty or income tax."

35 *W & P 1893*, p. 473.

36 *Seven Colonies 1901/2*, p. 766.

37 *Australia and N.Z. 1902/3*, pp. 323 f. Besides his estimates of national income, Coghlan published annual estimates of the national (private and public) capital of New South Wales from 1887 until 1893 and again for 1898 and 1900 *(W & P 1886/7 –1900/1)*.

38 *Australia and N.Z. 1902/3*, p. 325.

39 *Ibid.*, p. 322.

40 *W & P 1900/1*, p. 751, and earlier volumes. The 1894 volume, for instance, gives the following table (p. 570):

Total Production of NSW

	At 1871 prices	At 1894 prices
	£	£
1871	15,370,000	8,314,730
1888	29,415,800	14,994,110
1891	56,914,500	28,658,000
1894	59,044,900	30,100,660

41 *W & P, 1900/1*, pp. 774, 776.

13

The Impact of Immigration

This article explained the economic costs and benefits of Australia's post-World War II immigration program. Its purpose was to allay popular fears that immigration would cause unemployment. Immigration, it argued, on the contrary, through its budget costs and through its stimulus to private investment and consumption, was more likely to add to inflationary pressures.

Originally published as a Commonwealth Bank *Monograph*, October 1950.

Population growth has a twofold economic significance. On the one side, it adds to the number of consumers, and thus to demand (or at least need) for consumer goods and services, and for capital equipment necessary to produce these additional goods and services. On the other side, it increases a country's productive capacity, most obviously by adding to its labour force. But it cannot be taken for granted that the two effects balance, the improvement in productive capacity just sufficing to meet the additional claims on resources.

Although economic advantage is not the primary object of the immigration program, it is generally believed that, in the long run, rapid population growth will facilitate the economic development of Australia's resources and thus make possible higher living standards for old and new Australians alike. But it is also generally recognised that, in its early phase, the immigration program will impose—and has indeed already begun to impose—a severe strain on the Australian economy.

Some of the reasons for this will have become apparent from the preceding papers. Messrs Strong and Lewis have indicated the large demands which the food requirements of a rapidly growing population will make on our rural industries. Mr Lawler has given reasons to believe that the projected increase in population may require an annual rate of gross investment, over a decade, some 40 per cent, above the 1948/49 rate. The object of this concluding paper is to develop this aspect further, to attempt a very rough assessment of the extent of the strain which the projected population increase will impose on our resources, and to indicate how ends may be made to meet.

1951/60 – A Theoretical Model

At bottom, the problem involves a comparison between the probable claims on resources and the resources likely to be available to meet these claims during the next (say) ten years. Table I shows how these two sides to the equation, aggregate demand for goods and services and aggregate supply of goods and services, were in fact made to balance in 1949/50.

Table I Market supply and demand, 1949/50
(Population, 8 million; 1949/50 prices)

	£ (million)	£ Per capita		£ (million)	£ Per capita
Local production (gross national product)	2,649	331	Personal consumption (incl. financial services £24m.)	1,669	209
Imports	635	79	Communal consumption (public authority expenditure on administration, education, health, etc.)	155	19
			Total consumption	*1,824*	*228*
			Gross private investment (incl. all motor vehicles and housing)	574	72
			Gross public investment (new works and maintenance)	181	22
			Total investment	*755*	*94*
			Defence	65	8
			Exports	640	80
Total market supply	*3,284*	*410*	*Total market demand*	*3,284*	*410*

Source: National Income and Expenditure 1949/50.

It will be seen that total local production (gross national product) and imports provided £3,284 million worth of goods and services, of which £1,824 million went to satisfy personal and communal consumption demand, £755 million were used to maintain and add to the nation's capital equipment, £65 million were used for defence, and £640 million exported (£5 million more than were needed to pay for imports).

Using the 1949/50 balance as our starting point, we have to ask ourselves whether the aggregate supply of goods and services which is likely to be available in the next decade will be sufficient to meet consumption, investment and defence demands.

Table II presents a hypothetical answer to this question. It must be emphasised at the outset that it rests on grossly simplified assumptions and should not in any way be taken as a forecast. It is designed merely as a framework of reference for further discussion and to illustrate the nature of the problem.

Table II is constructed on the following assumptions:

(a) Australia's population will grow from 8 millions in 1919/50 at the rate of 250,000 per annum.

(b) Per capital real consumption will grow at the rate of 1 per cent, per annum.

(c) Gross investment will remain constant at a rate of £850 million per annum. This figure is based on Mr Lawler's estimate of £735 million required gross investment per annum, adjusted for an estimated 15 per cent rise in prices of capital goods between 1948/49 and 1949/50.

(d) Defence expenditure will remain constant at three times the 1949/50 rate.

(e) Per capita production (gross national product divided by the total population) will grow from the 1949/50 level at the rate of 1 per cent per annum.

(f) Exports and imports will balance in every year.

Table II Aggregate supply and demand, 1951/60
(Hypothetical model, 1949/50 prices: £ million)

	Demand				Supply		Difference
	Consumption	Investment	Defence	Total	GNP	Import surplus	Inflation/ deflation gap
1949/50	1,824	755	65	2,644	2,649	-5	
1951	1,900	850	195	2,945	2,759	0	-186
1952	1,977	850	195	3,022	2,872	0	-150
1953	2,055	850	195	3,100	2,986	0	-114
1954	2,135	850	195	3,180	3,102	0	-78
1955	2,217	850	195	3,262	3,220	0	-42
1956	2,299	850	195	3,344	3,340	0	-4
1957	2,383	850	195	3,428	3,462	0	+34
1958	2,469	850	195	3,514	3,587	0	+73
1959	2,556	850	195	3,601	3,713	0	+112
1960	2,644	850	195	3,689	3,842	0	+153

Before examining the plausibility of these assumptions, it will be worth considering briefly the general picture which emerges from the table. The significant conclusion appears in the last column. It shows that, on the assumptions here made, demand for goods and services would exceed supply in each of the next six years. The excess demand (inflationary gap) would be large in the first year and would then fall steadily, giving way to excess supply (deflationary gaps) in the last four years. (The trend follows, of course, simply from our assumption of constant investment and defence expenditure absorbing a diminishing share of a growing national output.)

It would imply that, for the next six years, our resources would be insufficient to meet the demands made upon them. One way or another, the coat would have to be cut to the cloth. If nothing were done, the excess demand in the early years (resulting from a sharp increase in resources claimed for capital expenditure and defence) would lead to severe inflation which would bring about the necessary balance, partly by preventing expenditure plans from being realised because of shortages of labour and materials, but mainly by reducing the real income and consumption of those sections of the community whose incomes are relatively fixed. Inflation, moreover, would almost certainly strike the balance at a lower level of total output because of its disorganising effect on production.

The alternatives would be either to increase the supply of goods and services, for instance by financing additional imports by borrowing from abroad, or to reduce demand, by adequate cuts in one or more of its components. If the burden of cuts were to be placed solely on consumption, it would mean an immediate reduction of average living standards (personal and communal consumption expenditure, other than on new houses) of nearly 10 per cent, below the 1949/50 level; over the remainder of the decade, the cuts could be gradually restored, leading to a level of per capita consumption about 10 per cent above the 1949/50 level by 1960 (or more, if the later "deflationary gaps" in the model could be taken seriously). Even a complete elimination of defence expenditure, even if this could be contemplated, would barely suffice to close the gap. If the burden of the cut were wholly placed on investment, gross investment would be reduced in the first year well below the 1949/50 level. This, in turn, would almost certainly make it impossible to achieve the increase in supply of goods and services assumed for the later years, since additions to capital equipment would be insufficient to support even a constant, let alone an increasing, per capita output for a rapidly growing population.

This is stating in crude fashion the implications of a crude model. How far do the model and its implications resemble the real problem of Australian economic development in the next ten years? We can make some attempt at a qualitative answer to this question by examining, one by one, the assumptions on which the model is based. Such an examination will, at the same time, throw some light on the range of choice of policies open to us in meeting the problem of the next five years.

1951/60 — The Australian Economy

(a) Population increase

An average annual increase in population of 250,000 is a conservative assumption if present immigration plans are realised. But difficulties in procuring suitable immigrants may prevent even the smaller rate of inflow here assumed. On the other hand, we should note that a deliberate scaling down of the immigration program would be one possible way of alleviating the short-term economic problem of rapid growth. A lower rate of immigration would contribute most immediately to a reduction in the inflationary gap by reducing the required rate of gross investment. (It might make little difference, for a time, to private and public investment plans. Both private and public capital expenditure plans in Australia today are based on long-term expectations of an expanding economy in which expected rapid population growth is an important, but not the only element. But it would certainly make it possible to hold the rate of investment at a lower level by deliberate restraint or control without serious consequences for the future.) Other implications of a lower rate of immigration will become apparent in discussing some of the other assumptions.

(b) Average real consumption

A rate of growth of average real consumption of 1 per cent per annum corresponds to that which Australians enjoyed between 1938 and 1948 and is perhaps not unrealistic. (Personal consumption grew a little more slowly, communal consumption a good deal faster but at a much lower level.) There is, for example, little reason to assume that the average consumption demands of the newcomers will differ significantly from those of the average Australian. A more important point is that the 1949/50 level of personal consumption which we have taken as the starting point fell considerably short of what Australians would have tried to spend on consumption out of their 1949/50 incomes had they not been restrained by taxation, rationing and shortages, and that even these restraints were insufficient to prevent excess demand from causing inflationary price increases in the course of that year. The successive levels of consumption demand shown in column 1, therefore, assume controls of consumption at least as severe as those exercised in 1949/50. Any deliberate curtailment of personal consumption below these levels would require correspondingly more stringent taxation or other methods of keeping down demand (including, of course, encouragement of voluntary saving).

(c) Constant gross investment

On the face of it, the assumption of a constant rate of gross investment of £850 million per annum seems the most unrealistic feature of the model. As we have seen, it is this which chiefly accounts for the large inflationary gap in the early years and the improbable deflationary gap towards the end of the decade. It may be suggested that, even accepting Mr Lawler's (adjusted) figure of £850 million as the average annual required rate of gross investment for the next decade, the sensible procedure would be to assume a gradual increase in the rate of investment, e.g., to assume that gross investment will absorb a constant percentage of the growing national product.

In relation to the later years, such a correction would be quite legitimate and probably realistic. There is very little reason to suppose that the rate of capital expenditure which private firms and public authorities would be willing to undertake (as contrasted with the required minimum rate of investment to which Mr Lawler's estimate refers) will be insufficient in the later years of the decade to maintain the Australian economy in full employment. But in relation to the first half of the decade to maintain the Australian economy in full employment. But in relation to the first half of the decade, such a correction would ignore the crux of the whole problem—the need for larger initial investment outlay, on housing and productive equipment, if the productivity and living standards of a growing population are to be maintained and increased. Recognition of this need was largely responsible for the sharp increase (by about 25 per cent) in real investment between 1948/49 and 1949/50 which, in turn, was the chief cause of inflationary pressure in Australia last year. The further 15 per cent, increase in real investment between 1949/50 and 1951 assumed in the model will almost certainly be attempted if present private and public investment plans are carried forward, and it will inevitably exert further inflationary pressure on the economy. But to attempt to prevent this inflationary pressure by curtailing investment drastically would merely be to postpone, and perhaps aggravate, the problem since it would reduce the volume of goods and services available in later years.

(d) Constant defence expenditure

The assumption that defence expenditure will be increased to three times the 1949/50 rate is quite arbitrary, but not out of line with government pronouncements on Australian defence needs in the present international situation. Increased claims on resources for defence are a new factor in the problem, not directly connected with the immigration problem. But if policy dictates that these defence requirements be met immediately on the scale here assumed, they very gravely increase the short-term economic problem which the immigration problem involves for Australia.

(e) Per capita production

It is the assumption of a 1 per cent per annum increase in per capita production which raises the largest issues. In principle, the rate of increase assumed is a modest one. Even during the inter-war period, output per man hour is thought to have increased by about 1.5 per cent per annum, and rapidly expanding economies have in the past achieved rates of growth as high as 3 per cent per annum for substantial periods. Nor are the assumptions of a fairly constant ratio of working to total population (cf. Mr Foxcroft's paper) and of equal productivity of new and old Australians necessarily unrealistic.

Yet, the margin of error surrounding this assumption is enormous. If we allow our economy to be disorganised by inflation or industrial conflict, or if we fail to make the best use of the additions to our labour force, of if the good seasons of the last few years should give way to a run of bad ones, per capita output could easily fall well below the 1949/50 level. On the other hand, a substantially higher annual rate of increase of productivity is not inconceivable. The immigration program will make its own contribution, by providing skilled labour which will be particularly valuable where it can make good current specific shortages, and more gradually, through the economies of scale which may be realised with a larger population.

At the same time, it is important to preserve a sense of proportion, particularly about the extent to which productivity could be increased. Harder work and more efficient organisation of industry (more scientific management, widening of "bottlenecks", and elimination of waste) would undoubtedly contribute much to a higher rate of production. But in a modern economy, productivity is primarily a matter of the volume of capital equipment per head of worker, and this depends on an adequate rate of investment. Moreover, even if we make the extremely optimistic assumption of a steady increase in productivity of 3 per cent per annum, this would merely advance the date by which the inflationary gap could be eliminated; it would not substantially diminish the problem in the early years. It is true that, on the by and large optimistic assumptions of our model, an immediate all-round increase in productivity in all Australian industries by 7 per cent would close the gap at one stroke. But when allowance is made for the important share of the export industries (which do not directly make additional goods and services available in Australia) and for the limits imposed on attempts to raise productivity by dependence on productive equipment and by technical obstacles to reorganisation, an immediate improvement of such dimensions is hard to imagine, even assuming the most wholehearted individual and collective effort by all concerned in Australian industry.

(f) Export–import balance

The assumption that exports and imports will automatically balance in every year is, of course, quite unrealistic. But it is perhaps no less plausible that any alternative assumption that could be made in the light of our present knowledge. The sharp rise in wool prices since 1949, and the prospect of increasingly inflationary conditions, based on defence economy, in the United States and elsewhere abroad, might suggest that Australia could reasonably expect her terms of trade to improve, allowing her to finance a larger volume of imports out of the proceeds of a given volume of exports. Such an improvement is, in fact, not unlikely for the next year or two and might make some contribution to the domestic problem in the first crucial years. But inflation abroad will, before long, raise Australian import prices, too. What is more important, it may renew the difficulties in procuring supplies of imports which have been partly responsible for the export surpluses of the post-war years. In that event, an improvement in the terms of trade would be a merely academic advantage.

The most significant aspect of the foreign balance, in fact, lies in the contribution which import surpluses could make in supplementing domestic production, on the one hand, and in the danger of further inflationary pressure from export surpluses, on the other. Import surpluses, financed out of international reserves (sterling balances) or by borrowing abroad, represent one of the most obvious ways in which the prospective inflationary gap could be reduced, particularly if imports were selected so as to widen bottlenecks caused by specific shortages of equipment and thus helped to raise productivity. This, indeed, has been the motive for the recent successful negotiations for a dollar loan by the International Bank. But the limits to this approach must be recognised. It is doubtful whether it would be wise to devote more than a small portion of Australia's sterling balances to this purpose; and the scope for additional borrowing abroad, over and above the dollar loan already granted, is unlikely to be large.

The danger which has arisen with the prospect of inflation abroad is that high world demand will raise our export prices and incomes while, at the same time, making imports more difficult to obtain. In that case, the problem may be, not how to finance beneficial import surpluses, but how to avoid a recurrence of substantial inflationary export surpluses.

Conclusion

It is time to sum up. The projected flow of immigrants will almost certainly yield substantial economic benefits to this country in the long run and will help to solve specific difficulties at once. But in its short-run effects on the economy as a whole, it confronts Australia with a serious problem. If the rapidly growing population is, over the years, to enjoy living standards improving at the rate to which Australians have become accustomed, an abnormally large proportion of Australia's resources must be devoted to additions to capital equipment. The past year has already shown the inflationary impact of this investment demand. If the required rate of capital expenditure is to be attained, inflationary pressure will increase further in the next few years.

The great difficulty of the problem arises from two special features of the situation. The first is that the Australian economy has no slack of unemployed resources which could be drawn into production. On the contrary, the economy has, ever since the war, been suffering from "over-employment" (though this, it should be recognised, has partly reflected a high rate of private and public investment stimulated by the very prospect of rapid population growth). The second is the sudden drastic increase in defence claims on Australian economic resources which the deteriorating international situation necessitates. It is the simultaneous impact on an already fully employed economy of the requirements of economic development and defence which makes the problem so serious.

Two other factors may add to our difficulties. One is that rising overseas demand may exert additional pressure on the Australian economy by raising export prices and incomes, and by making imports more expensive and difficult to procure. The other is the fact, which our discussion in real terms has not allowed for, that the increases in living costs of recent years have left a legacy of prospective demands for higher money wages which are bound to complicate the problem of keeping inflation under control.

It appears that, in order to meet defence and development needs over the next three years, current average living standards in Australia might have to be reduced by something like 10 per cent, or by a smaller percentage to the extent that aggregate supply can be rapidly increased by overall increases in productivity and capital imports. Such a cut in current consumption levels might well involve social and political repercussions which would defeat its purpose by reducing overall productivity. In practice, some scaling down of defence and/or investment plans may be inescapable.

Whichever way scarce resources are allocated to these three conflicting claims, it is essential that the broad principles of allocation be determined in advance and appropriate policies adopted. If defence, investment and consumption claims are pushed regardless of the adequacy of available resources, the allocation will, in effect, be left to the haphazard force of inflation. The consequence will be not merely social injustice, but a disorganisation of the economy which will permit even smaller proportions of each of these claims to be satisfied.

14

Overseas Borrowing: The New Model

During the 19th century most Australian capital inflow has taken the form of government borrowing in London. After World War II, direct foreign investment, in manufacturing and other industries, was becoming more prominent. This slightly abbreviated article examined the costs and benefits of the "New Model".

Originally published in the *Economic Record*, August 1957.

Introduction

The decade since the end of World War II has brought a much more substantial revival of international investment than most economists had expected. Australia has been one of the main importers of capital, her imports being comparable in scale to the great inflows of the 1880s and 1920s. The international movement of capital of the past decade, however, and Australia's imports of capital in particular, have been very different in important respects from most past experience.

First, Australia's nineteenth century and inter-war capital imports were predominantly portfolio investment, mainly government borrowing through overseas loan issues. Most of the recent inflow has taken the form of direct investment by overseas companies in branches or subsidiaries. Secondly, while such direct investment has always played some part in international investment, it was in earlier periods characteristically investment in extractive export industries, agriculture and mining. In the statistics of post-war American direct investment, about half is classified as in primary industries; but almost the whole of this has been oil investment; most of the other half, and much the greater part of overseas direct investment in Australia, has been in manufacturing industries. Thirdly, the economic climate in which this investment has occurred has been one of almost continuous inflation. Association between high capital imports and boom has long been familiar, and is no accident. But there is reason to believe that we are living in no mere transient boom of the old type, that acceptance of the full employment objective is likely to make some degree of inflation an almost chronic state of affairs henceforth.

It seems to me that these three features of the "New Model" overseas borrowing require a reconsideration of some of the traditional analysis of international capital movements, their costs and benefits to the borrowing country and their effects on internal and external balance. Such reconsideration will not answer any of the policy problems in the field which have been raised from time to time in Australia in recent years. But it may help to clarify some of the issues which policy judgments must take into the reckoning.

The thesis I want to argue is that a clear-cut answer is virtually impossible. Besides the direct benefits and costs of overseas direct investment in Australia, which can be compared relatively easily, there are indirect benefits and costs which may be very important but are almost incapable of quantitative assessment. The trouble is that, while the benefits, even the indirect ones, accrue currently and are widely felt and appreciated, the costs are largely deferred and some of the indirect costs may not even be suspected. It is in bringing the less obvious costs and benefits to light and broadly assessing their probable weight that theoretical analysis can be of use.

I want to begin with an aspect which is sometimes brought into the discussion but which is of relatively minor importance: the effects of direct investment on short-term external and internal balance.

Short-Term External and Internal Balance

During the first post-war inflation of 1949–51, the suggestion was sometimes heard in Australia that one way of filling the gap between investment and saving would be to attract more overseas capital to Australia. Again, in the balance of payments crisis of 1955, it was argued by some that a larger inflow of overseas capital would be helpful by supplementing current foreign exchange receipts. How sound or fallacious were these views?

Clearly, any capital inflow into a country, other things being equal, represents , in money terms, an addition to the country's current foreign exchange earnings and, in real terms, an addition to available market supplies. Other things (including domestic effective demand) being equal, therefore, any capital import improves the balance of payments position, and through the additional imports which it finances, exercises a deflationary (or disinflationary) effect on the level of domestic economic activity. The question is whether other things will remain equal, whether the inflow of capital will not, directly or indirectly, add to domestic demand for resources (including imports and exportables) as well as to supply.

If the question is put in this form, the answer is not really in doubt. It is very difficult to think of any forms of capital import which will not have some effect in raising the level of domestic spending. Almost the only example I can think of is an equilibrating capital inflow, such as a fall in international reserves or borrowing from the International Montetary Fund, designed to finance an existing balance of payments deficit. Even the inflow of hot money of the years 1949–51, by increasing the liquidity of banks and other sectors of the capital market, must have given some fillip to domestic investment. Government overseas borrowing, though ostensibly designed to finance a pre-determined public works program, almost certainly induces a higher level of domestic spending since the coat of domestic public investment tends to be cut in some measure to the cloth of available finance. Where, as in the case of the first International Bank loan, the money is deliberately spent on imports of capital goods which will widen bottlenecks in domestic production, the capital import may not merely raise public investment, but also pave the way for additional private investment which would not otherwise have been undertaken.

There is a similar range of possibilities in the case of direct investment by overseas companies. Some of this investment in post-war Australia may merely have replaced domestic investment projects. But it is probably a reasonable assumption that much of it has been additional. If General Motors–Holden, for instance, had not entered the field, there would probably have been more domestic Australian investment in the motor car industry (we must abstract here from fiscal or monetary restraints that might have been imposed on such investment); but total investment in the Australian motor car industry has surely been much larger, thanks to GM-H and other overseas investments, than it otherwise would have been. Australian experience, moreover, suggests that overseas direct investment in new industries, while perhaps in some degree inhibiting domestic investment in these industries, often has the effect of stimulating domestic investment in complementary industries supplying materials, parts or products in joint demand, providing retail outlets, or exploiting new techniques in other directions.

There is little doubt in my mind that direct overseas investment tends to make a substantial net addition to the level of domestic spending, probably more so than all other forms of overseas borrowing. The question, then, is whether this addition to demand is likely to be greater or smaller than the capital imported.

In the most favourable case, where the capital imported by an overseas company pays for the whole of its investment expenditure and this replaces an equal amount of domestic investment that would otherwise have been undertaken, the answer is straightforward: total domestic spending remains unchanged and the favourable net effect on external and/or internal balance equals the capital imported.[1] If the capital

1 The mechanism by which the favourable net effect is achieved is the subject of familiar "transfer problem" analysis. The simplest case is where the whole overseas investment project is undertaken with imported resources. Imports increase directly by the amount of the capital import. The overseas project makes no demand on domestic resources. But this demand falls owing to the elimination of the domestic investment project. How this fall in domestic spending is distributed between domestic resources and imports depends on the direct import content of the domestic investment and the marginal propensity to import. If the initial condition of the economy was inflationary, the marginal propensity to import will be near unity; most of the fall in spending will quickly be reflected in reduced demand for imports (or exportables).

In some of the imported capital (which we may assume to have taken the form of a remittance of, say, dollars to Australia) is spent by the overseas company on domestic resources, the mechanism depends on the exchange system assumed. Under free exchanges, the remittance itself causes the £A to appreciate; with domestic spending unchanged, the import surplus resulting from the appreciation represents the net disinflationary effect (though the appreciation will be smaller, if the overseas investment has a higher import content than the domestic investment it replaces). Under a system of fixed exchanges, the capital import, with unchanged domestic spending, in the first instance merely increases international reserves; the improvement in the balance of payments position would be converted into a disinflationary effect on internal balance if it made possible relaxation of existing import restrictions or if an import surplus were brought about by deliberate appreciation of £A. Here again allowance must be made for a possible offsetting increase in import demand resulting from the replacement of domestic by overseas investment.

import finances the whole of the overseas company's investment but this represents a net addition to domestic investment spending, the effects of the capital import on supply and demand cancel out, leaving internal and external balance unaffected at a higher level of investment and imports. (In an underemployed economy, this conclusion would need to be qualified to the extent that some of the additional income generated would be saved; in a fully employed economy, this qualification can be neglected, since most of the increase in demand quickly spills over into imports.) If, however, the import of capital causes the level of domestic spending to rise by a larger amount—whether because the overseas company tries to finance part of its investment by raising additional domestic capital or because the overseas investment stimulates more domestic investment (in complementary industries) than it replaces—then the net effect of the capital inflow on internal and or external balance is almost certain to be unfavourable. Far from helping to close an existing inflationary gap or restoring balance of payments equilibrium, the inflow adds to inflationary pressure on resources (or at least to pressure on existing fiscal and monetary controls of inflation) and/or to existing balance of payments difficulties. It causes a "transfer problem in reverse".[2]

What the position has been in Australia's case in the post-war years is anybody's guess. My own view is that, in this short-run sense, ignoring its long-run effect on the national product, overseas investment has had a net inflationary effect in both the post-war booms, 1949–51 and 1954–56.

Long-Term Growth of Real Income

Any assessment of the costs and benefits to the borrowing country of investment of overseas capital must concentrate, not on the short-term effects we have so far considered, but on the long-term effects. If we abstract from non-economic considerations, such as the possible undesirability of foreign control, the criterion must be the effects of the process of overseas investment on the long-term rate of growth of the borrowing country's real national income.

Traditional theory, with its eye primarily on long-term fixed-interest portfolio investment, has tended to focus attention on what we might call the "direct" benefits and costs to the borrowing country. The borrowing country benefits from the increase in the productivity of its resources which results from the additional capital supplied from abroad. The costs are represented by the overseas debt service: interest and repayment of principal. Provided the additional real income which results from overseas borrowing exceeds the amount that has to be paid to overseas creditors in interest and amortisation, there is a net gain to the borrowing country. (There is a net gain to the lending country, provided the interest rate on overseas investment exceeds the highest yield obtainable on domestic investment.) It has usually been recognised that overseas debt service confronts the borrowing country with a transfer problem. But it has generally been thought sufficient to point out that the borrowing country

2 C. P. Kindleberger, *International Economics*, p. 354.

must ensure an adequate increase in export production to enable it to service its overseas debt.

In the case of the nineteenth century type of government overseas borrowing, there might sometimes have been legitimate doubt as to whether the direct benefits were sufficient to cover the direct costs, since there was no direct accounting relationship between the yield of the investment in terms of additional real income and the costs of overseas debt service. In the case of private direct investment, it can be shown *a priori*, subject to relatively minor qualifications, that the direct benefits exceed the direct costs to the borrowing country.

The direct costs are simply the profits accruing to the overseas investors (since, in the case of direct investment, there is usually no expectation of repayment of principal, i.e. repatriation of equity capital); and these profits come out of the increase in real income produced in the industry in which the investment is made. The profits cannot exceed the increase in real income resulting from the investment unless the investment reduces the incomes accruing to residents of the borrowing country. This is, of course, possible. Competition by the overseas firm may squeeze out, and inflict losses on, existing domestic firms; large overseas companies may achieve monopolistic positions in which they are able to exploit labour or consumers. In all these cases, moreover, what matters is not merely an absolute loss, but a loss of resident income relative to what it would have been in the absence of the overseas investment. But while such offsetting losses are possible, they are not likely to be serious. There is every reason to believe that profits accruing to overseas investors absorb only part of the benefit which accrues through higher productivity in the enterprises established by overseas capital; that a substantial part accrues to consumers in the form of better quality products (and/or lower prices), to local factors of production in the form of higher real incomes, and to governments in higher tax-revenue.

As far as the direct costs and benefits of direct investment are concerned, therefore, the issue is not really in doubt: there is almost certainly a net gain to the borrowing country. The trouble is that the matter does not end here. Direct investment, in addition, involves indirect benefits and costs which blur the issue almost irretrievably.

The indirect benefits mostly fall under the general heading of technical progress. It is a well-known advantage of direct investment over portfolio investment that it brings to the borrowing country not merely capital but also technical and managerial know-how. There is no need to dwell on the very great advantages which Australian manufacturing industries have derived in the post-war years from the introduction of overseas, and especially American, enterprise, managerial skill, techniques, methods and new products. In so far as all these factors help to increase the efficiency and profitability of the overseas enterprises, they tend to increase the profits accruing to overseas investors at least as much as (and perhaps more than) these firms' contribution to the borrowing country's national income. They may, therefore, yield no great net gain to the borrowing country. But there is no doubt that, through the stimulus and example they give to domestic firms, through training of local labour at all levels in new skills, and through the pressure of powerful competition, the benefits of technological advance spread beyond the firms in which the overseas investment is made; they accrue as external economies to residents of the borrowing country and represent an additional net benefit which, though quite incapable of measurement, may be very substantial.

Against these indirect benefits must be set three forms of indirect or social costs of direct investment: the non-economic costs, if they are so regarded, of increasing foreign control of the borrowing country's industries; the economic and social costs of increased short-term difficulties in controlling inflation; and the long-term economic and social costs of balance of payments adjustment to which direct investment may give rise. The first is a matter of political opinion about which I have nothing to say. The second has already been discussed; I would regard it as an item of indirect cost but not a very important one. It is the third, the long-term balance-of-payments problem, that is by far the most serious and to which we must now turn.

Long-Term External Balance

The chief item of indirect social cost in relation to long-term external balance arises from the need to find foreign exchange for the remittance of profits accruing to overseas investors. That such a transfer problem may arise is well known, but its precise nature is not always understood.

For a developing national economy to remain in long-term external balance, in the absence of international capital movements, it is necessary that exports (or more generally current receipts of foreign exchange) rise in step with imports (or more generally payments due abroad). Domestic investment must be distributed between the various sectors of the economy in such a way that the value of exports keeps in step with national income or, if not, that enough replacement takes place to fill the gap.

Overseas investment must do more: it must have a sufficient bias towards increased export production or import replacement to ensure the long-term improvement in the balance of payments necessary to finance the transfer of dividend remittances abroad. The emergence of this problem may be postponed in two ways: either by retention and reinvestment of profits by the overseas companies themselves, or by a steady increase in new capital inflow which keeps pace with the growth in remitted profits on past investments. The former is intrinsically unlikely for any length of time; individual overseas investors will sooner rather than later want to see a return for their money. The latter is, in principle, conceivable. But for various reasons, some of which we shall consider later, it would be foolish to rely on it. Sooner or later the chickens will come home to roost. For all practical purposes, the growth in the borrowing country's dividend commitment on overseas direct investment, viewed on its own, is equivalent to the certain prospect of a long-term decline in its terms of trade.

The magnitude of the necessary bias towards export production or import replacement depends on the relative rates of growth of the profits accruing to overseas investors and the borrowing country's national income. Here Dr Penrose has given convincing reasons to expect that, in the very nature of the overseas firms, with their technical and managerial superiority and their advantages of new products and economies of growth, their profits are likely to grow faster than the national income.[3] As the figures I quoted earlier showed, they rose during the postwar decade from 1.4 to 1.8 per cent of Australian national income.

Thus far (except for the Penrose effect) the problem of debt service is common to direct and portfolio investment. Indeed, it is less for direct than for portfolio investment since repayment of principal can be neglected (though there may be difficulties of sporadic partial repatriation to which I shall revert later). In the past, moreover, direct investment, in its character, overcame the transfer problem. So long as most direct investment was in extractive export industries, plantation agriculture and mining, it had all the export bias that was needed and more.

This is no longer true of the New Model direct investment of the post-war years. Practically none of it has been in Australia's traditional export industries—none in rural industries and only a little in mining. The great bulk has been in manufacturing industries and a little in tertiary industries. (As Dr Penrose has pointed out, the pace of investment in manufacturing may actually have retarded growth in the export industries by depriving them of capital and other productive resources,[4] although the rural industries no doubt benefit in the long run from increased productivity in manufacturing.) There can be very little doubt that the inflow of overseas capital has been a factor, perhaps a major factor, in the disproportionately rapid growth of Australia's secondary industries, relatively to her traditional export industries. This establishes a strong *prima facie* case for the view that post-war direct investment, far from having had the necessary bias towards export production, has helped to give post-war Australian economic development a bias *against* export production. If this is true, it would imply that overseas investment would have contributed to a long-term balance-of-payments problem even if it had taken the form of free gifts.

Of course, I have so far substantially overstated the point. In the first place, some of Australia's manufacturing industries may gradually develop significant export markets. Secondly, the development of these secondary industries may be contributing towards long-term external balance through import replacement. This is a matter which has been much discussed recently[5] and on which I do not want to spend time. All I need to say is that I am not as sceptical as some about the possibilities of import replacement in the long run. If Australia is to follow in America's footsteps and develop from a primary producing and exporting into an industrial economy, this is the transformation in the pattern of her trade that must occur in the long run. But I think it would be optimistic to hope that these two factors will, for some years yet, offset (let alone outweigh) the disequilibrating bias of large-scale investment in manufacturing industries.

3 E. T. Penrose, *op. cit.*, pp. 228f.

4 *Ibid.*, p. 232 n.

5 C. D. Kemp, "The Import Replacement Theory", *IPA Review*, Melbourne, Oct–Dec 1955; R. J. Familton, "The Import Substitution Thesis", paper presented to Section G of ANZAAS, Dunedin, 1957.

A third, more esoteric, point which may be thrown into the scales in favour of the New Model direct investment is the converse of a traditional objection to the old type of overseas investment in primary industries. It used to be said that such investment tends to turn the terms of trade against the borrowing countries. On the same reasoning, the New Model investment might be expected to have a modest effect in improving Australia's long-term terms of trade. But this is true of almost any domestic structural change which worsens a country's balance of payments.

We must conclude, therefore, that direct investment of the post-war type is very likely to give rise to a long-run balance of payments problem because, while the transfer of remitted profits to overseas investors requires a long-run bias in the structure of the economy towards export production (or import replacement), the structural effects of this investment have so far, if anything, been in the opposite direction. It is reasonable to regard this as an indirect social cost of overseas investment since it will sooner or later require socially and economically costly measures of balance of payments adjustment, whether there are costs, in terms of productivity, of quantitative import restrictions, or social costs of currency depreciation in terms of its effects on internal balance, income distribution and necessary shifts of resources, or similar social costs of alternative measures. Unfortunately for the formulation of a rational policy on overseas investment, it is quite impossible to assess the likely magnitude of these costs; but the very fact that they lie in an uncertain future should put us on our guard against discounting them too generously.

To give just one highly speculative quantitative illustration. Between 1948/9 and 1954/5, the ratio of profits on US direct investments in Australia to Australian national income rose from 0.24 to 0.71 per cent; the corresponding ratio for UK investment from 0.72 to 0.89 per cent. If both ratios maintained their rates of growth to 1965, total profits accruing overseas would in 1965 represent 6.3 per cent of Australian national income (US 5 per cent, UK 1.3 per cent). Assuming Australian exports remain at about one quarter of national income, the 1965 profits accruing overseas would represent 25 per cent of Australian export income; by 1969, this ratio would overtake the average for the 1930s of 34 per cent. It is easy to make one's flesh creep with such crude extrapolations. But they should be examined critically, not simply ignored.

Apart from the transfer problem, there is a second indirect cost of overseas investment relating to long-term external balance which we must take into account. It is arguable that a high rate of overseas borrowing increases the social costs arising from instability in the balance-of-payments.

It used to be a commonplace that a large overseas debt exposes the debtor country to special risks of balance-of-payments trouble in the event of a slump in its export prices and earnings. Australia's inflexible interest commitments abroad represented one of the most serious aspects of the slump of 1929/30. It therefore used to be thought an important advantage of direct over portfolio investment that a slump automatically reduced the volume of profits payable abroad.

More recently it has been pointed out that this argument in favour of direct investment has lost some of its weight with the prospect that disastrous slumps and depressions of the 1930/33 type may be a thing of the past.[6] (Chronic inflation is likely to yield chronic boom profits, though if inflation in Australia is not paralleled by inflation elsewhere these profits are likely to be impaired from time to time by currency depreciation.) The force of the argument is further diminished if, as in post-war Australia, overseas investment is concentrated in secondary industries producing for the home market; for their profits will not be as sensitive to fluctuations in export earnings as were the profits on the old-type direct investments in export industries. Still, the fact that, despite a huge inflow in the preceding year, Australian profits accruing overseas remained constant in the recession year 1952/3 suggests that there is still something in this in favour of direct over portfolio investment.

There is, however, a second more serious threat to balance of payments instability to which the New Model overseas borrowing in no more immune than nineteenth century borrowing by overseas loan issues: the danger of sharp cyclical or other fluctuations in the rate of net inflows of new capital, including the possibility of repatriation of past investments. (Direct investment has a steadily growing base in reinvested undistributed profits; but these do not in any case affect the short-term balance of payments.) In the Great Depression, the sudden cessation of American investment overseas was as serious a cause of balance-of-payments trouble in the rest of the world as the slump in American imports.

Here again, the prospect that we may be able to avoid serious slumps and depressions in future also promises to reduce the risk of drastic cyclical fluctuations in the rate of overseas investment. But even minor recessions, in Australia or abroad, may give rise to quite substantial fluctuations in the rate of inflow of overseas capital. As I pointed out earlier inflow of new capital (excluding undistributed profits) fell from £62 m. in 1951/2 to £9 m. in 1952/3, the product of a fall in UK investments from £43 m to £20 m and an actual outflow of US capital £10 m. The combined effect of the relative inflexibility of profits due abroad (particularly, because of dividend stabilisation, of remitted profits) and the sharp fall in new capital inflow was that an excess of new capital inflow over dividend remittances of £46 m in 1951/2 turned into an excess of profits remitted over new capital inflow of £13 m in 1952/3.

These are still relatively puny figures compared with the huge swings in Australia's export earnings. But they will grow if new capital inflow keeps step with the rapid growth in profits due overseas, and the ups and downs may come at the most awkward times. I am not unduly concerned about this aspect of overseas investment. But it cannot be left out of the reckoning in assessing the social costs to the borrowing country.

6 E. T. Penrose, *op. cit.*, p. 231.

Conclusion

It is time to sum up.

I have tried to show that the direct benefits to Australia of investment of overseas capital almost certainly exceed the direct costs. But there are also indirect benefits and indirect costs which are very much more difficult, indeed quite impossible, to assess. I have said very little about the indirect benefits, increased productivity through the introduction of new ideas, skills, techniques, methods, products, because they are familiar. I have devoted much of my time to analysing the indirect costs, especially those arising from long-term balance-of-payments problems, because they have not, I think, received sufficient attention. I must therefore emphasise that the time I have spent on each in no way reflects my opinion of their relative magnitude. I think it is quite possible that the benefits, direct and indirect, of overseas investment during the past decade have greatly outweighed the costs, direct and indirect, and will continue to do so. My point is that I do not know and that I cannot see how anyone can find out. I would merely add the rider that I suspect that those who have to make the policy decisions, in common with every one else, may have been inclined to treat the indirect costs too lightly, partly because they have not been clearly recognised and partly because the bill for them will be presented in the future. But this does not greatly alter the picture. Anyone is entitled to the view that the benefits greatly outweigh the costs even when all the indirect costs have been brought fully to account.

I confess this conclusion bothers me as an economist. Here is a major issue of economic policy, yet it seems impossible to find a rational basis on which the economist can advise the policy-maker. Perhaps the rational course in such a situation is to make hay while the sun shines and cross one's bridges when one comes to them. Things may turn out all right, and in the last resort, the foreign debt problem has often enough in the past been "solved" by default or moratoria or restrictions on transfer. It is arguable that this is a risk of which overseas investors are, or should be, aware and for which they can be expected to allow in their investment decisions.

The alternative course, for those who conclude that the costs of an open door policy for direct investment by overseas companies are likely to outweigh the benefits in the long run, might be to seek ways of reducing the costs, if necessary by restricting the inflow. As all the efforts of recent years to clear away obstacles to overseas investment demonstrate, it should not be difficult to give *indiscriminate* discouragement to overseas investors. But that would be throwing out the baby with the bath water. A more sensible approach would be to see whether the costs could be limited.

Something might be done to give preferential treatment through taxation or in other ways, to investment in export or import replacing industries. Overseas investors might be required to grant a minimum share in the equity of new subsidiaries to local (private or public) capital. More attention might be given to the practicability of devices, such as management contracts, by which overseas technical know-how might be obtained without overseas capital and the dividend commitment limited in time. The corollary would be to obtain overseas capital, as far as possible, in the cheaper form of fixed-interest capital through government or even corporate bond issues.

I do not want to elaborate these very unoriginal suggestions, if only because I am not sure whether anything of the sort needs doing at all. But if anyone, after examining my arguments, should come to the conclusion that a revision of Australian policy on overseas investment would be desirable, these, I think are the sorts of measure that should be given consideration.

15

The Financial Year

The financial year ends on 30 June in Australia. So does the federal fiscal year in the USA. But in the UK and New Zealand it ends on 30 March. Some US states have fiscal years ending 30 September or 31 March. This note explains when these arrangements were adopted and why.

Originally published in *Australian Quarterly*, June 1963.

The financial year of the Commonwealth and all States of Australia ends on June 30th. In Great Britain and New Zealand the financial year ends on March 31st. In the United States, the federal fiscal year ends on June 30th; some states have fiscal years ending September 30th or March 31st. This note explains when these arrangement were adopted and why.

Great Britain

> The Budget statement (and all the accounts relating to the Exchequer and the Consolidated Fund) relate, not to the calendar year, but to a 'financial year' beginning on April 1st and ending on March 31st. From the times of the earliest financial records to 1751/52 each year's public accounts were made up to Michaelmas quarter-day, September 29th, and between that year and 1800 to October 10th ('New Style' for September 29th). For the Finance Accounts of 1800/01 the date was altered to January 5th, which was then the usual making-up day in commerce. In 1832 the Budget was presented for the year to April 5th, 1833, and the annual Supply grants began to be voted for the year ending March 31st. But the Finance Accounts kept to January 5th until 1854 when the Public Revenue and Consolidated Fund Charges Act of that year directed that they should in future be made up to March 31st each year, and the latter date has since been maintained as the end of the financial year...The year of assessment for income tax and surtax still ends on April 5th.[1]

An account of the circumstances of the change to March 31st in 1832 was given in the Victorian Parliament in 1870:

> Reasons...which influenced the British House of Commons to make a change in the financial year in 1832. It was found, just as we find it here, that, practically, it was almost impossible to call Parliament together until after the financial year had commenced. If Parliament was prorogued in autumn, it was almost impossible to commence a fresh session before the Christmas holidays. The consequence was that, in England, year after year, the

1 Sir Herbert Brittain, *The British Budgetary System*, London, 1959, p. 20.

expenditure began before there were any Supplies voted, just as has been the case here for a great many years. In 1832 Lord Althorp called attention to the matter and succeeded in inducing the House to acquiesce in making a change.[2]

United States of America

The beginning date and termination of the budgetary period—one, two or four years as the case may be—is determined by the fiscal year of the governmental unit. On this subject there is wide diversity in the United States. A few governmental bodies employ the calendar year. Some odd datings are found—October 1st to September 30th in Alabama and Maryland, April 1st to March 31st in Washington. Most state and local governments and the federal government use July 1st–June 30th fiscal years.

Two reasons—one obsolete, one currently pertinent—dictate this arrangement. The obsolete reason is that state and local governments used to rely predominantly on property tax revenues which were collected in the fall when farmers had cash from their crops. Thus a government with a fiscal year beginning on January 1st would have to wait nine months for most of its current-year revenue, while one with a July–June fiscal year would obtain funds early in its operating year. The second reason, which applies today and accounts for the recent changeover of Oregon to a July–June fiscal year, is that legislatures commonly convene in January. Thus they have six months' opportunity to debate and adopt budgets, which then go into effect a couple of months after adoption. Such smooth timing is not possible for calendar-year budgets.[3]

From 1789 to 1842, the fiscal year ended December 31st; from 1844 to date, on June 30th.[4]

Australia

Throughout most of the 19th century, the Australian colonies used the calendar as the financial year. New South Wales appears to have used the calendar year from very early days,[5] presumably because this was then English practice. The other Australian colonies followed New South Wales practice and continued to use the calendar year even when Great Britain changed to March 31st in 1832. (New Zealand, on the other hand, seems to have adopted March 31st from its beginnings in 1840.) South Australia used a financial year ending June 30th for a few years (1859/60 to 1865) but followed the general Australian practice of using the calendar year from 1866 until 1874.[6]

Victoria initiated the change from the calendar year to a financial year ending June 30th in 1870. South Australia followed in 1874, Queensland in 1875, Western Australia

2 *Victorian Parliamentary Debates*, vol. 11, 2nd session, 1870, p. 227.

3 W. J. Schultz, *American Public Finance*, New York, 1946, p. 139.

4 US Bureau of the Census, *Historical Statistics of the United States*, 1951, p. 298.

5 *Historical Records of Australia*, Series I, vol. III, p. 485, "Estimate of the charge of defraying the Civil Establishment of New South Wales from the 1st of January to the 31st of December, 1802".

6 N. G. Butlin, *Public Capital Formation in Australia*, Australian National University, Canberra, 1954.

in 1892,[7] New South Wales in 1895 and Tasmania in 1904.[8] The Commonwealth from the beginning adopted the (by then standard) financial year ending June 30th.

The change from the calendar year to a financial year ending June 30th was adopted in Victoria at the initiative of a private member, Mr Langton, who induced the government of the day to obtain parliamentary approval for the change. The reasons for the change were fully explained by Langton and others in the debate in the lower House:

> There can be no doubt that the change suggested would be greatly to the convenience of the House and to the advantage of the public. Looking back over the past ten or twelve sessions, I find that Parliament has almost invariably been in session during the months of May and June, whilst it has been found an exceedingly difficult matter to get Parliament together in November or December. Whilst under the present system, the consequence has been that payments required at the beginning of the year have not been provided for until after they were due, in the other case Parliament would have been in session just before the termination of the financial year; it would have been able, without difficulty, to make due provision for the requirements of the ensuing year, and the inconvenience inflicted on the civil servants and other public creditors would by that means have been avoided.[9]
>
> Parliament should assemble not later than October next. We know how difficult it is to do anything in the way of public business when the Christmas holidays approach. We know, also, how very inconvenient it is for those persons who regard that as the only season when there is a prospect of relaxation from work, to have to be called upon to attend to parliamentary duties. Moreover, it is the time of the year when those who are engaged in country pursuits desire to be at their homesteads. Shearing is going on, and those who follow agricultural pursuits have to look after their crops just at the time when, generally speaking, these two Houses are called upon to meet. By the proposed alteration in the financial year, all that will be got rid of...[We would] get rid of the necessity for sitting in summer.[10]

The Chief Secretary, Sir J. McCulloch, in moving the resolution, explained:

> The Government has no particular interest in having the financial year commenced at one period of the year or another... Whether the alteration was to be made or not was a matter resting entirely with honourable members...[It was] for them to say whether it would be more convenient...I believe that if we sit in the winter months, instead of the summer months, we can do our work more comfortably and with less irritation. It is very unpleasant to have to sit in the House during the hot months of January and February.[11]

In New South Wales, in 1894, the Colonial Treasurer of the day (Mr Reid) found it convenient to cover a revenue deficiency without immediate need for extra taxation by changing the financial year from a calendar year to a June 30th basis. The ostensible reasons he gave were similar to those advanced 25 years earlier in Victoria:

> I am going to give the Committee good reasons why we should change the date of the financial year...I ask honourable members to say whether, having in view the climate of

7 Statistical Register of Western Australia for 1938–39, *Statistical Review of 110 Years Progress*, p. 3.

8 *Commonwealth Year Book*, Vol. I, 1908, p. 663.

9 Mr Langton, *Victorian Parliamentary Debates*, Vol. 10, 1870, p. 432.

10 Mr Fellows, *ibid.*, p. 436.

11 *Ibid.*, pp. 178, 226.

the country and its industrial seasons, a session ranging from March or April to September is not a better session than a session from September to March or April?The bulk of the industrial work in this country inland is done between September and March, and not between March and September, which is the slackest time, and we should adjust our sessions as much as we can to preserve a genuine country representation; and I believe that this change will make our parliamentary session far more attractive to country members. I also consider that in doing this we are following very wise examples. They have altered the financial year in Victoria, South Australia, Queensland and the United States so as to date from the 1st July. In England and in New Zealand it dates from the 1st April, and the only country which imitates us—in these latitudes at any rate—is Tasmania where the climate is essentially different.[12]

Conclusion

It appears then that in all these countries the primary motive for the adoption of a particular financial year was the parliamentary timetable; in particular, to ensure that the last months of the financial year, during which financial measures would need to be debated and approved, would fall in a time of year convenient for parliamentary sittings. In all countries, the difficulty of getting parliaments to meet around Christmas argued against a calendar-year basis. But it does seem odd that a financial year ending June 30th came to seem convenient for climatic reasons both in the northern and in the southern hemispheres.

What is even odder is that in Australia the climatic argument for the financial year ending June 30 has boomeranged. The argument, it will be recalled, was that the budget and estimates ought to be passed before the beginning of the new financial year but that parliaments could not be expected to sit in the hot summer months of Melbourne and other capital cities. Today the reluctance of Commonwealth parliamentarians to hold a budget session in the grim Canberra winter is said to be one reason why the Commonwealth budget is not presented until August or September.

In fact, the original reasons for adopting a financial year ending June 30th have lost all relevance. The present practice of introducing the budget and estimates some weeks after the beginning of the financial year is not just a case of mismanagement or a whim of comfort-loving politicians. Governments in all countries find it difficult to formulate budget policy for the coming year until the financial results (and national income accounts) for the past year are available. In Australia, it is also an advantage to the Commonwealth Treasurer to have before him the financial claims of the states which are decided upon at the June Loan Council meeting. Finally, by August it is usually possible to assess the year's seasonal prospects for primary products which have an important bearing on the appropriate financial policies for the year. These advantages are held to outweigh the inconvenience to spending Departments in being unable to undertake substantial new expenditures in the first two months of the financial year and to taxpayers in not knowing until the budget the rates of income tax

12 *NSW Parliamentary Debates*, First Series, Vol. 73, 7th November, 1894, p. 2135.

to which their current income will be subject. The constitutional requirement by which no moneys may be spent until they have been appropriated by Parliament is met by the passage of a Supply Act each June which enables the government to carry on until the budget is passed.[13]

There does not therefore seem to be anything much wrong with the present financial year as the accounting period for government finances. Australia, however, is practically alone in the world in its present practice of using the financial year ending June 30th, also as the accounting period for all annual economic statistics.[14] Most other advanced countries, like Australia, have financial years that differ from the calendar year; but they publish their annual economic statistics on a calendar year basis.[15]

The Australian practice is a nuisance for two reasons. First, it is a bother to have to write and print "1962/63" millions of times when every other country can do with "1963". Secondly, Australian annual data can never be tidily used in international economic comparisons or aggregations. Until recently, there was perhaps some case for the present practice. For although most economic statistics are available monthly or quarterly and can therefore as easily be put together on a calendar year as on a financial year basis, this was not true of the important series for national income. Now that the Commonwealth Statistician publishes quarterly national income estimates there seems no good reason why we should not follow world-wide practice in giving annual economic statistics on a calendar year basis.

13 The whole question was examined in the 18th Report of the Joint Committee of Public Accounts, Commonwealth Parliamentary Papers, 1954.

14 Australian statistics on agricultural and pastoral production are still collected and published on the basis of a "season" ending March 31.

15 The only exceptions, beside Australia, appear to be India, Pakistan, New Zealand, South Africa, Hong Kong, Haiti and Puerto Rico.

Part IV
POLITICAL ECONOMY

16

Political Economy

A history of the term. Classical 'political economy' became economics. 'Political economy' came to be concerned with power relationships, combining analysis with advocacy, as exemplified by two schools, neo-Marxism and the libertarian Chicago School.

Originally published in the *Economic Record*, September 1984.

The term 'political economy' has a long and curious history, from its 17th-century meaning of statecraft to the classical economists' use of it for what later came to be called economics and its recent appropriation by neo-Marxists for social theory which, in contrast to 'orthodox' economics, goes into history, politics and sociology, focuses on power relationships and combines positive analysis with advocacy. This article points out that there are now at least two schools of political economy in this latter sense, the neo-Marxists and the Chicago school. The concluding section distinguishes sensible and not so sensible uses of the term.[1]

For almost two decades the term 'political economy' has been a battle cry, not least at one or two Australian universities. A historical review of the various uses of the term may help, if not to stop the fighting, at least to clarify what the fighting is about. This paper provides such a historical survey, beginning with classical political economy and ending with neo-Marxist and Chicago political economy. It concludes with an attempt to sort out uses and abuses.

The Science of Political Economy

The word 'economy', as is well known, derives from the Greek οικονομια or household management. When the adjective 'political', from πολιζ or (city) state, was first attached to the noun, the intention was to distinguish the rules of state management from those of household management. As Sir James Steuart put it in his *Inquiry into the Principles of Political Economy* (1767, cited Cannan, 1929, p. 40): "What economy is in a family political economy is in a state."[2]

1 For helpful comments on earlier drafts the author is indebted to R. M. Sundrum and D. M. Bensusan-Butt, as well as to three anonymous referees. The usual disclaimers are particularly called for.

2 Chapter II of Cannan's book, "The Name of Economic Theory", covers the story up to Marshall in great detail. For the earlier history, Cannan acknowledged his debt to Garnier (1852). Cf. also Stollberg (1977).

The first book with "political economy" in the title, Montchrétien's *Traieté de l'Oeconomie Politique* (1615), was a survey of the industries of France, interspersed with much advice to the king on how matters might be improved, but the emphasis on economic aspects of state management was almost incidental (Gray 1931, p. 80).[3] In the following century, the term was used as virtually equivalent with what we would call public administration. Rousseau's article on *Économie politique* in the *Encyclopédie* (1755) dealt with politics, not economics.

Superficially, this also applies to Adam Smith who referred to political economy as a "branch of the system of civil government", and there was still an echo of the mercantilist connotation in the fact that he specifically used and defined the term when he came, in Books IV and V of *The Wealth of Nations* (1776), to deal with public policy and public finance. But for Adam Smith, public finance was only one of the concerns of public policy and therefore of political economy.

> Political economy considered as a branch of the science of a statesman or legislator, proposes two distinct objects: first to provide a plentiful revenue or subsistence for the people, or, more properly, to enable them to provide such a revenue or subsistence for themselves; and secondly, to supply the state or commonwealth with a revenue sufficient for the public services. It proposes to enrich both the people and the sovereign (1776, p. 643).

And to devise a public policy which will enable people to provide a plentiful revenue for themselves requires an understanding of the working of a market economy. For Adam Smith, therefore, political economy embraced all of economics, positive and normative. In fact, in one passage he equated the subject matter of political economy with that of his book, the study of the nature and causes of the wealth of nations (Vol. II, pp. 176 f.).

It was in this sense, as concerned with "the entire universe of discourse of economic science and the theory of economic policy" (Robbins, 1976, p. 1), that the term was used throughout by the British classical economists. Most treatises of economics, from Ricardo and Malthus to J. S. Mill and W. S. Jevons, had *Political Economy* in the title, and the "science of political economy" was generally understood to include both analysis and policy prescription. Even when Nassau Senior insisted that the political economist's "conclusions, whatever be their generality and truth, do not authorise him in adding a single syllable of advice", he would seem to have been voicing not so much the scruples of the modern welfare economist as the view that policy requires a knowledge of other disciplines besides economics:

> That privilege belongs to the writer or statesman who has considered all the causes which may promote or impede the general welfare of those whom he addresses, not to the theorist who had considered only one, though among the most important, of those causes (p. 3).

3 Schumpeter (1954, p. 167) said unkindly that the innovation in the title of Montchrétien's book was "its only merit".

Economics

The usual name of the discipline in English, 'political economy', was displaced by 'economics' towards the end of the 19th century. Marshall's was the first major treatise to be called *Principles of Economics* (1890), though the new term had appeared a little earlier in two forgotten books, by J. M. Sturtevant (1877) and H. D. Macleod (1878).

The new term had also been used by Alfred and Mary Marshall in their joint work *Economics of Industry* (1879). As they explained, they thought it best to drop the term "political economy" because 'political' was misleading since 'political interests generally mean the interest of some part of parts of the nation' (p. 2). As Cannan plausibly surmised, they were probably thinking of 'political' in the sense of party politics (p. 43). Ironically, the adjective which was originally adopted because it referred to the state or community as a whole was now abandoned because it had come to denote the struggle for power between factions.

Other writers gave other reasons for preferring 'economics' to 'political economy'. Jevons explained in the preface to the second edition of his *Theory of Political Economy* (1879) that, although it was too late to alter the title, he had discarded "the old troublesome double-worded name of our science" on grounds of convenience; the adjective, after all, was 'economic' not 'politic-economic', and there was the analogy with other disciplines, such as mathematics, ethics, aesthetics (p. xiv). Later, D. H. Robertson, in his lectures, used the same analogy, but now more pointedly with natural sciences—"the termination -ics indicates that our study is or aspires to be a science, like physics, dynamics and so forth" (Vol. I, p. 16). He also thought that "the dropping of the word 'political' emphasises that our ultimate concern is with individual human beings, not with 'States'" (Vol. I, p. 16).

Oddly enough, Wicksell, great economist and great radical, gave a similar reason for, on the contrary, retaining the older term in the title of his *Lectures on Political Economy* (1901–6). He argued that the term 'political economy', while appropriate in the age of mercantilism when it was regarded as a duty of the state itself to exercise an extensive influence over the affairs of individuals, had become less so with the advent of physiocratic ideas and the ascendancy of *laissez-faire*. He had nonetheless decided to retain the old name because "in accordance with the modern outlook, the subject matter of political economy is becoming more and more the doctrine of economic phenomena in their interrelations, seen as a whole" (pp. 1f.). At first glance, this might be thought to refer to macroeconomics in the Wicksellian–Keynesian sense. But Wicksell immediately went on to explain that he had something else in mind.

> i.e., in so far as they uniformly affect whole classes of the community...As soon as we begin seriously to regard economic phenomena as a whole and to seek for the conditions of the welfare of the whole, consideration of the interests of the proletariat must emerge; and from thence to the proclamation of equal rights for all is only a short step. The very concept of political economy, therefore, or the existence of the science with such a name, implies, strictly speaking, a thoroughly revolutionary programme (p. 4).

This, as we shall see presently, could be taken as foreshadowing some 20th-century usage rather than as harking back to the 18th and early 19th centuries. But it requires an important caveat. Wicksell's lectures were first published in German, and he used the German term *Nationaloekonomie*. While traditional German usage never sharply differentiated between the state and the nation, Wicksell's notion that 'the whole' refers to all classes of the community, including the proletariat, is more plausible for 'national' than for 'political' economy, the term used by his English translator.

Most 20th-century economists have preferred 'economics' to 'political economy' as the name of their discipline because they have thought it important to distinguish clearly between description and analysis of economic phenomena, on the one hand, and prescription and advocacy of policies on the other. As Robbins (1976, p. 2) has recently put it once again,

> Economics, as a positive science, has no status as ethical or political prescription...Political economy in my vocabulary is not scientific economics, a collection of value-free generalisations about the way in which economic systems work.

There has, of course, been much debate about the possibility of 'value-free' economics (e.g. Myrdal, 1932, and Schumpeter, 1954, pp 34–47), and much questioning of the claim of mainstream economists, neoclassical and other, that their theories are politically or ideologically neutral (e.g. Myrdal, 1969). There has also been a sustained effort by economists, under the name of welfare economics, to find ways of making value-free statements about economic policy. But the great majority of the profession have explicitly or implicitly accepted Robbins' terminology and his case for it.

Economists' Political Economy

This has left them free to use 'political economy' to cover some of the ground which methodological scruple requires them to exclude from 'economics'. Robbins called his recent book *Political Economy: Past and Present* because he devoted at least part of it to "a discussion of principles of public policy in the economic field" (1976, p. 3). The authors of a recent book on *The Political Economy of the Welfare State* explain that

> the preference for the term 'political economy' in the title of this book must not for a moment be taken to imply that political economy can somehow resolve the difficulties of welfare economics and provide clear-cut answers, untroubled by...interpersonal comparisons or by conflicts between basic value judgments. The term 'political economy' has been used, rather, to imply an extension of interest, where appropriate, to other fields, and in the present context the relevant field is social ethics...Some of the main propositions of moral philosophers can be taken up and their implications explored from the economist's point of view (T. & D. J. Wilson, 1982, p. 28).

Schumpeter, in his *History of Economic Analysis*, was more explicit. Distinguishing sharply between economic analysis which allows for "scientific progress in economics" and "our emotional or aesthetic preferences for the various schemata of life", he referred to "systems of political economy" as resting on what more recently have been called paradigms:

> By a system of political economy I mean an exposition of a comprehensive set of economic policies that its author advocates on the strength of certain unifying (normative) principles, such as the principles of economic liberalism, of socialism and so on (1954, p. 38).

His own *Capitalism, Socialism and Democracy* (1943), regarded by many as the most perceptive work in political economy of the 20th century, was obviously not political economy in this sense—it did not advocate anything—and he never referred to it as such.

Sometimes, 'political economy' has been used when nothing more precise would do. Thus the editors of a new journal, *History of Political Economy*, justified the choice of title in their Avant Propos by saying that it

> indicates the catholicity of our interest. We wish to count among our contributors not only those devoted to unravelling the intricacies of the development of economic analysis but also scholars who explore the relations of theory and analysis to policy, to other disciplines, and to social history generally (1969, p. 1).[4]

Marxist and Neo-Marxist Political Economy

While mainstream economists after Marshall called their subject 'economics' and kept 'political economy' up their sleeves to be available when they wanted to put forward views on public policy involving value judgements and interpersonal comparisons, 'political economy' was resurrected as a banner of the Radical left. The revival of political economy was the chief contribution of the neo-Marxist New Left to the radical protest movement of the 1960s.

Marx himself, the classical economist, always used 'political economy' in exactly the same sense as the other classical economists. *Das Kapital* was sub-titled *Kritik der Politischen Oekonomie*, and Marx continued to use the term even when other German economists used *Nationaloekonomie* or *Volkswirtschaftslehre*. But Marx was a follower of Ricardo rather than of Adam Smith. Where Adam Smith had seen the primary task of political economy as being to study "the nature and origins of the wealth of nations" or, as we would say, the determinants of economic growth, Ricardo said that "to determine the laws which regulate this distribution [of national income] is the principal problem of political economy" (1817, Vol. I, p. 5); and the distribution he had in mind was that between social classes, landlords, capitalists and workers. It was this Ricardian emphasis that became the centrepiece of Marx's economics (though intimately linked, in his view of the dynamics of capitalist development, with the forces of production). Marx, however, was not merely an economist; he was also a sociologist, philosopher of history and revolutionary.

4 The term 'political economy' also survives in the title of a distinguished Chicago journal and continues to be used by some universities such as Glasgow, University College London and Johns Hopkins, in preference to 'economics' in the names of their departments. But whether this is a pleasant antiquarianism or a profession of wider interests than scientific economics is not certain. One suspects that it means more to some than to others.

When 'political economy' was resurrected by the Radical Left in the 1960s, it was with these three connotations: an emphasis on distribution, rather than on productivity or growth; an emphasis on power relations between social classes as the main determinant of distribution; and a refusal to confine the subject to positive social science as contrasted with advocacy.[5]

The neo-Marxist critique of economics under the banner of 'political economy' is not easy to paraphrase. The literature is vast and contains many keenly disputed variants. Its three main lines of attack are perhaps best indicated by three sets of quotations (not all from professed neo-Marxists):

> Orthodox economics tries to show that markets allocate scarce resources according to relative efficiency; political economics tries to show that markets distribute income according to relative power (Nell, 1972, p. 35).
>
> As used by the classical French and British economists, the term 'political economy' referred to a study of the social laws governing the production and distribution of goods, and thus social classes and their conflicts were the economist's legitimate concern (Mermelstein, 1970, p. 3).
>
> The search for the laws of motion of society was largely abandoned to be replaced by the investigation of market processes and their allocative properties' (Barber, 1967, p. 123).
>
> Issues involving class and power have been relegated to the disciplines of sociology and political science (Mermelstein, 1970, p. 4).

> Retreating from 'subjective' value judgments...welfare theorists no longer believe that interpersonal judgments and comparisons can by made, at least by scientists...This nonsense conclusion...Marginalism is conservative for the reason that it deliberately abstracts from history and institutional specifications and centers its gaze upon the mechanism of choice...taking as given the existing distribution of income and wealth (Lekachman, 1970, p. xii).

> As economics is currently defined, little in the subject lends explicit support to institutional change...What the times require is a return to open partisanship in economics as well as in other social sciences (Lekachman, 1970, p. xi).

The institutional change advocated by most exponents of neo-Marxist political economy was, of course, the replacement of capitalism by a more efficient and equitable socialist system.

This is not the place to discuss the merits of neo-Marxist political economy in any detail. The neo-Marxist critics were clearly correct in their charges that orthodox economics had abandoned the interest of the classics in the "laws of motion of society", that it had no very satisfactory theory of the distribution of income and wealth, and that no such theory is possible without attention to the role of power of social groups. But it did not necessarily follow that laws of change of whole economic systems, such

5 For similar reasons, 'political economy' has seemed an appropriate label to some of the Cambridge 'post-Keynesians'; one of them, J. A. Kregel, called his introduction to post-Keynesian economics *The Reconstruction of Political Economy* (1973, p. xvi) because post-Keynesian theory, like that of Ricardo and Marx, emphasised social relations and the distribution of income, as well as changes and growth over time.

as those which Marx claimed to have discovered, can in fact be found and that either the search for such laws (as contrasted with analysis of the determinants of secular economic growth and structural change) or the study of power relationships among social groups and their effects on the distribution of income and wealth, is a job for economists. Similarly, neo-Marxists certainly touched a tender spot when they chided economists for their disclaimer to be able, as economists, to make statements about the desirable distribution of income or other policy pronouncements involving value judgments, of the kind most of them in fact made throughout their professional lives. But in doing so, neo-Marxists simply ignored the methodological problem whether such statements can be either proved or refuted, in other words, whether they represent anything more than, in Schumpeter's words, "our emotional or aesthetic preferences". Finally, it is evident that most professional economists have failed to be converted to 'political economy' in the Marxist sense of doctrine favouring the replacement of capitalism by socialism. And this points to the most intriguing irony of this story.

Chicago Political Economy

While Marxists have continued to denounce economics in the name of political economy, a large literature has grown up which, without claiming the label 'political economy', does very much what Marxists demand of social scientists but comes to very different conclusions, with very different policy implications. This is what might be called the literature of Chicago or libertarian political economy, provided it is understood that much of it derives from centres other than the University of Chicago, such as the Virginia Polytechnic, that many Chicago economists would not espouse it, and that not all those who use its methodology are necessarily libertarian in their politics.[6] W. C. Mitchell (1968) proposed the term "the new political economy" for part of this literature but, as will be explained later, it was the part for which the term was least appropriate.

Like the Marxists, the Chicago political economists are interested in the "laws of motion of society", but they attribute the rise of capitalism not so much to technological change in the process of production as to the emergence of a system of property rights which gave adequate and secure rewards to innovation. Like the Marxists, the Chicago political economists believe that income is distributed according to relative power, but unlike the Marxists they believe that power depends on control rather than on ownership of the means of production. They therefore see as the chief source of privilege, not concentration of ownership in the hands of capitalists, but concentration of power in the hands of the state and those who control it. Like the Marxists, they recognise market failure as a source of inefficiency and inequity under capitalism but they believe that there is much greater likelihood of inefficiency and inequity arising from the operation of the "political market" and that this grows as the role of the state grows, in western welfare states and under socialism. Contrary to the

6 For a popular, but comprehensive and readable, summary, see Lepage (1982).

Marxists, therefore, they tend to favour free markets and a reduction in the role the state.

For our purposes, it does not matter much that this summary over-simplifies the views of both these schools. The interesting fact is that there are now at least two schools of political economy in the Marxist sense, that is to say, social theory which goes beyond economics into history, and politics and sociology, which focuses on power relationships and which combines theoretical analysis with advocacy of policies.

Chicago political economy has given the story another ironic twist. In much the same way as Marx is said to have turned Hegel upside down, so Chicago has turned Marx upside down. By emphasising power and distribution, the zero-sum game aspects of social relations, in preference to economic efficiency and growth, Marx politicised economics. The Chicago school, with its economic theory of democracy, of the family and philanthropy and, more generally, its economic approach to human behaviour (cf. Downs, 1957; Becker, 1976, 1981; Lepage, 1982), has "economised" politics. But this analogy needs to be handled with some care.

There has for long been an ambiguity in the definition of economics, between definitions by subject matter and by method. When Marshall defined economics as "the science which investigates man's action in the ordinary business of life" (p. 95) and Pigou economic welfare as that part of social welfare that "can be brought directly or indirectly into relation with the measuring rod of money" (p. 11), they were broadly indicating the subject matter. In contrast, when Robbins defined economics as "the science which studies human behaviour as a relationship between ends and scarce means which have alternative uses" (p. 15) and, more obviously still, when Schumpeter adopted "Mrs Robinson's unsurpassably felicitous phrase, economic theory is a box of tools" (p. 15), they were focusing on the method.

The theory of rational choice was developed by economists to deal with economic problems (in Marshall's sense), but it has been found to have wider application. Fundamentally the same theory of maximising behaviour is applicable whether the maximand is utility (or real income) or prestige (as in Fred Hirsch's (1977) "positional competition") or power (as in Macchiavelli or Lenin) or the salvation of the soul (as in St Thomas Aquinas). But it is this approach—called 'economic' only because it is in relation to economic behaviour (in Marshall's sense) that it was first developed and most successfully applied—which the Chicago school has tried to apply to other aspects of human behaviour. In doing so, it does not claim that the assumption of rational maximising behaviour under conditions of perfect foresight is realistic in politics, family life or philanthropy, any more than in the economic sphere (cf. Bensusan-Butt, 1978). Their claim is merely that the economic approach has a wider power of explanation and prediction than any other simple model, and wider application beyond the economic sphere than had previously been realised (Lepage, 1982, p. 41). This part of Chicago political economy is social science, susceptible at least in principle to proof or refutation. Beyond this, the Chicago political economists, like the Marxists, advocate policies which are frankly based on value judgments, with the difference that much weight is given to individual freedom, in the liberal sense, as well as to efficiency and equity.[7]

Abuses and Uses of 'Political Economy'

Our historical survey suggests some conclusions about sensible and not so sensible uses of the term 'political economy' on which it may be possible to secure fairly general agreement. Let us begin with the inappropriate ones.

First, 'political economy' is no longer an appropriate term for economics as a positive social science. This includes economics at its most scientific, that is, as a discipline which seeks to explain economic behaviour through the formulation and empirical testing of hypotheses or models with predictive value. It also includes non-econometric applied economics, the study of economic institutions and other not easily quantifiable aspects of economic life. It may also be taken to include welfare economics, that is, the corpus of normative propositions concerning the most efficient means of achieving given ends relevant to economic policy. These descriptions still require some such criterion as Pigou's "relation to the measuring rod of money" to delimit economics from other social sciences, such as sociology, politics or social psychology. But this is not crucial to the line to be drawn between economics and political economy.

Secondly, 'political economy' is not a sensible umbrella term for any sort of interdisciplinary work among social scientists. While there is obvious scope—some would say need—for interdisciplinary studies, it makes little sense to call all cooperation between economists and political scientists 'political economy', any more than one would want to call cooperation between economists and psychologists 'psychological economy'.

Thirdly, the term 'political economy' is not really appropriate (*pace* W. C. Mitchell) for the positive social science component of what we have called Chicago political economy, that is to say, the use of the model of Economic Man outside the area of economic behaviour as normally understood. The theory of rational choice should not be regarded as a branch of economics (or as an 'economic theory') merely because it represents a generalisation of a model first developed in relation to economic behaviour; nor should it be regarded as a kind of political economy, merely because it uses economic concepts for the explanation of political behaviour (as in 'political market'). It is perhaps best viewed as a contribution to sociology in the broadest sense.

This seems to leave three uses of 'political economy' which can be justified.

There is, first, the unobjectionable, if not very rigorous, use of 'political economy' as illustrated by our quotations from Robbins and the Wilsons. Economists may feel they need a term for "discussion of principles of public policy in the economic field" which falls well short of advocacy but in which they openly avow their personal value

7 Marx, the Hegelian, valued 'positive' freedom (in the sense of participation) but despised 'negative' freedom (in the sense of absence of constraint), (Walicki, 1983).

judgments about trade-offs between ends. If they take the austere view that such discussion is beyond the proper bounds of economics, 'political economy' serves the purpose.

There is, secondly, Schumpeter's use of "systems of political economy" as expositions of comprehensive sets of economic policies which their authors advocate "on the strength of certain unifying (normative) principles, such as the principles of economic liberalism, of socialism and so on". Political economy in this sense is a pursuit common to contemporary neo-Marxists and contemporary Libertarians. Advocacy based on ideology is a wholly legitimate and important activity. But it is not in any sense a science, and it is not appropriate in a university curriculum. If what the advocates of university courses in political economy have in mind is "a return to open partisanship", it should be firmly resisted, and that applies to marketeers, environmentalists, feminists and peace-campaigners, as much as to Marxists.

There is, finally, the study of power as a determinant of economic phenomena, and particularly of the distribution of income and resources (cf. Rothschild, 1971). Since power is which politics is about, it makes sense to call this aspect of positive social science 'political economy'. In this circumscribed sense, political economy is an important field for more research and entirely suitable for study in the classroom. Indeed, it is only in this sense that political economy deserves a place in a university curriculum, not as a subject or discipline with its own department—it is hardly big enough for that—but as a unit in an economics and/or political science course. For the most part, it calls for the skills of the political scientist rather than the economist. Since political economy in this sense was largely developed by Marx, the contributions of Marxist thought must be expected to figure prominently in such studies. But a scholarly approach to political economy will also give due weight to Tullock, Buchanan and others of what we have called the Chicago school, as well as to Weber, Parsons and other sociologists.

References

Barber, W. J. (1967), *A History of Economic Thought*, Penguin, Harmondsworth.

Becker, G. S. (1976), *The Economic Approach to Human Behaviour*, University of Chicago Press, Chicago.

—— (1981), *A Treatise on the Family*, Harvard University Press, Cambridge, Massachusetts.

Bensusan-Butt, D. M. (1978), *On Economic Man*, Australian National University Press, Canberra.

Cannan, E. (1929), *A Review of Economic Theory*, P. S. King, London.

Downs, A. (1957), *An Economic Theory of Democracy*, Harper & Row, New York.

Garnier, J. (1852), 'De l'origine et de la filiation du mot economie politique', *Journal des Economistes*, vol. 32, pp. 300–16; vol. 33, pp. 11–23.

Gray, A. (1931), *The Development of Economic Doctrine*, Longman, London.

Hirsch, F. (1977), *Social Limits to Growth*, Routledge & Kegan Paul, London.

History of Political Economy (1969), vol. 1, p. 1.

Jevons, W. S. (1879), *Theory of Political Economy*, 2nd edn, Macmillan, London.
Kregel, J. A. (1973), *The Reconstruction of Political Economy*, Macmillan, London.
Lekachman, R. (1970), 'Special Introduction' to Mermelstein (1970).
Lepage, H. (1982), *Tomorrow, Capitalism: The Economics of Economic Freedom*, Open Court, La Salle, Illinois.
Macleod, H. D. (1878), *Economics for Beginners*, Longman, London.
Marshall, A. (1890), *Principles of Economics*, Macmillan, London.
Marshall, A. & Marshall, M. P. (1879), *Economics of Industry*, Macmillan, London.
Mermelstein, D. (1970), *Economics: Mainstream Readings and Radical Critiques*, Random House, New York.
Mitchell, W. C. (1968), 'The New Political Economy', *Social Research*, vol. 35, pp. 76–100.
Myrdal, G. (1932), *The Political Element in the Development of Economic Theory*, Routledge & Kegan Paul, London.
—— (1969), *Objectivity in Social Research*, Pantheon, New York.
Nell, E. (1972), 'Economics: The Revival of Political Economy', in R. Blackburn (ed.), *Ideology in Social Science*, Fontana, London.
Pigou, A. C. (1920), *Economics of Welfare*, Macmillan, London.
Ricardo, D. (1817), *On the Principles of Political Economy and Taxation* (ed. Sraffa), Cambridge University Press, Cambridge.
Robbins, L. (1932), *An Essay on the Nature and Significance of Economic Science*, Macmillan, London.
—— (1976), *Political Economy: Past and Present*, Macmillan, London.
Robertson, D. H. (1963), *Lectures on Economic Principles*, Staples, London.
Rothschild, K. W. (1971), *Power in Economics*, Penguin Economics Readings, Harmondsworth.
Rousseau, J. J. (1755), 'Économie politique', *L'Encyclopédie*, Paris.
Schumpeter, A. J. (1943), *Capitalism, Socialism and Democracy*, Allen & Unwin, London.
—— (1954), *History of Economic Analysis*, Oxford University Press, New York.
Senior, N. (1836), *An Outline of the Science of Political Economy*, Augustus Kelly, New York, 1951.
Smith, A. (1776), *The Wealth of Nations* (ed. Cannan), Methuen, London.
Steuart, Sir J. (1767), *Inquiry into the Principles of Political Oeconomy*, Millar & Cadell, London.
Stollberg, G. (1977), 'Zur Geschichte des Begriffs "Politische Ökonomie"', *Jahrbücher für Nationalokonomie*, vol. 192, pp. 1–35.
Sturtevant, J. M. (1877), *Economics or the Science of Wealth*, Putnam, New York.
Walicki, A. (1983), 'Marx and Freedom', *New York Review*, no. 18, 24 November.
Wicksell, K. (1901–6), *Lectures on Political Economy*, Routledge, London, 1934.
Wilson T. & D. J. (1982), *The Political Economy of the Welfare State*, Allen & Unwin, London.

17

"Reaganomics"

Everything you wanted to know about Reaganomics but were afraid to ask

A review of P.C. Roberts, *The Supply-Side Revolution*, which sought to defend President Reagan's "voodoo economics". The supply-siders wanted to shift the emphasis from Keynesian demand management to incentives to productivity, but the huge expansion of money supply (for which the "Laffer curve" provided an alibi) caused an unprecedented double (budget and current account) deficit.

Originally published in *Quadrant*, March 1987.

The Supply-Side Revolution

For a quarter of a century after World War II, economic policy in Western countries was dominated by the combination of Keynes's macroeconomics and Beveridge's welfare state. To maintain full employment without inflation was the function of demand management through monetary and fiscal policy, while government spending financed by progressive taxation was to enhance social security and welfare. During the 1970s this edifice came apart. The Phillips curve trade-off between unemployment and inflation become more and more unfavourable. "Stagflation", combining high unemployment with high inflation, became the norm. At the same time, unceasing sectional pressures for more government welfare expenditures ran into increasing taxpayer resistance, reflected in threatening breakdown of tax systems through evasion and avoidance and in rising budget deficits.

In the United States, "supply-side economics" emerged as a way out of this dilemma. Between 1975 and 1978, it gained adherents in Congress. In November 1980, Reagan was elected President with a supply-side economic program. In June 1981 Congress enacted the first large tax cuts which were the core of the program. This book,[1] by one of the original supply-siders who played an influential role, first as economic adviser to Congressmen and as a *Wall Street Journal* columnist, and later as Assistant Secretary of the Treasury during part of the first Reagan Administration, admirably expounds supply-side economics, brilliantly if subjectively describes the political battles over it within the Administration, in Congress and in the media, but

1 Paul Craig Roberts, *The Supply-Side Revolution: An Insider's Account of Policymaking in Washington*; Harvard University Press, Cambridge, Mass., 1985.

quite inadequately explains the failure of supply-side economics to achieve its objectives.

Supply-Side Economics

Supply-side economics was well summed up in a statement by a sympathetic Harvard economist, Otto Eckstein, quoted by Roberts:

> The mistake we have made over the last twenty years is that we have always looked at the short-run demand effects, and have thereby ignored what we are doing to the long-run growth potential of the economy. (p. 64)

Keynesian theory explained the economy's performance in terms of the level of total spending. The focus of Keynesian macroeconomics was on demand management, regulating the level of aggregate spending so as to maintain full employment without inflation. The Keynesian emphasis was on fiscal policy, budgeting for deficits to raise total spending, and thus economic activity and employment, in periods of recession, and for surpluses to counter inflation through restraint on spending. On this view of fiscal policy the role of taxation was to reduce taxpayers' ability to spend—"tax cuts affect the economy only by affecting demand".

> Supply-side economics brought a new perspective to fiscal policy. Instead of stressing the effects on spending, supply-siders showed that tax rates directly affect the supply of goods and services. Lower tax rates mean better incentives to work, to save, to take risks, and to invest. As people respond to the higher after-tax rewards, or greater profitability, incomes rise and the tax base grows, thus feeding back some of the lost revenue to the Treasury. The saving rate also grows, providing more financing for government and private borrowing. (p. 25)

In demanding across-the-board tax cuts, and especially cuts in marginal rates of income tax, to stimulate incentives, supply-siders had to battle on at least five fronts.

Keynesians, looking only at the effects on demand, assumed that tax cuts would cause budget deficits and, while not in principle opposed to deficit finance, rejected them in current conditions as inflationary. Supply-siders countered by arguing that the incentive effects of tax cuts would limit deficits by expanding the tax base and bring down inflation by increasing supply of goods and services.

Egalitarians and others concerned with social welfare opposed cuts in progressive income tax as inequitable, cutting "taxes on the rich". Supply-siders countered by arguing that "there are more important ways to benefit from a tax cut than from the money it hands back. Better incentives meangreater labour productivity, greater growth in real wages, and more and better opportunities through which people can benefit themselves."

Traditional Republicans, such as Senator Goldwater, insisted on balanced budgets, partly because they condemned deficit finance as unsound, but mainly because they counted on the unpopularity of taxes as the most effective restraint on growth of government spending. Supply-siders played down the likely magnitude and adverse effects of budget deficits, but mainly insisted that the way to cut government spending was through growth of jobs and private sector income, not by attacking the government's budget with a paring knife in a static or declining economy. The way to reduce the burden of government spending was to have it decline as a percentage of national income as the economy grew.

There was also monetarism, associated especially with the name of Milton Friedman. Monetarists, like Keynesians, focused on demand management, but in opposition to Keynesians saw the root cause of inflation in excessive growth of money supply. In place of a counter-cyclical fiscal policy, they advocated a monetary policy aimed at moderate and steady money supply growth. Monetarists, too, tended to be wary of deficit finance, as traditionally one of the main causes of excessive monetary expansion, but were of course happier with deficits due to tax cuts than with deficits due to increases in government expenditure. Supply-siders therefore saw monetarists generally as allies, but viewed monetary restraint merely as an adjunct to their supply-oriented policy of tax cuts.

Finally, there was Arthur Laffer with his famous curve. "Laffer, an economics professor at the University of Southern California with a fondness for parrots and cacti" (p. 25), was a thorn in the side of supply-siders because he discredited their case by overstatement. He claimed that tax cuts would pay for themselves by stimulating the economy so strongly that rising tax revenues would quickly eliminate the budget deficit. The supply-siders, at least in their more sober moments, merely claimed that the incentive effects on the tax base would gradually reduce the deficit. The question was not whether tax cuts paid for themselves but whether they were more effective in promoting economic growth than were increases in government spending.

The Political Battle

Four middle chapters of Roberts's book are entitled "Prelude to Victory", "Victory and Defeat", "The Unravelling of Reaganomics" and "Assessing Reagan". They deal with the politics of the story, they give Roberts's view of what went wrong, and they provide a fascinating, and rather gruesome, account of the working of the American political system in Washington.

What went wrong, according to Roberts, was that supply-side economics was never given a fair test. From the start Reaganomics was a compromise between supply-side economics, monetarism, and traditional Republican budget-balancing. Reagan, while proclaiming himself a supply-sider and pushing through "the largest tax cut in history" in 1981, agreed to "the largest tax increase" in 1982.

Roberts's explanation is conspiratorial. "The President, who resisted higher taxes, finally succumbed to pressures from his aides and political rivals in the Senate." Roberts's *bête noire* is David Stockman, Reagan's Budget Bureau Director, who, he believes, in league with White House Chief of Staff James Baker and a small group of Senators, sabotaged the supply-side program from inside. Stockman, he thinks, driven by ambition and bemused by a mixture of Keynesian and traditional budget-balancing thinking, "intended from the beginning to replace the President's program".

The argument was: deficits cause inflation and high interest rates; high interest rates cause recession; to avoid recession we must raise taxes to lower the deficit.

The mystery, to which Roberts has no real answer, is why "the President has surrounded himself with people who did not believe in his program". Part II of this article looks at the other side in this argument, in Stockman's own autobiography.

Apart from this in-fighting within the Administration and Congress, the supply-siders had to contend with bitter hostility from what Roberts calls the "liberal establishment" (in the American sense of liberal), as represented within the Administration by Vice-President Bush who labelled their program "voodoo economics" and by the media, especially CBS-TV, the *New York Times* and *Washington Post*. In the course of his reflections on the reasons for Reagan's "policy reversal", Roberts devotes a page to what he calls the "denunciatory ethic" of the American intellectual élite, the tendency "to blame ourselves for everything that goes wrong in the world". I cannot resist the temptation to quote a paragraph on this phenomenon which has its echoes in Australia:

> One of the most successful nations in history, the United States projects abroad the image of a country totally dissatisfied with itself. Consider a typical member of our intellectual élite. His commitment to society is conditional upon pushing through the changes in institutions and policies that he thinks are necessary to bring about the desired improvements. Therefore, his allegiance at any point in time is weak; to satisfy his desire for progress, he feels he must remain an opponent of existing society. He does not see his country's gifts of foreign aid as attesting to its moral sense, but the insufficient amount is evidence to him of an immoral foreign policy. He justifies foreign nationalisation of his fellow citizens' property as a necessary remedy for neocolonial exploitation. He does not see lack of progress in arms limitations as a reflection on the opponent's intentions but, instead, on his own country's lack of good faith. A strong defense posture is not a justifiable response to an external threat, but is provocative and the cause of the arms race. He responds to warnings about a Soviet threat with stiff and strident protests against jingoism and, invariably, with that lead letter in the *New York Times* explaining the Soviet point of view. He reminds the alarmist of America's own sins and chides him for indifference. On the domestic scene he champions the failures as victims of society, and he explains the successful in terms of ill-gotten gains... (p. 256)

Patriotism has come to imply a lack of objectivity, where 'anti-American' has taken on certain positive connotations. At times the designation is almost a badge of honour. To be anti-American is to be against imperialism, neocolonialism, racism, sexism, commercial exploitation (particularly of the environment and the Third World), pollution, poverty, inequality, and war. In short, anti-American implies broadmindedness, a person who can transcend the anachronism of narrow national interest to represent the world, humanity and history's best impulses.

Success and Failure

Politics apart, Roberts's account of the supply-side revolution in the end fails to convince on the economic evidence. The reason is partly that it was written too soon.

From the vantage point of 1986, it is apparent that the 1982 tax increase was only a temporary reverse. Reagan persisted, and in 1986 achieved another large tax reform, including substantial cuts in marginal rates of personal and company income tax. In some respects, Reaganomics has been successful beyond all expectations. In other—crucial—respects, it has failed, with a legacy of problems as yet quite unresolved.

Roberts claims in the last chapter of his book that events had after all vindicated supply-side economics against its opponents within and without the Administration.

> His advisers had told him that the deficits would keep inflation high, but the inflation rate had collapsed. They had told him that the deficits would keep the interest rates high, but a fantastic rally began in the financial markets. They had told him there would be no recovery, but one appeared. They had told him it would be weak and faltering, but it grew in strength. (p. 299)

The latest OECD annual survey of the US economy substantially confirms these claims. The recovery from the 1981/82 recession was very rapid.

> In the first two years of the recovery (1983/84) output growth was stronger than in past upturns, inflation came down to one of the lowest rates in the OECD area, while unemployment also fell substantially. This situation stands in marked contrast to that in Europe, where disinflation has been accompanied by modest economic growth and rising unemployment. (OECD, *United States*, 1985)

Total civilian employment in the USA increased by 7.6 million in two and a half years. A surge of entrepreneurship, especially among small firms and self-employed, responded to investment opportunities, particularly in computers, electronics and biotechnology, but also in a host of other industries.

> It is estimated that approximately 600,000 new companies are started each year, double the rate in the 1960s. Although new firms have a high failure rate, they have also provided the bulk of new employment.

How much of this success is attributable to the supply-side program, the tax cuts with their hoped-for effects on incentives to work, save and invest? The answer is we do not know. There can be little doubt that high marginal tax rates affect incentives adversely while tax cuts affect them favourably. But such effects are so intangible and diffused that they are incapable of measurement. It seems quite likely that Reagan can take much of the credit for the good performance of the US economy, but perhaps less on account of the tax cuts than of the aura of optimism and self-confidence that he spread around the country, and the stimulus this gave to what Keynes called the "animal spirits" of capitalist entrepreneurs. But Keynesians have another simple explanation: the huge budget deficits which, they would say, directly, and indirectly through induced private investment, propelled the economy forward by expanding aggregate demand.

What we do know is that the supply-side program signally failed in two of its ostensible objectives. A tax base rising with rising income did not reduce, let alone eliminate, the budget deficit which nearly doubled between 1982 and 1985, rising from $US 128 to 210 billion; and the tax cuts failed to stimulate domestic saving and thus to provide the means to finance the deficits. Roberts never comes quite clean on the deficit issue. While conceding that large budget deficits are not good for the economy, he diverts attention from their adverse effects by questioning whether "higher taxes are preferable to higher borrowing". And while he more than once dissociates himself from Laffer, he also more than once comes close to Laffer's position by claiming that the improved economic performance resulting from tax cuts "would bring the budget into balance".

The facts are that increases in defence expenditure and debt interest payments quite outweighed the reductions in non-defence spending that Reagan achieved, and the ever increasing budget deficits have been largely financed, not by increased domestic saving, but by capital inflow, largely from Japan, attracted by high US interest rates and investment opportunities. Capital inflow also financed the ever increasing US current account deficit which reflected declining international competitiveness of many American industries and, by keeping the dollar strong, aggravated the decline in competitiveness. In consequence, the USA, until not long ago the world's largest creditor, has become the largest debtor country. The Chairman of the Federal Reserve Board, Mr Volcker, in recent evidence to a Congressional committee, spoke of the USA living in a "false paradise". Stressing the huge interest burden which is accumulating with rising foreign debt, he said:

> Unfortunately, given our Budget deficit, savings patterns, and the trend of plant and equipment spending, the evidence suggests that most of the funds available from abroad have indirectly supported consumption, rather than adding much to our productivity or productive capacity...The strains are now showing economically and politically. Looking ahead, the relevant question is whether the large shift in resources, implicit in reducing our trade deficit, and the surpluses of others, can be accomplished in a framework of non-inflationary growth, here and abroad. (Quoted by Paul Kelly, *The Australian*, 11 October 1986)

The 1986 depreciation of the US dollar is a first step towards the necessary adjustment.

It is a striking feature of Roberts's book, and its chief weakness, that there is hardly a single reference to the US balance of payments or exchange rate. The facts summarised in the preceding paragraph are totally ignored, partly perhaps because they had not yet become so obvious when the book was written. This, incidentally, makes the book less relevant to Australia's current economic situation which, on a much smaller scale, resembles that of the USA in precisely these respects. But what the book does deal with most instructively and readably, the issues raised by supply-side economics, is also relevant to Australia. Roberts's book therefore deserves more attention in this country than it has yet received.

The Triumph of Politics

David Stockman was Reagan's Director of the Budget until he resigned in August 1985 and the man whom Paul Roberts accused of having sabotaged Reagan's supply-side revolution. Stockman has now written his own *apologia*.[2]

Clever young David was brought up on a middle western farm, entered Michigan State University as an orthodox Republican, became a radical student leader during the campus rebellion of the 1960s, tried a spell as a Divinity student, took a PhD in Political Science, at 28 got himself elected as Congressman for Michigan and was converted to supply-side economics by the group around Jack Kemp and Irving Kristol just in time for Reagan's election in November 1980. Most of the book is an agonised and ill-tempered account of his vain attempts to stem the Gadarene rush to disaster by an Administration caught between "voodoo economics" and "the politics of American democracy".

The book is not easy or pleasant reading. Stockman writes in the breathless, vulgar style of smart-aleck American political journalism. Three hundred pages of the book are taken up by tedious ball-by-ball description of wrangling among advisers in the first year of the Reagan Administration. Stockman's technique of heaping abuse on all his former friends and colleagues—and not least on President Reagan—by disingenuous confessions of what blind fools "we all were" does not endear him to the reader. The years 1983–85 are virtually ignored. The really important facts about the American economy are presented on one page of an Epilogue which appears to have been written long after the rest of the book. And there is no index to help the reader. But the book deserves some attention because it clarifies aspects of Reaganomics which were ignored or played down by Roberts and which are ominously relevant to Australia.

Stockman never really was a supply-sider, although for a while he was prepared to make common cause with them. He was a "hard-core anti-spender". His prime objective was "an enormous shrinkage of the vast expenditures that the Congress pumped into illicit and inappropriate functions of the state", the whole gamut of the welfare state, of farm subsidies and industry bail-outs, of the pork barrel of urban development, job corps, rapid-transit programs and other "statist abominations". He passionately believed that most of these programs did not really help the poor. The political process tended to shift the benefits to "middle-class entitlements" and to the welfare bureaucracy. "As with so many of the Great Society programs, the ones who profited from the Job Corps were the people who ran it." Spending cuts would permit lower taxes, and "capitalist dynamism also required lower taxes". But Stockman was from the beginning totally unconvinced by the Laffer "magic" or even by Roberts's moderate version and was therefore adamantly opposed to tax cuts unless they were accompanied, or preferably preceded, by corresponding cuts in spending. For he believed in balanced budgets as staunchly as the most orthodox Hoover Republican.

Until page 405, Stockman is virtually silent on why deficits are "disastrous". He hints at "cheap unsustainable debt creation", at "runaway inflation" and at high interest rates as inevitable consequences. But these arguments cut little ice when, as Roberts triumphantly pointed out, during the years 1982–85 Reaganomics seemed to attain substantial economic growth with falling inflation and falling interest rates, despite rising deficits. Stockman did score one telling point which quite escaped Roberts. The

2 David A. Stockman, *The Triumph of Politics*; The Bodley Head, London, 1986.

supply-siders' projections of a rapid rise in the tax base with rising GNP (and therefore moderate budget deficits) extrapolated from years of high inflation. It was bracket-creep based on high marginal rates of income tax plus inflation, rather than accelerated real growth due to supply-side response to tax cuts, which would yield the extra revenue. Hence, the hoped-for slowdown of inflation would automatically expand the budget deficit, as did indeed happen.

From the first days of the Reagan Administration, Stockman, with a few like-minded collaborators in and out of Congress, fought for spending cuts—against politicians and bureaucrats, each determined to protect his fiefdom. The modest cuts here and there to which they managed to get the President to agree were generally swamped by increases in other programs, especially defence. When adequate cuts in spending proved unattainable, Stockman pushed for deferment of the tax cuts and in response to the 1981/82 recession for a tax increase—the "sabotage" which, in Roberts's view, robbed the supply-side revolution of its initial impetus.

Stockman attributes his failure to "the triumph of politics".

> The sovereign state ended up on open bazaar, its fiscal and legal resources plundered by organised interest group by means of political muscle, bargaining and logrolling. (p. 33)

At times he is inclined to see a gulf between the "interests" and the people.

> Government was no longer accountable to the people because the instruments of government had been seized, the better to serve the parochial ends of society's modern-day guilds and syndicates: the trade associations, unions, professions and other organised interests. (p. 33)

But in the end, he sees the root cause of the trouble in the nature of the democratic process and is ready to exonerate the politicians:

> The electorate...is interested in getting help from the government to compensate for a perceived disadvantage. Consequently the spending politics of Washington do reflect the heterogeneous and parochial demands that arise from the diverse, activated fragments of the electorate scattered across the land. What you see done in the halls of the politicians may not be wise, but it is the only real and viable definition of what the electorate wants. (p. 228)

Not until the very last pages of the Epilogue does it dawn on him for the first time that the crucial malaise of the American economy after six years of Reaganomics is not merely, or primarily, that "a trillion dollars has already been needlessly added to our national debtto pay for a tax cut we could not afford" (p. 379), but that much of this debt is foreign debt.

> We have...borrowed enormous amounts of foreign capital to make up for the shortfall between our national production and our national spending. (p. 379)

The savings that have been used to finance the deficit have largely been Japanese rather than American savings.

> By turning ourselves into a debtor nation...we have sacrificed future living standards in order to service the debts we have incurred. (p. 379)

Capital inflow, in turn, by keeping the dollar strong until 1986, covered up but also aggravated a serious decline in the international competitiveness of many US industries. Stockman ends with the profoundly gloomy prognosis that "repudiating the debt through inflation will soon be revealed as the inevitable consequence of the course we are now set on".

The sad story of Reaganomics has at least four important lessons for Australia. First, the supply-siders had a sound instinct when they rejected the almost exclusive reliance on demand management that had dominated macroeconomic policy thinking in Western countries since World War II and advocated policies, such as reduction of high marginal rates of income tax and deregulation, which would strengthen incentives to produce, save and invest.

Secondly, the supply-siders proved mistaken in thinking that the effects of tax cuts on incentives would be strong and quick enough to keep budgets balanced through a rising tax base.

Thirdly, Stockman was therefore right in arguing that tax cuts must be accompanied by cuts in spending, although his emphasis on balanced budgets was probably excessive. But Stockman's account of his total failure to persuade the Administration and Congress to make such spending cuts, the "triumph of politics", points to the fundamental problem of the Western democracies, the relentless and increasingly organised demands on government for more and more government spending to meet more and more "needs".

Fourthly, the worst course in this predicament is the line of least resistance which both American and Australian governments have followed in recent years—of financing large budget deficits by borrowing abroad. A major difference between the USA and Australia is that the US budget deficits have risen so rapidly partly because inflation has been virtually halted in the USA. In Australia, growth of budget deficits has been restrained partly because a high rate of inflation has continued to expand government tax revenue through bracket-creep.

18

Keynes and Churchill

Keynes and Churchill, arguably the two greatest British figures of the century, were contemporaries. They had social contacts and for twenty years worked with (and sometimes against) each other. Yet the vast literature on both contains no account of their relationship. To give such an account is the purpose of this essay.[1]

Originally published in the series "Working Papers in Economic History", No. 186, May 1995, The Australian National University, Canberra.

In June 1944, the British economist, Lionel Robbins, having observed Keynes negotiating with the Americans at the Bretton Woods conference, confided to his diary:

> I often find myself thinking that Keynes must be one of the most remarkable men that ever lived—the quick logic, the birdlike swoop of intuition, the vivid fancy, the wide vision, above all the incomparable sense of the fitness of words, all combine to make something several degrees beyond the limit of ordinary human achievement. Certainly, in our own age, only the prime minister [Churchill] is of comparable stature. He, of course, surpasses him. But the greatness of the Prime Minister is something much easier to understand than the genius of Keynes. (Howson-Moggridge 1990, p. 158)

More recently, the American economist, J. K. Galbraith, has drawn the same comparison in his usual caustic manner: In 1936 "Keynes, like his great contemporary Churchill, was regarded [in US official circles] as too clear-headed and candid to be trusted" (Galbraith 1975, p. 133).

Keynes and Churchill stand out as arguably the greatest British figures of this century. They were near contemporaries, Churchill born in 1874, Keynes in 1883. Although born into and belonging to very different segments of British society—Churchill the aristocrat and politician, Keynes the middle class intellectual—they had social contacts through most of their lives and for over twenty years worked with (and sometimes against) each other. Yet the vast literature on both of them contains no account of their relationship. To give such an account is the purpose of this essay.

1 For helpful comments on an earlier draft I am indebted to Professor D. Moggridge and Dr L. D. Thomson.

Parallel Lives

From 1906 until 1908, Churchill was Under-Secretary at the Colonial Office in the Liberal government, while Keynes was a clerk in the India Office. But the two government departments were quite distinct, and there is no evidence, nor likelihood, that the Minister and the junior civil servant had anything to do with each other. From 1908 until 1910 Churchill was President of the Board of Trade and, in close collaboration with Lloyd George who was Chancellor of the Exchequer, initiated a radical program of social reform. Spurred on by Beatrice Webb and assisted by the young William Beveridge, he introduced labour exchanges, unemployment and infirmity insurance. But during the very years while Churchill was "one of the founders of the welfare state" (Addison 1994, p. 57), intensely concerned with the problem of unemployment which twenty years later would preoccupy Keynes, the latter was a young don at Cambridge, moving from philosophy to economics, but living the congenial life of an "Apostle" among like-minded friends. 1909 was the year of Lloyd George's radical budget, the constitutional crisis over the House of Lords and troubles in Ireland. Keynes, we are told, "was aware of these things, tangentially involved in some of them, but was basically indifferent to them" (Skidelsky 1985, p. 232).

In 1911, after a spell as Home Secretary, Churchill became First Lord of the Admiralty, and "his radicalism faded" (Addison 1994, p. 65). For the next decade, he was wholly absorbed by political and military affairs, naval rearmament, the Dardanelles, active service in France, the Ministry of Munitions and the War Office. Thus, although Keynes, from the outbreak of World War I in August 1914, played an important role in the Treasury under the government of which Churchill was a member, their official paths did not cross, and this remained the case even during the Versailles peace conference of 1919. Keynes was in Paris as Treasury representative on the British delegation from January 1919, and Churchill visited Paris in February, but, as Keynes later mentioned, "Churchill was little concerned with the conference" (Keynes *Collected Writings X,* p. 64; hereafter cited as CW) and there is no evidence that they met there. When Keynes published his passionate denunciation of the Versailles settlement in his *The Economic Consequences of the Peace,* he sent a complimentary copy to Churchill, but we do not know whether it was acknowledged.

Until 1924, therefore, when Churchill became Chancellor of the Exchequer in Baldwin's Conservative government, Keynes and Churchill lived parallel lives, almost fortuitously unconcerned with each other's business. But this is not to say that they did not know each other and meet socially. Churchill's political and society circles and Keynes's Cambridge and Bloomsbury ones overlapped at a few points. One may have been the Webbs. Beatrice first met Churchill in 1903 when she dismissed him in her inimitable way as "bumptious, shallow-minded and reactionary", but came to be much more favourably impressed when in 1908 he swallowed Sidney's scheme for labour and unemployment (MacKenzie 1977, p. 355). Keynes was on the fringe of Fabian activity at Cambridge. In 1909 he spoke to the Fabians on foreign investment, in 1911 at the Union in support of Sidney Webb (Moggridge 1992, p. 190). Among the Cambridge Fabians was his friend Rupert Brooke who once, with Lytton Strachey, "tried to explain Moore's ideas to Mrs Webb while she tried to convince us of the efficacy of prayer" (MacKenzie 1977, p. 381). It is difficult to believe that, through Brooke and the Webbs, and later in Bloomsbury, Keynes did not have social contact with Shaw, Wells and others who in turn must have encountered Churchill, the Liberal politician.

The other possible *point d'appui* is Lady Ottoline Morrell, who liked to play hostess to Bloomsbury, on Thursday evenings at the Morrells' house at 44 Bedford Square and later at their Garsington country home. On 18 May 1911, she gave a party in honour of Churchill who "looked very fine in full-dress uniform"—he was going on to a ball at Buckingham Palace (Seymour 1992, p. 131). Keynes visited her for the first time a month later, though he had no doubt seen and heard of her before, and in the following years saw much of her, staying at Garsington many times, including for quite a while to recuperate after his appendicitis operation in July 1915 (Moggridge 1992, p. 247). Again there is no record that Churchill and Keynes met through Lady Ottoline but it is not unlikely. During the war, in 1916, we are told,

> Keynes continued to labour at the Treasury and his letters to his parents were full of a busy social life studded with the names of the Asquiths, the McKennas, Lady Ottoline Morrell and Mr Winston Churchill. (Keynes, CW XVI, p. 177)

In March 1916, he told his mother he had "dined twice at Downing Street in the past fortnight" (Skidelsky 1985, p. 326). Whether at No. 10 or 11 he did not say, but Churchill may well have been present.

Between 1922 and 1924 Churchill was out of office and Parliament and divided his time between fighting elections unsuccessfully, journalism and other writing. Keynes, intermittently involved in reparations and war debt diplomacy, commuted between Cambridge and Bloomsbury and divided his time between teaching, journalism and other writing. This phase ended dramatically when Baldwin resumed office as Prime Minister in November 1924. To Churchill's own and everyone else's surprise, he offered him the Chancellorship of the Exchequer. Churchill later explained, "I should have liked to have answered 'Will the bloody duck swim?' but as it was a formal and important occasion I replied 'This fulfils my ambition'." (Gilbert 1976, p. 59)

Churchill's Chancellorship

Ever since he left the Treasury in 1919, Keynes had been much concerned with the central problem of British financial policy: whether Britain should return to the gold standard at the pre-war parity for sterling. At the end of the war, a Committee on Currency and Foreign Exchanges headed by the former Governor of the Bank of England, Lord Cunliffe, had recommended such a return. The Lloyd George government had accepted this recommendation in principle and had passed legislation which, following questions in Parliament, set 31 December 1925 as the deadline. Keynes's views fluctuated. In the early 1920s he had favoured a policy of securing domestic price stability by maintaining a flexible exchange rate and thus avoiding the deflationary policy needed to raise sterling to parity, with the adverse effects of such a policy on money wages and/or unemployment. He argued this case in the *Tract on Monetary Reform* (1923) and in numerous articles. He again presented his views in July 1924 to a committee under Austen Chamberlain appointed by Snowden, the Chancellor in the short-lived first Labour government. He now argued that there was no need for a deflationary policy since rising prices in the USA would see sterling rise to or above par. The Committee seemed to agree with Keynes, rather than with the Treasury and the Bank of England which regarded return to gold at the old parity as essential to the standing of London as the world's financial centre. But before they completed their report, the Labour government fell, and general elections in October 1924 brought Baldwin to power with Churchill as his Chancellor of the Exchequer (Moggridge, ch. 17).

Churchill came to the Chancellorship without any formal training in economics and without any strong views except for a liberal attachment to free trade and sympathy for the unemployed. It is probably true, as Skidelsky has claimed, that "Churchill understood modern no better than old-fashioned economics" (Skidelsky 1992, p. 197), but he had an acute intelligence and great power of application to any problem he had to deal with. Within weeks of assuming his new office he was presented by Montagu Norman, the Governor of the Bank of England, with a plan to prepare for a return to gold at par before the end of 1925. He was worried about the domestic implications of which Keynes had warned in articles in *Nation* with which he was familiar. By 29 January he had written a substantial paper, dubbed "Churchill's Exercise", setting out the objections to a quick return to gold. It led the head of the Treasury, Bradbury, to comment that "he appears to have his spiritual home in the Keynes–McKenna sanctuary" (Skidelsky 1992, p. 426). There has been some doubt whether Churchill was expressing his own view or was merely provoking his official advisers into stating their case for the return to gold more forcefully. In this he was certainly successful, eliciting long and trenchant replies. But there is also no doubt that Churchill was genuinely perplexed and torn between the pros and cons. On reading another article by Keynes on "The Return Towards Gold", Churchill complained in another memorandum:

> The Treasury have never, it seems to me, faced the profound significance of what Mr. Keynes calls "the paradox of unemployment amidst dearth". The Governor shows himself perfectly happy in the spectacle of Britain possessing the finest credit in the world simultaneously with a million and a quarter unemployed. (Moggridge 1992, p. 428)

In another attempt to resolve his doubts, Churchill arranged for a dinner on 17 March to which he invited, besides his private secretary (P. J. Grigg), Bradbury and Niemeyer for the Treasury and Bank and Keynes and McKenna for the opposition. Till midnight and beyond, Keynes and McKenna argued that at the pre-war parity sterling would be overvalued by 10 per cent and that the adjustment to the higher rate would mean additional unemployment and industrial unrest over wage cuts, while Bradbury and Niemeyer again put their case. Churchill, "ready to and anxious to be convinced as far as my limited comprehension of these extremely technical matters will permit" (Rose 1994, p. 174), asked McKenna:

> This is not entirely an economic matter; it is a political decision, for it involves proclaiming that we cannot, for the time being, complete the undertaking which we acclaimed as necessary in 1918, and introduced legislation accordingly. You have been a politician; indeed you have been Chancellor of the Exchequer. Given the situation as it is, what decision would you take? (Grigg 1948, p. 182f)

McKenna is said to have replied: "There is no escape; you have to go back; but it will be hell." (*ibid.*).

On 19 March Churchill agreed with Norman on the return to gold at the old parity and on 28 April he announced the decision in the Budget. In July Keynes published his pamphlet, *The Economic Consequences of Mr Churchill.* Keynes was not now opposed to a return to the gold standard as a fixed exchange-rate system. His ferocious attack was directed at the overvaluation of sterling implied in the return at pre-war par, because of its effects on unemployment and the balance of payments. Nor was it directed at Churchill personally. Churchill, he said, had made the disastrous decision partly because he

> has no intuitive judgement to prevent him from making mistakes; partly because, lacking this intuitive judgment, he was defeated by the clamorous voices of conventional finance; and, most of all, because he was gravely misled by the experts. (CW IX, p. 212)

Neither did Churchill resent Keynes's criticisms. In Parliament, he charged Snowdon with inconsistency in first urging the earliest possible return to gold and then attacking the government for taking this course and contrasted Snowdon's line with

> the position of Mr Keynes, who is, I suppose, by far the most distinguished and able exponent of opposition to the return to gold. He is the great advocate of a managed currency, the most powerful and persuasive advocate. (Churchill Speeches, p. 3595)

On the day in September 1931 when the pound went off gold—an event which Keynes greeted with delight, "chuckling like a boy" (C. H. Rolphe, cited in Skidelsky 1992, p. 397)—Keynes had lunch with Churchill. That evening the Webbs visited the Keyneses at Tilton, their country house. Keynes told Beatrice, as she later recorded in her diary, that during lunch Churchill had claimed he had never been in favour of the return to the gold standard (Mackenzie 1985, p. 260). He called it his "biggest blunder" for which he blamed Montagu Norman (Boyle 1967, p. 190).

Keynes's warnings about the economic and social consequences of the return to gold at par were soon borne out by the problems of the coal industry which led to the general strike of 1926. When the coal owners, in the face of declining international competitiveness, sought to reduce wages, Keynes objected, and Churchill, as Chancellor, also adopted a conciliatory position, offering a subsidy which, he hoped, would maintain industrial peace. But once the miners secured the support of the TUC for a general strike, Churchill turned militant. Keynes had little sympathy with the rabid tone Churchill adopted as editor of the government's official strike journal, the *British Gazette,* and indeed with Churchill's increasingly conservative positions in the last three years of his chancellorship. In 1928, we find him writing a rude letter to Churchill: "Dear Chancellor of the Exchequer, What an imbecile Currency Bill you have introduced!" Churchill replied courteously: "My dear Keynes, Apologies for not replying sooner...I will read your article enclosed and reflect carefully, as I always do, on all you say" (CW XIX, p. 749f.). In 1929, Keynes criticised Churchill's opposition to the program for combating unemployment through public works put forward by Lloyd George and supported in a Liberal Party pamphlet, *We Can Conquer Unemployment*, to which Keynes had contributed. Churchill in his last budget speech of April 1929 had put the orthodox "treasury view" that deficit financed public investment would create little employment because it would crowd out private investment through higher interest rates. Keynes's refutation was the main theme of his *Treatise on Money* on which he worked during those years.

From May 1929, when the Baldwin government fell, until September 1939, when Churchill once again became First Lord of the Admiralty, he was out of office and almost devoid of interest in economic matters, preoccupied first with India and then with Germany. Professional contacts with Keynes were few and far between. When Keynes in 1930 proposed a 10 per cent tariff on all imports, as an alternative to a devaluation of the pound, Churchill, in a dramatic departure from his attachment to free trade, expressed sympathy, converted, according to Grigg, "by the blandishments of Keynes" (Grigg 1948, p. 233). When Churchill visited the USA in the following year, Brendan Bracken briefed him on events at home, sending him the views of Keynes on the world monetary situation (Lysaght 1979, p. 132).

There is no published record of Churchill taking any interest in the Keynesian revolution of the 1930s. Keynes, on the other hand, was all with Churchill in his onslaught on appeasement. In March 1938 he wrote to him: "I have shared the general admiration of your magnificent speeches in the House of Commons" (Gilbert V, p. 955) and a few months later he referred in a letter to Kingsley Martin to "anti-Chamberlain candidates supported by all of us, e.g. Winston" (C W XXVIII, p. 123).

But if professional contacts after 1925 were few, social contact was frequent, chiefly through the Other Club.

The Other Club

The Other Club was founded by Churchill and F. E. Smith (the later Lord Birkenhead) in 1911 when, it is said, both had applied for membership of The Club, the exclusive club that went back to Samuel Johnson's day, and had been blackballed (Campbell 1983, p. 268). The object of the new club (as of the old) was "dining and wagering". It was to consist of not more than 50 members, of whom not more than 24 should be Members of the House of Commons. The rules, whimsically drafted by F. E. Smith, specified that the club was to meet on alternate Thursdays "at 8.15 punctually" when Parliament was in session. The names of the Executive Committee "shall be wrapped in impenetrable mystery". "Nothing in the Rules of Intercourse of the Club shall interfere with the rancour or asperity of party politics." Dinners were generally held in the Pinafore Room of the Savoy and could go on late into the night. Churchill's chauffeur had many happy memories of these occasions when interviewed by Churchill's biographer: "Winston never missed this if it was possible to attend, and he always enjoyed himself there, always coming out at around 2 am, give or take an hour, in a very happy frame of mind" (Gilbert V, pp. 63, 506). Churchill's last public appearance in December 1964, aged 90, was at a dinner of the club (Rose 1994, p. 141).

Membership was by invitation. If a particularly eminent member was to be recruited, Lloyd George would join Churchill in issuing the invitation (Hazlehurst 1995). The list of members over the years reads like a *Who's Who* of Britain's political and intellectual élite, from Lloyd George, Smuts and Reading, to high brass, such as Kitchener and Roberts, to press lords, such as Beaverbrook and Camrose, writers such as H. G. Wells, Arnold Bennett and P. G. Wodehouse, artists such as Lutyens and Munnings, scientists such as Lindemann (Lord Cherwell) and Cockroft, and judges (Coote 1971). But the chief qualification for membership appears to have been that "Winston thought well of them" (Gilbert V, p. 63).

Keynes was invited in 1927, the invitation demonstrating that Churchill bore him no grudge over his *Economic Consequences.* Keynes attended the dinners whenever time allowed. "It was a place of good talk and pleasant intimacy, more worldly in tone than the Bloomsbury gatherings in which he usually found recreation" (Harrod 1951, p. 396). Arnold Bennett encountered the new member at dinner in 1927 and found him "very agreeable and rather brilliant" (Bennett 1933, p. 962). In 1929, Keynes lost £160 in bets on the general elections but won £10 from Churchill, no doubt at the club. When Churchill during his visit to New York in 1931 was run into and severely hurt by a car, several of his Other Club friends, including Keynes, contributed to a £2,000 gift of a car. On another occasion, in 1940, Churchill's Other Club companions, including Keynes, presented him with a silver-gilt snuffbox that had belonged to Nelson (Gilbert VI, p. 853).

Dinners at the Other Club gave Keynes opportunities to talk to Churchill and, particularly after the outbreak of World War II, to raise policy matters, by-passing official channels. In October 1939, he tried (unsuccessfully) to persuade Churchill, then First Lord, to remove wheat from the list of contraband goods, partly to influence German and world opinion and partly to dissipate Germany's foreign exchange reserves (Moggridge 1992, p. 628). In July 1942, Keynes became concerned about the large sterling liabilities Britain was accumulating. When the India Office rejected any suggestion of blocking these balances, Keynes took his case to Churchill, now Prime Minister, at a meeting of the Other Club. The result was an "Action This Day" minute to the Chancellor which began: "Lord Keynes mentioned to me the other night" and asked for discussion in Cabinet (Moggridge 1992, p. 638). Keynes attended one more dinner of the club, exhausted after strenuous negotiations in the USA and amidst numerous other commitments, three weeks before his death on 20 April 1946 (Rose 1944, p. 341).

World War II

From May 1940, Churchill led the country's war effort, daily preoccupied with national defence, domestic politics and high diplomacy. For most of the time, according to Austin Robinson, he was "sublimely unaware in all but very occasional detail of what happened on the economic front" (Robinson 1975, p. 19). Brendan Bracken claimed he was "always bored by unheroic money matters" (Lysaght 1979, 250). Keynes was sometimes inclined to agree with this view. In July 1941, he wrote to the Chancellor of the Exchequer, Kingsley Wood:

> The President [F. D. Roosevelt] ought to be left free to concentrate on issues of strategy, diplomacy and politics without having to consider the pressing and difficult details of economic policy, which he does not really care for any more than our own Prime Minister. (CW XXIII, p. 155)

But there were many times when he found Churchill attentive to economic policy issues he put to him and at least once he gave him top marks. In April 1945, reporting in a personal letter on a dinner Churchill gave to a lot of finance people, including the Chancellor of the Exchequer and the Governor of the Bank of England to hear the views of Roosevelt's emissary, Bernard Baruch, Keynes said:

> Winston was quite magnificent throughout, in his best form, taking a profound interest in our Treasury problems for once, thoroughly understanding the points at issue. (CW XXIV, p. 302)

Keynes spent the first months of the war mainly at Cambridge, plagued by ill health after a severe bout of influenza, writing about "How to Pay for the War" and other aspects of war-economic policy. But he was soon drawn into official business and from August 1940 had an office and a secretary in the Treasury. Churchill soon made use of him. When Sir John Anderson was appointed Lord President of the Council with responsibility for overall control of the country's economic resources for the war effort, Churchill directed him: "You should summon economists like Keynes to give their views to you personally" (Wheeler-Bennett 1962, p. 260). In June 1940 Keynes drafted for Churchill a statement of encouragement to the French (CW XXII, p. 180). In July 1941, just preceding the Roosevelt–Churchill meeting that yielded the Atlantic Charter, Keynes saw a draft of Article VII which, by proclaiming non-discrimination in trade as one of the Allies' war aims, appeared to preclude the maintenance of imperial preference. Keynes may have had a hand in the subsequent insertion of the saving clause "with due respect for their existing obligations" (Amery 1988, p. 707f.) which later became the 'grandfather' clause in the GATT.

During the war years, Keynes visited the USA five times on official business, in 1941 to help mobilise US financial resources for Britain, including Lend-Lease; in 1943 for preliminary negotiations about the Keynes and White plans for the IMP and World Bank; in 1944 for the Bretton Woods conference, and in 1946 for discussions on the terms and conditions of the US loan to Britain, and each time also on much else. Churchill was undoubtedly aware of these issues, though not closely involved. A draft of Keynes's plan for a clearing union was put to Cabinet in April 1942

(Moggridge 1992, p. 678). When it came to finding a name for the new international currency unit, Keynes proposed 'bancor' but at one point suggested that

> our Prime Minister and President Roosevelt could between them do better than most of us at this game, as at most other games, if they had the time to turn their minds to writing a new dictionary as well as a new geography. (CW XXV, p. 272)

D. H. Robertson suggested 'winfranks' (CW XXII, p. 302). On one occasion, Churchill and Keynes travelled back from America together (Gilbert VIII 1988, p. 526). During the tense discussions of plans for post-war world trade early in 1944, Cherwell reported to Churchill that there were two factions in Treasury, one headed by Keynes, the other by Henderson, "an economist with Schachtian aspirations" (CW XXV, p. 302). Again, early in 1945, Churchill asked Keynes to attend a meeting on the same issues with the Governor of the Bank of England and senior Ministers (CW XXVI, p. 323).

There is little published evidence of other contacts between them during the war years, apart from dinners at the Other Club. The Prime Minister undoubtedly had a say in the appointment of Keynes as a director of the Bank of England in September 1941 and his elevation to the peerage in June 1942. Professor Moggridge tells me that Keynes's Appointments Book mentions, for 17 June 1942, "10 Downing Street"—to celebrate the latter event? Harrod refers to Keynes "staying with Mr Churchill during the war", presumably at Chartwell (Harrod 1951, p. 471). In May 1946, a few weeks after Keynes's death, Churchill, almost as exhausted as Keynes had been, wrote to Cherwell: "I am at what poor Keynes called in the last weeks of his life 'saturation point'." (Gilbert VIII, p. 234).

Two Great Men

Public figures as prominent, clever, opinionated and combative as Churchill and Keynes inevitably attracted criticism all their lives. Margot Asquith once said: "Winston has a noisy mind" (Leith-Ross 1968, p. 30). A recent biography of Churchill is a compendium of every criticism and abuse ever levelled at him (Rose 1994). Keynes was fiercely attacked over his *Economic Consequences of the Peace* and later by economists who disagreed with him. Montagu Norman referred to him as a "clever dilettante" (Boyle 1969, p. 160), Lloyd George in his war memoirs as "an entertaining economist whose bright but shallow dissertations on finance and political economy when not taken seriously, always provide a source of innocent merriment to his readers" (Lloyd George 1933-36, p. 684). But even at the time, and certainly on a longer view, these aspersions were overwhelmingly outweighed by praise and admiration.

One of Churchill's senior officials in Treasury reminisced about his

> vitality, his keen imagination and critical appreciation of any proposal put to him and his grasp of administration in the office, together with his generous temperament and genial expansiveness at Chartwell [which] won him the affection of all of us. (Leith-Ross 1968, p. 118)

One of his successors as Prime Minister described the Churchill of 1924–29: "Unique, wayward, exciting, a man with a peculiar glamour of his own, that brought a sense of colour into our rather drab political life" (Macmillan 1966, p. 176). These testimonies could be multiplied from the large literature.

Panegyrics on Keynes, no less whole-hearted, abound. Bertrand Russell: "The sharpest and clearest intellect that I have ever known" (Skidelsky 1983, p. 124). At the Bretton Woods conference: "On our side, one name stands quite alone. Maynard's performance was truly wonderful... His industry was prodigious, his resilience and continuous optimism constant wonder to those inclined to pessimism, while I doubt whether he has ever spoken with more lucidity and charm" (Lee 1975, p. 220). And, finally, one of his former Cambridge students:

> He was so much ahead of the field in wisdom, intellect and power, wit, in art, in generosity, in his range, and in the ease, gaiety and simplicity that went with all this, that I have never had any reverence left for any other famous men, economists or not, that I have since encountered. (Bensusan-Butt 1980, p. 26)

In the heat of debate, Churchill and Keynes could be disparaging about each other. During the 1929 election campaign Churchill once referred to "Professor Keynes" as "the proprietor or controller of an extreme radical weekly newspaper" (Churchill Speeches, p. 6442), and Keynes once declared a statement by Churchill to be "feather-brained" (Keynes CW IX, p. 240). But through most of their public lives, they expressed mutual regard. "Keynes had not only an intellectual appreciation of Mr Churchill's gifts, but also: a certain warmth of sympathy for one whose type of mind was very different from his own" (Harrod 1956, p. 360). Keynes was not merely being polite when, in his review of Churchill's *The World Crisis,* he declared that "Mr Churchill was, perhaps, the most acute and concentrated intelligence which saw the war at close quarters from beginning to end" and that "Mr Churchill writes better than any politician since Disraeli" (Keynes CW X, p. 53). Nor was Churchill merely being polite when he referred to Keynes in 1925 as "by far the most distinguished and able exponent of the opposition to the return to gold" who has argued his case in "a series of searching and brilliant articles, formidable and instructive" (Churchill Speeches, p. 3595).

Churchill and Keynes's backgrounds, personalities and interests were very different. Their two major periods of substantial professional interaction, Churchill's Chancellorship and World War II apart, the published literature allows us only glimpses of personal contact between them. But, as Skidelsky has said, "the relations between the two men were friendly" (Skidelsky 1992, p. 690), and to know this, and to learn something about the relations between these two great men, cannot fail to give one pleasure.

References

Addison, P. (1994), "Churchill and Social Reform" in P. Blake and W. R. Louis (eds), *Churchill,* Oxford University Press.

Amery, L. (1988), *The Empire at Bay: The Leo Amery Diaries, 1929–1945*, ed. J. Barnes and D. Nicholson, Hutchinson, London.

Baruch, B. (1960), *The Public Years*, Oldhams, London.

Bennett, A. (1935), *Journal 1896–1928,* Viking, New York.

Bensusan-Butt, D. M. (1980), *On Economic Knowledge*, Australian National University, Canberra.

Boyle, A. (1967), *Montagu Norman*, Cassell, London.

Campbell, J. (1983), *F. E. Smith: First Earl of Birkenhead,* Cape, London.

Churchill, W. S. (1974), *Complete Speeches*, (ed. R. R. James) 8 vols. Heinemann, London.

Coote, C. R. (1971), *The Other Club,* Sidgwick & Jackson, London.

Galbraith, J. K. (1975), "How Keynes Came to America" in Milo Keynes (ed.), *Essays on J. M. Keynes,* Cambridge University Press.

Gilbert, M. (1966–88), *Winston S. Churchill.* 8 vols, Heinemann, London.

—— (1967–82), *Companion Volumes (CV),* 6 vols, Heinemann, London. (Vols 1-2, author is Randolph S. Churchill.)

Grigg, P. J. (1948), *Prejudice and Judgment,* Jonathan Cape, London.

Harrod, R. F. (1951), *The Life of John Maynard Keynes*, Macmillan, London.

Hazlehurst, C. (1995), "Who founded The Other Club?: an alternative history", Canberra.

Howson, S. and D. Moggridge (eds) (1990), *The Wartime Diaries of Lionel Robbins and James Meade, 1943–45*, Macmillan, London.

Keynes, J. M. (1971–89), *Collected Writings (CW)*, ed. A Robinson & D. Moggridge, 30 vols, Macmillan, London.

Keynes, Milo (ed.) (1975), *Essays on J. M. Keynes,* Cambridge University Press.

Lee, F. G. (1975), "The International Negotiator" in Milo Keynes (ed.), *Essays on J. M. Keynes,* Cambridge University Press.

Leith-Ross, F. (1968), *Money Talk: Fifty Years of International Finance,* Hutchinson, London.

Lloyd George, D. (1933–36), *War Memoirs,* Nicholson & Watson, London.

Lysaght, C. E. (1979), *Brendan Bracken*, Allen Lane, London.

MacKenzie, N. and J. (1977), *The First Fabians,* Weidenfeld & Nicolson, London.

—— (eds) (1985), *The Diary of Beatrice Webb, (1924–43),* Vol. IV, Virago, London.

Macmillan, H. (1966), *Winds of Change, 1914–1939,* Macmillan, London.

Manchester, D. (1983), W. S. *Churchill: Visions of Glory, 1874–1932,* Little Brown, London.

Moggridge, D. (1992), *Maynard Keynes,* Routledge, London.

Robinson, A. (1975), "A Personal View" in Milo Keynes (ed.), *Essays on Keynes,* Cambridge University Press.

Rose, N. (1994), *Churchill: An Unruly Life*, Simon & Schuster, London.

Seymour, M. (1992), *Ottoline Morrell: Life on a Grand Scale*, Hodder & Stoughton, London.

Skidelsky, R. (1983), J. *M. Keynes: Hopes Betrayed, 1883–1920,* Macmillan, London.

—— (1992), John *Maynard Keynes: The Economist as Saviour, 1920–1937,* Macmillan, London.

Wheeler-Bennett, J. W. (1962), *John Anderson,* Macmillan, London.

19

Globalisation

'Globalisation' became a fashionable term in the 1990s. Enthusiasts spoke of the "borderless world". No more national frontiers, the whole world one market. This essay attempted to put globalisation in a more sober perspective. Liberalisation of markets has played as important a part as the "information revolution", and it is important to distinguish between short and long-term capital movements.

Originally published by the Australia–Japan Research Centre at The Australian National University in their series "Pacific Economic Papers", No. 275, January 1998.

Introduction

'Globalisation' has become fashionable. A few years ago, the term 'globalisation' took over from 'globalism' (Arndt 1996). Still unknown to the Oxford English Dictionary or spell checkers, it has spread like wildfire through the political economy literature: see "The borderless world" (Ohmae 1990); "No more national frontiers" (Reich 1991); "The end of the nation state" (Ohmae 1995); and "The whole world one market" (Radius Prawiro *forthcoming*).

These extravagant slogans clearly belong to fantasy land. The world still consists of nation states; there are nearly 200 members of the United Nations (UN). They all have national frontiers attended by immigration and customs officers. Politically, the trend is all the other way. Separatists—such as Kurds, Basques, Chechens, Tamil Tigers, Bougainvilleans (not to mention Quebecois and Scots)—are out to break up nation states.

Certainly, the world is one market in the sense that goods and services produced in one country can be sold in all other countries, subject to government-imposed trade barriers and transport and transaction costs. But this was also true in 1900 and 1800.

What has changed is the ease and speed with which goods and services, and capital, can move from one country to another. Governments have reduced trade barriers, while technical progress has greatly reduced the cost of transport by road, sea and air and increased the speed of communication by means of the phone, the fax and the Internet.

The world has experienced a marked opening up of national economies and an increasing degree of internationalisation.

This is an important fact, with important implications for economic policy. But it needs to be examined with a sense of proportion and some effort to sort out the various phenomena that have been lumped together in the literature of globalisation. To make such an examination is the object of this paper.

Causes

There is a tendency in the literature to attribute 'globalisation' simply to technological change (e.g. Ohmae 1995, p. vii). This is unconvincing. The crucial change in recent decades has been the liberalisation of international trade and payments by all developed, and many developing, countries.

The present century has witnessed a paradigm shift, from increasing government regulation and control of the economy in the first half to deregulation of trade and financial markets in the second half. It would take a separate paper to try to explain these profound changes. The strengthening of political democracy and organised labour in the wake of industrialisation in the 19th century; the emergence of socialist movements; the Great Depression of the 1930s, and consequent widespread pessimism about the future of capitalism; the imposition of direct controls over all aspects of the economy during World War II; and the distortions of production and trade which resulted from these developments all played a part in the first half of the century (Arndt 1944). The campaign of the USA for freer trade and non-discrimination; the mounting evidence for the inefficiency of state enterprises and direct controls in the Soviet Union and elsewhere; and the unexpected conjunction of full employment and sustained economic growth in the 25 years from 1945 presumably have been the chief factors in the second half (Maddison 1997).

Whatever the explanation, it is primarily this shift towards market-oriented and outward-looking policies that has propelled the internationalisation of national economies. Rapid growth of modern technology in transport and communications has undoubtedly played an important part; "The free flows of information, capital, expertise, technology and ideas have made the world smaller" (Gurung 1995). Liberalisation and technical change have interacted.

But that interaction has mainly taken the form of liberalisation being facilitated by changing technology. The result has been a very large increase in the international flow of goods and services. In the past two decades, world trade has grown twice as fast as world output (Howe 1994, p. 116). International long-term capital flows have increased much faster still and the daily volume of short-term international capital movements is being counted in trillions of dollars.

Liberalisation has taken four main forms. There has been a marked reduction in government-imposed trade barriers, including but not limited to tariffs, and a decline in transaction, transport and communication costs. In exchange rate policy, there has been a shift from fixed (or at least stable) exchange rates towards floating exchange rates. Domestic financial systems have been liberalised. Industrialising countries have sought to attract direct foreign investment through tax incentives and in other ways.

The increase in the volume of international trade is readily explained by the combination of growth of GDP, not least in the developing countries of East Asia, and opening up of national economies. The huge increase in the volume of international capital movements is more puzzling. The increase, in the course of world economic development, in the number of countries with significant domestic financial systems is part of the explanation. But where has all the money come from? Part of the answer is probably to be found in the expansionist monetary policies pursued by some countries, especially the United States, during the 1970s and early 1980s (cf Arndt 1995). The ease with which liberalised financial markets have come to be able to generate pyramids of liquidity, especially in the form of Eurodollars, has undoubtedly been another factor, and here the increased speed of telecommunication has played a part.

Some of the literature links 'globalisation' with 'regionalisation' (e.g. Chen and Kwan 1997), an equally ugly word but one with more substance. As long ago as 1959, the Executive Secretary of UNECLA (United Nations Economic Commission for Latin America), Raul Prebisch, promoted the idea of free trade areas—the "internationalisation of protection", as Harry Johnson called it (Arndt 1996, p. 377). Since then, regional preferential trading arrangements (PTAs) have proliferated, from the European Common Market to the European Free Trade Agreement, the North American Free Trade Agreement, the ASEAN Free Trade Agreement and more. The object here has been limited trade liberalisation, widening the protected market from national to regional boundaries. Technical progress has had virtually nothing to do with it.

Effects

Short-term International Capital Movements

> Since the early 1980s, the domestic financial markets of many economies have been increasingly globalised in the wake of liberalising policy initiatives implemented by governments around the world... Assisted by significant improvements in information technology and falling transaction costs, this has resulted in record growth in international monetary flows in the 1990s. (Makin 1997, p. 31)

Volatility of international short-term capital movements is a problem that goes back to at least the 1930s. (Indeed, financial crises caused by domestic and international flights from a currency are as old as capitalism; cf. Kindleberger 1996.) It was suggested more than fifty years ago that:

> the rapid and unpredictable movements of huge volumes of capital from one country to another which played a large part in the breakdown of the gold standard during the years 1931–3 and which were largely responsible for the unprecedented instability of exchange rates during the 1930s, were an altogether new phenomenon of the inter-war period. (Arndt 1944, p. 285f)

In the 1960s the problem recurred in a form later associated with the name of Robert Mundell:

> High interest rates calculated to enforce domestic monetary restraint, induced inflows of short-term funds which increased domestic liquidity. In other words...an active interest policy for domestic objectives is liable to be rendered partly self-defeating through its effects on international short-term capital movements. (Arndt 1996, p. 174)

The effect, it came to be argued, was loss of national monetary autonomy. In the past decade, the problem has recurred dramatically, in Mexico in 1994 and in Southeast Asia recently.

At the 1944 Bretton Woods conference, which re-established the gold standard system of stable exchange rates in the modified form of adjustable pegs, Keynes advocated one exception to the accepted objective of abolition of exchange controls: short-term capital movements. These, he said with the experience of the 1930s in mind, could wreck the new system. In the following years exchange control over international capital movements came to be increasingly recognised as impracticable, if only because leads and lags on current accounts could achieve large outflows of funds. Indonesia was the first major developing country to accept this fact, by opening its capital account in 1970.

The abandonment of gold convertibility of the dollar by US President Nixon in 1971 signaled the end of the Bretton Woods system of stable exchange rates. The decision was induced not by actual flows of "hot money" but by the increasing risk of potential outflows (chiefly Japanese withdrawals of funds) arising from US unwillingness to carry out the domestic macroeconornic adjustment required to sustain the old exchange rate.

The US decision to deal with the disequilibrium in its balance of payments not by a devaluation, as envisaged by the Bretton Woods system, but by in effect allowing the dollar to float, was influenced by a change of outlook about exchange rate policy that had developed for some time, associated chiefly with the name of Milton Friedman. He argued in favour of a system of flexible exchange rates on the grounds that it would minimise the costs of adjustment and that speculation in foreign exchange markets could be relied upon to be stabilising. As a currency depreciated beyond a point, an increasing proportion of speculators would bet on appreciation.

The issue has dominated debate about exchange rate policy ever since. The European Union has opted for a single currency (in effect, fixed exchange rates among member currencies) chiefly for political reasons, but is still struggling to overcome formidable adjustment costs in member countries. Most developing countries have tended to "anchor" their currencies to a major currency (or to a trade-weighted average), at best operating a managed float. But the Thai financial crisis of 1997, with its contagion effects on other East Asian currencies, demonstrated once again that, in the absence of the necessary domestic adjustment, destabilising currency speculation renders the maintenance of a fixed exchange rate impracticable.

Behind this debate lies a more fundamental issue. The classical gold standard, as it operated during 1870–1914, was designed to achieve international equilibrium automatically by imposing international discipline upon domestic macroeconomic policies. A deficit in the balance of payments would be corrected automatically by outflow of gold which compelled a reduction in domestic money supply and thereby a fall in domestic prices (including wages). The basic reason for the final collapse of the gold standard in the 1930s was that money prices, and especially money wages, had ceased to be sufficiently flexible downward (Hicks 1953).

Allowing currencies to float suspends the international discipline imposed by fixed exchange rates. In its place, international discipline is imposed by the market. The market reacts to imprudent domestic macroeconomic policy, excessive expansion of money supply through budget deficits or unsound bank lending by speculation against the currency. Sooner or later, corrective action to obviate the adverse effects of currency depreciation on domestic price stability and foreign trade becomes unavoidable.

International discipline is resented. In the 1930s, in Britain and other countries which were suffering from unemployment and balance of payments deficits imposed by the domestically generated US depression, the gold standard prescription of deliberate further deflation was regarded as quite unacceptable (Arndt 1944, p. 97). In the recent Southeast Asian crisis, the Prime Minister of Malaysia, Dr Mahathir used strong language against Soros and other speculators, the "beasts":

> I say openly these people are racists. [They are] not happy to see us prosper. They stab us. They say we are growing too fast, and when we do not listen to them they initiate action to make us poor. (Mahathir 1997)

The immediate reaction by the market was a further sharp fall in the ringgit. Prime Minister Mahathir's reaction may have been extreme, but there is no doubt that his resentment of the discipline imposed by speculators—mainly rich, foreign capitalists— is widely shared.

Long-Term Capital Movements

Portfolio capital Throughout the 19th century long-term capital movements predominantly took the form of portfolio capital, chiefly consisting of funds raised in the London bond market by colonial and other governments to finance railway and other infrastructure development (Arndt and Drake 1985). Huge flows of capital were effected internationally by the issue of bonds, and to a lesser extent equities, floated principally in London. Such flows generally eclipsed direct foreign investment (Arndt 1996; Bloomfield 1968). Foreign direct investment (FDI) was in the main confined to primary industry.

In the second half of this century, the situation has been transformed. During the long post-war boom, FDI expanded rapidly, accompanying and promoting development in industrialising countries, especially in East Asia. Portfolio investment also grew substantially in volume; some statistics suggest that it increased faster than FDI (Argy 1996, p. 3). But, under the impetus of financial innovations—securitisation and development of financial derivatives—and the emergence of new financial centres, such as Hong Kong and Singapore, the distinction between long-term portfolio and short-term capital movements has become increasingly blurred. Bonds and equities are now transferred internationally with the same volatility as bank funds.

International flows of portfolio capital, therefore, now have much the same effects as short-term capital movements. They respond to changes in interest and exchange rates in the same way and tend in the same way to diminish national monetary autonomy. But in so far as the distinction between short- and long-term capital movements can still usefully be made, the suggestion that "increased availability of credit and reduced liquidity constraints have produced a sustained reduction in private saving" (Argy 1996, p. 2) in capital-importing countries would apply primarily to portfolio capital. As an aspect of globalisation, the increased volume of international portfolio capital flows, like that of short-term capital movements, reflects interaction between deregulation of financial markets and improved information technology.

Foreign Direct Investment Until World War II, FDI was largely limited to mining and plantations. Railway companies financed their investments mainly by issuing their own bonds. This began to change soon after the end of the war. The impetus came from decolonisation and industrialisation in what was then beginning to be called the Third World. For three decades, industrialisation in developing countries relied almost entirely on import-substitution. Direct foreign investment by developed country (DC) manufacturers was involved in two ways.

One was the phenomenon of "tariff factories". Developing (formerly "less developed", hence "LDC") country governments protected their infant industries through tariffs and in other ways. Rather than lose their export markets altogether, DC manufacturers established subsidiaries behind the tariff walls. The objective was import substitution—for many years there were virtually no exports of manufactures—and the initiative was with the DC manufacturer.

The other impetus to FDI came from the desire of LDC governments to attract foreign capital and technology. From the 1960s they offered tax and other incentives. Since they competed with one another, the benefits accrued mainly to the foreign multinationals. Few felt able to avoid providing costly incentives, but the ones that did best were those, such as Singapore, which were able to offer attractive conditions, including good port, rail and other infrastructures, law and order and minimal corruption (Hughes and You 1969).

During this phase, FDI had little to do with globalisation. It involved little international movement of capital—much of what was needed was raised by the overseas parent company in the host country—and it involved no significant new technology. The multinationals generally transferred existing technology, often technology that was beginning to be obsolete in the home country, with at best some adaptation to local conditions and some training of local staff (cf. Santikarn 1981). (Some industrialising countries, especially Japan following the Meiji Restoration in 1868, and Korea in the period after World War II, secured transfer of technology without FDI, through imitation and reverse engineering, with or without patent rights.)

The role of FDI changed in the 1980s for two main reasons. One was the almost universal shift from inward to outward-looking industrial development and trade and financial liberalisation. Manufacturing multinationals in the advanced industrial countries formed joint ventures with state or private enterprises in developing countries, to produce for export as well as home markets. The "national cars" in Malaysia and Indonesia are examples. The same increasingly occurred in service industries such as banking and other financial services, sea and air transport and hotels.

It is arguable that this trend represented globalisation, but while the spread of FDI in financial markets owed a good deal to the rapid improvement in information technology, the driving force here was opening up of national economies, rather than technical change.

The other factor was changing comparative advantage. As income and unit labour costs rose in the industrialising countries—first in Japan, then in the newly industrialising economies (NIEs) of East Asia and elsewhere—the labour-intensive industries which were the core of the first phase of industrialisation became increasingly uncompetitive. In the 1970s, many Japanese manufacturers transferred their plants to lower-wage countries in East and Southeast Asia, largely to produce for export, particularly back to Japan but also to third countries.

From the mid-1980s the NIEs, especially Hong Kong and Singapore, began to follow in Japan's footsteps, transferring their labour-intensive industries to lower-wage neighbouring countries, and "moving up the technology ladder" into skill and technology-intensive industries, partly on the initiative of domestic manufacturers but chiefly by encouraging such investment by multinationals (Goh 1995). Towards the end of the decade, the countries of the Association of South-East Asian Nations (ASEAN), in turn, were concerned that they were losing their competitiveness in these industries to China and Vietnam (ASEAN Secretariat 1997). This "flying geese" pattern of changing comparative advantage (Okita 1989)[1] owed little if anything to technological change or even to opening up. Manufacturers, domestic and multinational, were responding to changes in relative cost that came with economic and industrial development, in much the same way as had happened when Britain lost her comparative advantage in cotton textiles to India in the first decades of this century. In moving from labour-intensive to skill and technology-intensive industries, Singapore and other NIEs took advantage of technology available in DCs, but technical change was not the motive force.

The same applies to another new facet of international trade and investment which has attracted much attention in the literature: competitive advantage, which is associated especially with the name of Michael Porter (Porter 1990). It derives from the view that non-price competitiveness has played a major part in Japan's success in export markets. Japanese manufacturers, it is claimed, compete primarily through quality, not price. Stringent quality control, attention to consumer tastes, flexible adjustment to changing market trends (aided by a "just in time" inventory policy), product innovation and skillful marketing: all these, it is said, enable Japanese producers to compete internationally on reputation rather than price, with the implication that other producers must follow the Japanese example if they are to hold their own (Arndt 1996, p. 52). Warr has suggested that, in the course of economic development, the emphasis shifts from price to non-price competition (Warr 1992), but has also emphasised that, while competitive advantage may be relevant for the performance of firms, comparative advantage remains as relevant as ever for the performance of nations (Warr 1994).

1 Okita gave credit to Akamatsu as the originator of the idea in 1935, cf Akamatsu 1961.

These are important trends in world trade and economic development, but they have little if anything to do with globalisation, being the internationalisation of national economies promoted by opening up and/or technological change. A much stronger case for globalisation rests on the role of the product cycle in international trade, as first propounded by Vernon (Vernon 1966) and subsequently amended by him and others. In its first version, the product cycle theory sought to explain the factors responsible for one country (specifically the USA) being the innovator, and how other countries gradually overcome the hurdles to imitation until the product becomes standardised and is produced in large-scale, highly capital-intensive plants for the mass market (Harris 1992; p. 30–1).

By 1980, Vernon himself came to think that the product cycle theory no longer explained trade patterns. The reason was the new role of multinationals:

> As the multinationals grew, and extended production and sales around the globe, there began an inevitable change in the perception of the management of these firms. Rather than viewing themselves as creatures of the United States' (or other countries') market system, they view themselves as part of an integrated world economy. All decisions were taken with an eye to maximising the overall economic efficiency of the world firm. This meant locating production, sales, R&D and management wherever profitable opportunity and the constraints of competition dictated... Modern technology reduced the information and communication problem of multinationals to the point where it was possible to run a firm with day-to-day monitoring of the activities of globally dispersed divisions. (Harris 1992, p. 33)

This is undoubtedly the most persuasive case for the globalisation thesis. The behaviour of many major multinationals fits this description. But how much of world production and trade conforms to it? No statistical estimates seem available, but it is unlikely that more than 10 per cent of world trade and more than five per cent of world production is "globalised" in this sense.

Another feature of globalisation that has attracted some anxious comment is what has been called "hollowing out" or "outsourcing". The relocation abroad of uncompetitive labour-intensive industries is said to have "hollowed out" the Japanese and Hong Kong manufacturing sectors, and DC manufacturing companies, it is claimed, are shifting their purchases of equipment and parts from locally produced products to those of industrialising countries. There is little evidence that this is a serious problem. In so far as hollowing out and outsourcing are happening, both are incidental to changing comparative advantage within manufacturing, and to the structural change from manufacturing to service industries which is a universal feature of the most developed—"post-industrial"—economies. Opening up has undoubtedly accelerated this process by intensifying international competition, presumably with favourable effects on productivity and growth.

It has also made it easier for manufacturing and other companies to move, or threaten to move, abroad to escape what they regard as government policies damaging to their interests. More often than not, the threat is bluff, but it is obvious that government policies sometimes deter inflow and induce outflow of investment. Similarly, movement of financial capital to tax havens abroad, openly or through transfer pricing and other forms of tax avoidance, is an old story, going back decades, though financial liberalisation may have made it more difficult to counter.

Trade and financial liberalisation has greatly facilitated and promoted FDI in production of goods in much of the world. This is much less true of services. There are multinationals in banking and insurance, shipping and civil aviation, and media and other service industries operating in different countries, but trade liberalisation has here come up against strong resistance in many countries, based on national interest concerns, which the General Agreement on Trade in Services initiative under the World Trade Organisation's auspices has not yet been able to overcome.

International Mobility of Labour

Globalisation, we are told, has made capital much more mobile internationally. What about labour? It is not obvious that the international mobility of labour is greater now than it was in the 19th century. Certainly, there have been great movements of people in the aftermath of war, in Germany and India for example. Migrant workers have been attracted from Turkey to Europe, from Mexico to the USA and from North Africa to France. There have been waves of refugees, including boat people from Vietnam and Rwandans from Zaire. But, with the partial exception of post-war migrant labour and the Mexican flow across the US border, these have all been crisis phenomena, not evidence of international mobility of labour in response to market forces. There is some international mobility, especially short-term mobility (such as conferencing and consultancies) among professional people, scientists, business executives and others. But in striking contrast to liberalisation of trade and finance, national governments still prohibit, restrict, or at best regulate, immigration. Here globalisation has made virtually no impact.

Reactions

Many of the developments that have been brought under the portmanteau description of globalisation have been unpopular: consider "Has globalisation gone too far?" (Rodrik 1997); "One World Ready or Not: the manic logic of global capitalism" (Greider 1997); and "The Globalisation of Poverty: impacts of IMP and World Bank reforms" (Chossudovsky 1997). A recent UN Committee on Trade and Development (UNCTAD) report attributes to globalisation all manner of ills: slow growth; rising inequality and widening income gaps between North and South; hollowing out of the middle class; rapid expansion of private and public debt; and increased job and income insecurity. The UNCTAD Secretary-General, Rubens Ricupero, has warned there is:

> a real threat of political backlash which could wipe out gains of recent economic reforms, perhaps rolling back economic integration. The 1920s and 1930s provide a stark and disturbing reminder of just how quickly faith in markets and openness can be overwhelmed by political events. (UNCTAD 1997)

Some of these complaints about globalisation merely echo the old socialist critique of capitalism, reinforced nowadays by the Green critique based on environmental grounds. Some voice the grievances of less developed countries which found expression in the 1970s in demands for a New International Economic Order. Others raise traditional objections to power being exercised by foreigners. The distinguished historian, Arthur Schlesinger, believes that technology and globalisation pose a threat to the future of democracy (Schlesinger 1997). Then there are the exponents of what Paul Krugman has recently called the doctrine of "global glut": the view that, under the impact of technology in an environment of increasingly free trade, the world is flooded with an oversupply of goods (Krugman 1997). But these concerns, reminiscent of the Keynes–Hansen thesis of "secular stagnation", have little to do with globalisation.

Opposition to globalisation in the specific sense of the increasing internationalisation of national economies derives, at bottom, from economic nationalism and protectionism, both reinforced by a widespread sense of insecurity (justified or not). It focuses on fear of cheap labour competition and on the two main forms of international mobility of capital described above: short-term international capital movements and FDI. Neither is new, but both have been extended and accelerated by technology and deregulation.

Mention was made before of the ferocious reaction of Prime Minister Mahathir to the currency speculation which forced a severe depreciation of the ringgit in the aftermath of the Thai financial crisis in September 1997. But Prime Minister Mahathir was not alone. There was much concern expressed throughout Southeast Asia about the crisis and its likely effects in slowing down economic growth in Southeast Asia and, indeed, throughout the world, when it spread to Northeast Asia, Wall Street and Europe. The sharp fall on world stock exchanges was seen as an overdue correction of a boom that had got out of hand. But in East Asia the crisis threatened a serious slowdown of economic growth. While it was generally admitted that unsound macroeconomic policies and banking practices were the chief cause of trouble, there was general agreement that the volatility of short-term capital movements had ignited it.

Some limit to national monetary autonomy is inevitable. No country can for long pursue reckless macroeconomic policies. International discipline is imposed either by a fixed exchange rate regime, as existed under the pre-1914 gold standard and now exists in the European Monetary Union, or by the market. The case for leaving it entirely to the market, in the form of a floating exchange rate regime, is that it allows for gradual adjustment in response to warning signals, instead of a sudden collapse when the fixed or anchored rate can no longer be held.

While this has, in the past two decades, become the orthodox view, a floating exchange rate regime has by no means universal support. McKinnon, among other economists, has long argued for pegged rates (McKinnon 1981). "Flexibility", it has been pointed out, "has disadvantages...":

> The most important are that exchange rates can be volatile and, on occasion grossly misaligned. This can hinder trade. If trade is a large share of GDP, then the costs of currency instability can be high. This suggests that small, open economies may be best served by fixed exchange rates. (*Economist* 1997)

The next step along this line of thinking may be a revival of Mundell's idea of "optimum currency areas" (Mundell 1961).

The Southeast Asian crisis has pointed to another risk of floating exchange rates: a repetition of the competitive depreciation following the breakdown of the gold standard when "the process of exchange depreciation spread through...the desire of each country to protect its export trade" (Arndt 1944, p. 100; cf League of Nations 1944). Strictly speaking, competitive depreciation occurs only in an adjustable peg system; but managed floats tend to follow the same pattern, and even clean floats may do so if the market anticipates such management.

Tobin has suggested "sand in the machine" in the form of a tax to moderate hot money movements (Tobin 1974), but it is doubtful whether such a tax could be effectively administered. At the September 1997 meeting of the International Monetary Fund (IMF) and World Bank in Hong Kong, the case for freely floating rates was strongly challenged, with some arguing for closer IMF involvement to introduce order into the international capital turbulence (*Straits Times* 1997). In a crisis such as that which befell Southeast Asia in September–October 1997, the most urgent need is to restore confidence, and that is probably the chief role of IMF involvement.

The debate on exchange rate policy remains unresolved. But the issues have not really changed in the past 100 years, even if international short-term capital movements have become larger and faster. Globalisation throws no light on the problem.

The other main objection advanced by critics of globalisation is related to protectionism. "The forces of globalisation are increasingly associated with an inability on the part of national governments to tackle deep-seated problems of long-term unemployment" (Beeson 1997). Resentment of technical change as a cause of unemployment is as old as the Luddite destruction of textile machinery in Britain in the second decade of the 19th century, and the fear that resumption of free trade after the Napoleonic wars would cause unemployment in the United States and France (Arndt 1996, ch. 21).

There is no doubt that technical change and trade liberalisation impose adjustment costs by displacing labour in particular jobs, but these are temporary, given a reasonably flexible labour market and good economic growth. Relocation of industries in response to changing comparative advantage did not cause unemployment in Japan, Hong Kong or, more recently, Singapore; labour displaced from labour-intensive industries was readily absorbed by service and other industries higher up the "technology ladder". Whatever the explanation for the high rates of unemployment experienced by many Organisation for Economic Cooperation and Development (OECD) countries in recent years, there is no evidence that the opening up of national economies has made a significant contribution, even when wage rigidity and labour immobility have impeded adjustment.

A more plausible target for critics of globalisation is, as we have seen, the "world firm, the multinational company which views itself as part of an integrated world economy and locates production, sales, R&D and management wherever profitable opportunity dictates" (Harris 1992). The injury, however, is not so much to the national economy, or even to exposed sectors—the decisions of multinationals will as often be beneficial as harmful, if only by encouraging economic reform—as to national pride. But the vulnerability of small nations to external pressure is not obviously worse if this pressure is exercised by powerful multinationals rather than by powerful states.

Finally, there will be some who, with George Soros, lament the social effects of globalisation: the spread of pop music, standardised fast food, pornography and drugs, undermining national or ethnic social values and traditions. Similar laments, about the spread of vulgar films and dances, short skirts and clean-shaved faces, were heard in the 1920s, though not much in the less developed parts of the world. But globalisation has also brought modern medicine, literacy and access to other cultures. Once the bounds of economic discourse are transcended, the answers must be left to subjective judgment.

References

Akamatsu, S. (1961) "A theory of unbalanced growth in the world economy", *Weltwirschaftliches Archiv*, 86(2), pp. 19–217.

Argy, F. (1996) "The integration of world capital markets: some economic and social implications", *Economic Papers;* June.

Arndt, H.W. (1944) *The Economic Lessons of the Nineteen-Thirties*, London: Oxford University Press.

—— and P. J. Drake (1985) "Bank loans or bonds: some lessons of historical experience", reprinted in Arndt (1996).

—— (1995) "Dollar shortage—yen shortage?" Pacific Economic Papers No. 244, Canberra: Australia–Japan Research Centre.

—— (1996) *Essays in International Economics 1941–1994*, Aldershot: Avebury Press.

ASEAN Secretariat (1997) *ASEAN Manufacturing Competitiveness* Singapore.

Beeson, W. (1997) "In the grip of global finance", *Australian*, 25 October 1997.

Bloomfield, A. (1968) "Patterns of fluctuations in international investment before 1914". *Princeton Essays in International Finance*, No. 21, Princeton.

Chen, E. and Kwan Chi Hung (1997) *Asia's Borderless Economy: the emergence of subregional zones*, Sydney: Allen & Unwin.

Chossudovsky, M. (1997) *The Globalization of Poverty: impacts of IMP and World Bank reforms*, London: Zed Books.

Dunning, J. H. (1995) "The role of foreign direct investment in a globalizing economy", *BNL Quarterly Review*, June.

Economic Planning Advisory Commission (1995) *Globalisation: issues for Australia*, Canberra: Australian Government Publishing Service.

Economist (1997) "Peg or float—is there a magic solution?", 22 October 1997.

Greider, W. (1997) *One World Ready or Not: the manic logic of globalisation*, New York: Simon & Schuster.

Goh Keng Swee (1996) "The technology ladder in development: the Singapore case", *Asian-Pacific Economic Literature*, 10(1), pp. 1–12.
Gurung, H. (1995) "Foreword" in S. H. Salleh and L. V. Carino *Globalisation and the ASEAN Public Sector*, Kuala Lumpur: Asian Pacific Development Centre.
Harris, R. G. (1992) "New theories of international trade and the pattern of global specialisation", in Liemt (1992).
Hicks, J. R. (1953) "An inaugural lecture", *Oxford Economic Papers*, June.
Howe, J. (1994) "Industrialisation, trade and foreign direct investment" in P. Lowe and J. Dwyer (eds) *International Integration of the World Economy*, Sydney: Reserve Bank of Australia.
Hughes, H. and You Poh Seng (1969) *Foreign Investment and Industrialisation in Singapore*, Canberra: Australian National University Press.
Kindleberger, C. P. (1996) *Manias, Panics and Crashes: a history of financial crises*, 3rd ed., Basingstoke: Macmillan.
Krugman, P. (1997) "Is capitalism too productive?", *Foreign Affairs*, September/October.
League of Nations (R. Nurkse) (1944) *International Currency Experience*, Princeton: Princeton University Press.
Liemt, G. van (ed.) (1992) *Industry on the Move: causes and consequences of international relocation in the manufacturing sectors*, Geneva: International Labour Office.
Makin, T. (1997) "Financial globalisation: ceding sovereignty or safeguarding growth?", *Policy*, 13(2), pp. 31–34.
Maddison, A. (1997) The Nature and Functions of European Capitalism, Groningen: lecture 1 October 1997.
Mahathir, Moh. (1997) quoted *Australian*, 5 September 1997.
McKinnon, R. I. (1981) "The exchange rate and macroeconomic policy: changing perceptions", *Journal of Economic Literature*, June.
Metal Trades Industry Association. (1997) *Make* or *Break*, Melbourne.
Mundell, R. A. (1961) "A theory of optimum currency areas", *American Economic Review*, vol. 51, September, pp. 657–64.
Ohmae, K. (1990) *The Borderless World*, London: Harper Collins.
—— (1995) *The End of the Nation State*, London: Harper Collins.
Okita, S. (1989) *Japan and the Developing World in the 1980s* Tokyo: Tokyo University Press.
Porter, M. (1990) *The Competitive Advantage of Nations*, New York: Free Press.
Prawiro, Radius (forthcoming) *Indonesia's Struggle for Economic Development*, Kuala Lumpur: Oxford University Press.
Reich, R. B. (1991) *The World Work of Nations: preparing ourselves for 21st century capitalism*, New York: Knopf.
Rodrik, D. (1997) *Has Globalisation Gone too Far?*, Washington: Institute for International Economics.
Santikarn, Mingsarn (1981) *Technology Transfer: a case study*, Singapore: Singapore University Press.
Schlesinger, A. Jr (1997) "Has democracy a future?", *Foreign Affairs*, September/October.
Straits Times (1997) 30 September, Singapore.
Tobin, J. (1974) *The New Economics One Decade Older*, Princeton: Princeton University Press.
UNCTAD (1997) Report cited *in Australian Financial Review*, 11 September 1997.
Vernon, R. (1966) "International investment and trade in the product cycle", *Quarterly Journal of Economics*, No. 80.
Warr, P. G. (1992) "Comparative and competitive advantage in manufactured exports", *EDI Working Papers*, Washington: World Bank.
—— (1994) "Comparative and Competitive Advantage", *Asian-Pacific Economic Literature*, 8(2), pp. 1–14.

20

From State to Market

The first half of this century brought a striking increase in the role of the state in the economy, the second half an equally pronounced move towards the market. The object of this paper is to try to explain this paradigm shift.

Originally published in the *Asian Economic Journal* 1998, Vol. 12, No. 4.

I. Pre-History

During the hundred years before 1900, the industrial revolution and the rise of the middle class had promoted emancipation from absolutism and mercantilism, with Britain in the lead. The origins of liberalism as a political philosophy go back further—to Locke and the Glorious Revolution of 1688 in Britain, to the Declaration of Independence of the United States and to Voltaire, Rousseau and the 1789 Revolution in France. But economic liberalism is a nineteenth century phenomenon. On the theoretical foundations laid by Adam Smith and Ricardo, the Reform Act of 1832 and the abolition of the Corn Laws of 1846 signalled the ascendancy of manufacturing over rural interests. *Laissez-faire* and free trade became the dominant ideology for the next fifty years, challenged but not significantly weakened by Chartists and other critics. Even on the European continent the socialist movement remained in opposition for the rest of the century.

II. 1900–1950: To State

Growth of the Welfare State

The intellectual climate began to change, and impinge on public policy around the turn of the century. The depression of the 1890s widened concern about urban poverty and unemployment, and strengthened the newly enfranchised working class and growing trade unions. The first moves towards the welfare state came in Germany in 1888, when Bismarck, to take the wind out of the sails of the social-democratic party, introduced health and other social insurance. In Britain, the Fabian socialists began to influence policy in the first decade of this century. Beatrice Webb's 1905 minority report of the Royal Commission on the Poor Law led Lloyd George in 1908 to introduce a modest unemployment insurance scheme designed by a young William Beveridge. The next three decades saw only minor advances in government provision of housing and other social services in western countries, but public support for a full-blown welfare state grew under the impact of cataclysmic political and economic developments. Welfare economists, Pigou and others, developed the theoretical underpinning by distinguishing the social from the personal marginal product (Myint 1948).

A Period of Prolonged Upheaval

The outbreak of World War I put a sudden end to the relatively untroubled peace and prosperity of the nineteenth century. It initiated what has been called a 'period of prolonged upheaval' (Kindleberger 1996). Mobilization of the economy for war brought unprecedented state intervention. The economic consequences of the war shifted world hegemony from Britain to the United States and those of the peace treaty sowed the seeds of Nazism in Germany. The Bolshevik Revolution in Russia dramatically suggested an alternative to capitalism. The severe post-war depression promoted the first Labour government in Britain and after a few years of seemingly normal prosperity, the 1929 US slump led into the Great Depression, a catastrophic decline in economic activity and massive unemployment. Pessimism about the future of capitalism became widespread. The upheaval reached its climax with World War II and Hiroshima.

The Great Depression The collapse of the boom of the 1920s assumed dimensions far exceeding a normal cyclical downturn. Among the reasons were structural disequilibria left over by the war—primary product prices sustained too long by commodity agreements, British loss of industrial competitiveness aggravated by restoration of the gold standard at the pre-war parity in 1925, and European balance of payments deficits financed by US capital outflows suddenly reversed in 1929—and adherence, even as economic activity and employment declined year by year, to the doctrine of "orthodox finance" that budget deficits are inflationary. Governments reacted in various ways without any clear understanding of the problem. "Hot money" flows forced Britain off the gold standard in 1931, followed by abandonment of free trade. In Germany, Hitler embarked successfully on a policy of full employment through rearmament. In the USA, President Roosevelt, elected in the depth of the depression, after tackling the banking crisis and devaluing the dollar, launched the New Deal. Its "pump priming" effect was quite inadequate to restore full employment, but it involved a pervasive increase of government intervention in the economy (Arndt 1944).

Keynes The Keynesian revolution profoundly changed thinking about the capitalist economy. In the *General Theory of Employment, Interest and Money* (1936) Keynes argued that macroeconomic equilibrium—full employment without inflation—cannot be left to the market. The neo-classical view that the rate of interest maintains a balance between saving and investment is wrong because, unlike the expected rate of profit, it cannot be negative and because investment in any case tends to be interest-inelastic.

Wage policy cannot restore full employment because (at least in a closed economy) cuts in money wages do not reduce real wages. What is needed is an active counter-cyclical macroeconomic policy, demand management; and the appropriate instrument is not monetary policy but fiscal policy, budget deficits to stimulate economic activity and employment, and budget surpluses to counter inflation. Keynesianism did not significantly influence policy before World War II and impinged only slightly on war finance, but by the time the war ended it had come to dominate western economic thought. "All of us were Keynesians" (Henderson 1986, p. 4).

World War II Mobilization of the economy for total war quickly required the imposition of direct controls over virtually all economic activity. Price and allocation controls, rationing, and foreign trade and exchange controls largely suspended the operation of the market in all belligerent countries. Most business remained under private ownership and management, but in other respects the Western capitalist economies came to resemble that of their Russian ally. The overriding single objective of victory in the war made planned resource allocation a relatively simple task.

The end of the war brought substantial decontrol and a much smoother shift of resources back from war to peace production than after World War I. But in Britain and other Western countries, a good many direct controls remained in place for some years, and the triumph of the welfare state and Keynesianism was signed and sealed by the two immensely influential Beveridge reports on *Social Security* and *Full Employment* and in official documents such as the British White Paper on *Employment Policy* and the US *Employment Act.* Already, however, there were whiffs in the air which suggested that a new wind might blow in the second half of the century.

III. 1950–2000: To Market

Towards Freer Trade

It was in the arena of international trade that the first, most sustained and relatively most effective moves were made. The initiative came from the USA which, with its new-found competitive superiority, and as a surplus country most exposed to discrimination, had the strongest interest in freer trade and payments. Roosevelt's Secretary of State, Cordell Hull, as a Southerner predisposed to free trade, had in 1934 secured the passage through Congress of a Reciprocal Trade Agreements Act which empowered the President to conclude reciprocal agreements with foreign countries for the reduction of tariffs and other trade restrictions, subject to unconditional MFN (most favoured nation) treatment. "Equal access to trade" through non-discrimination became one of the Western Allies' war aims, proclaimed by Roosevelt and Churchill in the Atlantic Charter of 1941, and the basic principle of the Havana Charter of 1946 from which emerged, as residual legatee of the still-born International Trade Organisation, the GATT (General Agreement on Tariffs and Trade).

Meanwhile, the Bretton Woods Conference of 1944 had established the International Monetary Fund, with the object of restoring stable (but adjustable) exchange rates and (gradually) free convertibility of currencies, and the International Bank for Reconstruction and Development (later the World Bank) which, through the provision of long-term credit to war-damaged and less-developed countries, would promote the flow of trade.

In the following decades, the GATT staunchly pushed trade liberalisation in successive rounds of multilateral negotiations, yielding, in 1997, the establishment of the World Trade Organization. As Japan and other East Asian countries gained in competitiveness, the USA and Europe put pressure on them to open their protected markets. Regional trading arrangements, mostly preferential, such as the European Common Market, EFTA, NAFTA, AFTA and APEC, contributed to a rate of expansion of world trade twice as fast as growth of world GDP.

Domestically, change came more slowly. In the UK, some of the economists who as wartime civil servants had gained first-hand experience of the inefficiency of bureaucratic controls, such as Jewkes and Wilson, proclaimed the virtues of a free market economy (Jewkes 1948; Wilson 1950, 1964). Others, such as James Meade (1948) and Arthur Lewis (1949) looked for a middle way. In Germany, Ludwig Erhard, a convert to Roepke's economic liberalism, spectacularly demonstrated its merits in guiding the country's rapid economic recovery (Erhard 1958).

For nearly two decades, the world enjoyed full employment without any apparent need to resort to Keynesian demand management. There was no repetition of the post-World War I depression. Catch-up of consumption and investment demand deferred during years of depression and war, reinforced by new technology (cars, planes, TV etc.) and heavy military expenditure, sustained a long boom. First Marshall Aid and then Korean War US deficits overcame "dollar shortage" in the rest of the world. Unemployment rarely exceeded 2 per cent. There was a striking revival of optimism about the future of capitalism, though not without often shrill dissent on the Left.

The End of Keynesianism

The Keynesian consensus lasted into the 1970s. In 1958 it was embodied in the Phillips curve: the crux of macroeconomic demand management was the trade-off between unemployment and inflation. A reduction in unemployment could be purchased at the price of higher inflation, and vice versa. In the UK the 1950s brought increasing wage–price pressures; price stability became the chief concern, not least to maintain the exchange rate at the Bretton Woods sterling parity. In the USA, economic policy came to be increasingly dominated by the Cold War. The Soviet Sputnik in 1957 sparked anxious questioning whether US economic growth would be sufficient to sustain US hegemony. In both countries growthmanship became the economic fashion, in the UK (influenced by a misreading of French experience under de Gaulle) with a penchant for "indicative planning" (Arndt 1987, p. 61).

For two decades after 1945, the OECD economies (as they came to be called) maintained fairly steady macroeconomic balance, unemployment and inflation both remaining most of the time below 2 per cent. The break came in 1965 with President Johnson's tax cuts and increase in military expenditure on the Vietnam war. It was the beginning of the US double (budget and current account) deficit which in 1971 led President Nixon to abandon gold convertibility of the US dollar, in effect jettisoning the Bretton Woods system. Freed from the international discipline of stable exchange rates, the double-deficit-propelled expansion of money supply, reinforced by the OPEC oil price increases of 1973/4 and 1979/80, turned the 1970s into a decade of high inflation.

The combination of wage–price pressures and monetary expansion gave rise to a phenomenon unprecedented and totally at odds with Keynesianism and the Phillips curve—stagflation. From around 1970, inflation accelerated in Western countries, but simultaneously unemployment rose. The explanation put forward by Milton Friedman constituted a doctrinal revolution as fundamental as the Keynesian revolution of the 1930s.

Friedman's macroeconomics consisted of two main propositions:

(a) The crucial macroeconomic variable is not aggregate spending but money supply; governments therefore have to rely on monetary rather than on fiscal policy, and since unpredictable lags rule out fine tuning either in monetary or in fiscal policy the safest rule is to aim at a constant rate of growth of money supply.

(b) Unemployment in market economies is mainly structural, caused by rigidities in the labour market, and therefore not amenable to demand management; any attempt to reduce unemployment below its "natural" rate—in effect, a vertical Phillips curve, later called NAIRU (the non-accelerating-inflation rate of unemployment)—merely causes inflation.

Since the early 1970s macroeconomics in Western countries has been monetarist rather than Keynesian in complexion. Fiscal policy, while still employed to assist in the maintenance of internal and external balance, has been subordinate to monetary policy. Central banks—*pace* Friedman—have continued to attempt fine tuning and have relied on the short-term rate of interest as the main instrument. But control of inflation has been the chief objective of macroeconomic policy. While unemployment has increased tragically in most Western countries, Friedman's view that it is a microeconomic problem, chiefly due to ill-adjusted and inflexible labour markets and requiring microeconomic measures, has come to be generally accepted.

But Friedman's influence extended well beyond macroeconomics, though in the role of missionary rather than innovator. Ever since the 1930s, a minority among economists and other intellectuals had spoken out against the growth of the state, socialism and Keynesianism. Prominent among them were the Austrian school, represented by Mises and Hayek. The latter's *Road to Serfdom* (1944) was a trumpet call, widely derided but influential.

In England, economists such as Robbins spoke out for private enterprise, competition and free markets, philosophers such as Popper for the open society. In the USA, the University of Chicago, which Friedman joined in 1945, became the Olympus of economic liberalism. Knight, Viner, Simons, Becker, Schultz, Stiglitz and others developed new theoretical foundations for economic liberalism—theories of human capital, public choice, property rights, new ways of looking at consumer behaviour, institutions and nineteenth century industrialization (Lepage 1978). From around 1960, think-tanks, such as the Institute of Economic Affairs in the UK and the Centre for Independent Studies in Australia, propagated the gospel.

Economic Rationalism

By the end of the 1970s, this outlook—economic liberalism (in the English sense)—had gained majority support among the voting public in the USA and England and in varying degree in other Western countries. With the elections of Margaret Thatcher in England in 1979 and Ronald Reagan in the USA in 1980, it came to dominate public policy.

The long boom had ended in stagflation, high rates of inflation, growing unemployment and slowdown of economic growth. The relentless expansion of government expenditure on welfare and other services met increasing opposition from taxpayers, particularly once declining rates of inflation deprived governments of easy access to income tax revenue through "bracket creep". Efforts to contain inflation through price and other direct controls were resented. Wage pressures made industrial relations more than usually contentious. What to socialists and Keynesians appeared as a "conservative revolution" was greeted by followers of Friedman, Thatcher and Reagan as an overdue affirmation of *Capitalism and Freedom* (Friedman 1962), individual choice, private enterprise and competitive markets.

During the two decades from 1980, governments adopted a broad range of market-oriented economic policies. Macroeconomic management gave priority to control of inflation through monetary policy and left exchange rates largely to the market. Microeconomic policies were designed to reduce the size of the public sector and to deregulate the private sector. Taxes were cut—by Reagan under the influence of the bizarre "Laffer curve" theory that revenue would grow through supply-side response thus keeping the budget in balance—and the tax structure shifted from income to consumption (value-added or goods & service) taxes. Nationalized industries and public utilities were privatized, banks and capital markets were substantially decontrolled, attempts were made to impose competition policies on business and enterprise bargaining on trade unions, and under the aegis of successive GATT rounds, foreign trade and payments were freed up to an extent that would have been thought impossible (and indeed undesirable) thirty years earlier.

Nor was this shift to the market confined to Western industrial countries or in these countries to the conservative side of politics. Developing countries, first in East Asia but later also in Latin America and South Asia, moved from import-substitution to export-oriented industrialisation, encouraged capital inflow and technology transfer through direct foreign investment and cautiously deregulated their financial systems. This integration of national economies into the world market economy, furthered by liberalisation of trade and capital movements and by technical progress in transport and communication, came to be known as globalisation. With Gorbachev's *perestroika* and the collapse of Communism in the Soviet Union, the end of the Berlin Wall and Deng Xiao Ping's reform in China, the market made conquests that nobody would have predicted in 1950 or 1960.

In Japan and throughout East Asia (with the conspicuous exception of Hong Kong), the shift towards export orientation and trade liberalisation did not greatly reduce the role of the state in the domestic economy. What came to be known as "industry policy" relied on state intervention to promote hoped-for growth industries—"picking winners"—and phasing out declining industries; financial deregulation also made limited progress, and in most countries domestic industry remained heavily protected. Even in Singapore which, next to Hong Kong, most fully embraced free trade, the government retained substantial control over the directions of industrial development. In varying degree, this applied to most other developing countries (Arndt 1987).

How far this interventionist approach to development in East Asian countries accounts for their spectacular economic growth during the 1980s, as some have contended (cf. Johnson 1982; Amsden 1989; Wade 1990) or for their troubles in the latter 1990s, remains a contentious question. In most other developing countries (Chile, Mexico and one or two other Latin American countries are becoming significant exceptions) intervention in the economy by relatively inefficient and frequently corrupt governments remains just one aspect of underdevelopment.

The paradigm shift from state to market is therefore in the main a feature of twentieth century economic history in Western, and indeed chiefly the Anglo-Saxon, countries. On the European continent, in France, Germany, the Netherlands and Scandinavia, the shift has occurred but has been qualified by retention of collectivist ("social market") elements of economic and social policy.

In 1976 the last British Labour Prime Minister before Mrs Thatcher, James Callaghan, told the Labour Party conference: "We used to think that you could just spend your way out of recession and increase employment by cutting taxes and boosting government spending. I tell you in all candour that that option no longer exists, and that insofar as it ever did exist, it worked by injecting inflation into the economy" (Brett 1985, p. 165). What came to be called "economic rationalist" policies of trade liberalisation and deregulation, policies aimed at economic efficiency and growth, were pursued, or at least not reversed, by left-of-centre governments such as the Blair "New Labour" government in the UK. In fact, the spectrum from pro to anti market-oriented policies cut across the traditional political spectrum from Left to Right. In Mrs Thatcher's derisory terminology, many on the Right were "wet" and many on the Left "dry".

III. Reaction

What the distinguished Keynesian economist J. K. Galbraith has called "the poison of economic rationalism" (Galbraith 1997) is vociferously condemned from the Left and from the Right. Left-of-centre voices complain that "both Labour and non-Labour governments regard heavy unemployment as inevitable and ignore the human and social consequences...Both favour large-scale cutbacks in the public sector. The results are a chronically sick economy, declining industries, widespread social breakdown and pervasive human misery" (Mathews and Grewal 1997). A right-wing commentator speaks of the "blind ideology" which "operates through budget balancing, in great part by selling off every marketable public utility...through continuous 'downsizing' and constant attempts to cut real wages and social services" and predicts that "the anger of the ordinary people will continue to grow" (Santamaria 1997). Denunciations similar to these Australian ones could be cited from the UK and USA.

The gravamen of such criticisms of economic policy is the Keynesian objection to the "obsession with inflation". "The shift to the Right in macroeconomic policy during the past two decades has deliberately used the blunt instruments of slow economic growth and high unemployment to fight inflation" (Bell 1997). The critics refuse to accept the Friedman thesis that unemployment cannot be significantly reduced by deficit spending. In so far as they accept the view that most unemployment in Western countries is structural, they advocate wage subsidies or even a negative income tax, rather than a reduction in minimum wages. The 1997 Economic Report to the US President questioned whether there was any need to go for zero inflation; "a little bit of inflation is probably good for you" (quoted in *Australian Financial Review*, 14/2/97).

The trade liberalisation agenda has predictably been subjected to criticism by ideological protectionists and by the lobbies of protected industries. Financial liberalisation has come under attack, particularly in the wake of the 1997/8 Asian crisis. The abandonment of the Bretton Woods system of stable exchange rates, it is claimed, has removed international discipline over domestic macroeconomic policy and has thus contributed to inflation; failure to control short-term international capital movements, "hot money", has had the same disastrous effects as in the 1930s; failure by central banks to exercise prudential surveillance has left a legacy of insolvent banks throughout East Asia; and globalization is subordinating national interests to those of foreign multinational companies.

Such specifically economic criticisms have been reinforced by root-and-branch onslaughts against "economic rationalism" on non-economic grounds. Deflationary budget-cutting and deregulatory policies, it is claimed, have by widening income disparities benefited the rich at the expense of the poor. Some churchmen and spokesmen for welfare lobbies have, in almost Marxist terms, demanded a distribution of income "to each according to his need". More generally, economists and other supporters of "economic rationalism", have been criticized for focusing too narrowly on economic objectives, efficiency and growth, and ignoring, or giving insufficient attention to, non-economic objectives—equity, social welfare, the environment, community or national identity (Meade 1995; Argy 1998). Some, in the spirit of King Canute, denounce "consumerism".

IV. Conclusion

Does all this clamour mean that the paradigm shift to the market is being reversed? Is the pendulum swinging back?

The first point to note is that economic rationalism has been sailing against the wind. All the push for smaller government has quite failed to halt the inexorable increase in the size of the public sector and the role of government in the economy. In 1979, the year Mrs Thatcher became Prime Minister, the share of government expenditure in British GNP was 38.0 per cent; by the end of her term, in 1990, it was 38.2. In the USA, it rose during Reagan's Presidency from 33.7 in 1980 to 36.1 per cent in 1988. Between 1980 and 1991 the share rose in all western countries except in the Netherlands where it had already reached 52.5 per cent in 1980 (World Bank 1993). Judging by the volume of legislation passed or by the number of regulatory agencies installed, deregulation has at best slowed down the growth in government regulatory activity. In all Western countries, social welfare expenditure has inevitably risen with increasing unemployment, the cost of pensions with ageing of the population, hospital and other health expenditure with more costly skills and technology.

International trade and payments have undoubtedly grown rapidly with liberalization. But the Common Agricultural Policy of the European Union, ubiquitous resistance to (or circumvention of) Uruguay Round commitments, and safeguarding of domestic industries through visible and invisible tariffs are evidence that protection remains entrenched in most parts of the world.

But the picture is by no means all black. The Western countries, especially the USA and UK with their relatively flexible labour markets, have experienced sustained growth and fairly moderate unemployment for the past decade. Statistics suggest that income distribution has deteriorated; some rich people have become a lot richer, and (mainly because of unemployment) an increasing number live below the poverty line, especially among immigrant and other ethnic minorities. But the great majority are enjoying living standards rising with economic growth. Economic development in much of Latin America has benefited greatly from the adoption of export and market-oriented policies, and there is every reason to believe that the countries of East Asia will return to quite high growth rates as the effects of the 1997/8 crisis are overcome in the next two to three years.

Economic prophecy is risky. But it is perhaps not unrealistic to expect support for market-oriented policies to continue to moderate the pressures for state intervention in the economy, to prevent the pendulum swinging back too far.

Postscript

And now a postscript: What light has the Asian financial crisis of 1997 thrown on the relative roles of state and market in the economy? Three points stand out.

First, the crisis has highlighted the enormous problem presented by the volume and volatility of international short-term capital flows. The near-consensus of professional opinion in favour of open capital accounts—if only because of doubt whether capital exchange controls are enforceable—has been questioned by prominent economists, such as Stiglitz (1994) and Bhagwati (1998), and even the IMP appears prepared to contemplate at least greater scrutiny of international short-term flows.

Secondly, the role of the banks in the crisis has led to reconsideration of financial deregulation. The collapse of the Indonesian banking system and the formal or *de facto* insolvency of major banks in Japan and Korea have made banking reform the most urgent step in crisis management. The preferred answer is not reimposition of direct government controls of the kind in operation before deregulation, but bail-out and reconstruction in the short term and a new regime requiring greater transparency and some form of prudential surveillance in the longer term. Banking reform does not impinge on the larger malaise of the financial system, the investment and stock exchange boom which has endangered economic stability in Japan and may yet do so in the USA. But this is a problem for monetary policy which, by general agreement, is a legitimate field of state intervention in the economy.

Thirdly, the threat of worldwide recession or even depression, spreading from Japan, has led to renewed discussion of demand management. World Bank Vice-President Severino has advocated "Keynesian expansionary measures" in Japan (Severino 1998). Those who take this view argue that there has never yet been scope for Keynesian full employment policy. From 1939 until 1970 the problem was to contain inflation; after 1970 expansionary measures were inappropriate, since unemployment in western Europe was mainly structural and not amenable to demand management, so that expansionary measures would merely cause inflation and balance of payments problems. Japan in the 1990s presents the first opportunity since the 1930s for a Keynesian full employment policy because Japan's balance of payments position is not vulnerable.

References

Amsden, A. 1989, *Asia's Next Giant: South Korea and Late Industrialization.* Oxford University Press, New York.

Argy, F. 1998, *Australia at the Crossroads.* Allen & Unwin, Sydney.

Arndt, H. W. 1944, *The Economic Lessons of the Nineteen-Thirties.* Oxford University Press, London.

—— 1978, *The Rise and Fall of Economic Growth.* University of Chicago, Chicago.

—— 1987, "Industrial policy in East Asia". *Industry and Development* (22), pp. 1–66.

—— 1996, *Essays in International Economics 1944–1994.* Avebury, Aldershot.

Australian Financial Review 1997, 14 February, p. 12.
Bell, D. S. 1997, *Ungoverning the Economy.* Oxford University Press, Melbourne.
Bhagwati, J. 1998, "The capital myth". *Foreign Affairs,* May-June, pp. 7–12.
Brett, E. A. 1985, *The World Economy since the War.* Macmillan, London.
Drake, P. J. and J. P. Nieuwenhuysen 1988, *Economic Growth for Australia.* Oxford University Press, Melbourne.
Erhard, L. 1958, *Prosperity through Competition.* Thames and Hudson, London.
Friedman, M. 1962, *Capitalism and Freedom.* Chicago University Press, Chicago.
—— 1975, *There's No Such Thing as a Free Lunch.* Open Court, LaSalle, IL.
Galbraith, J. K. 1994, *The World Economy since the War.* Sinclair-Stevenson, London.
—— 1997, *The Good Society: The Humane Agenda.* Houghton Mifflin, Boston, MA.
Hayek, F. V. 1944, *The Road to Seridom.* Routledge, London.
Henderson, D. 1986, *Innocence and Design.* Blackwell, New York.
Jewkes, J. 1948, *Ordeal by Planning.* Macmillan, London.
Johnson, A. Chalmers. 1982, *MITI and the Japanese Miracle: The Growth of Industry Policy 1925–1975.* Stanford University Press, Stanford, CA.
Keynes, J. M. 1936, *General Theory of Employment, Interest and Money.*
Kindleberger, C. P. 1996, *World Economic Primacy 1500-1900.* Oxford University Press, New York.
Leeson, R. 1996, "The rise and fall of the Phillips Curve in British policy-making circles". *History of Economics Review* (25), Winter-Summer, pp. 232–59.
Lepage, H. 1978, *Tomorrow, Capitalism.* Open Court, LaSalle, IL.
Lewis, W. A. 1949, *The Principles of Economic Planning,* Allen & Unwin, London.
Maddison, A. 1995, *Explaining the Economic Performance of Nations.* Elgar, Aldershot.
Martino, A. 1998, "Monetary and fiscal rules". *Policy,* 14(1), pp. 3–9.
Mathews, R. and B. Grewal, 1997, *The Public Sector in Jeopardy.* Victoria University, Melbourne.
Meade J. E. 1948, *Planning and the Price Mechanism.* Allen & Unwin, London.
—— 1995, *Full Employment Regained?* Cambridge University Press, Cambridge.
Myint, H. 1948, *Theories of Welfare Economics.* Longmans, London.
Olson, M. 1982, *The Rise and Decline of Nations.* Yale University Press, New Haven, CT.
Pigou, A. R. 1920, *The Economics of Welfare.* Macmillan, London.
Rawls, J. 1971, *A Theory of Justice.* Bellknap Press, Cambridge, MA.
Santamaria, B. A. 1997, "Revolt of the neglected". *The Australian,* 22 June, p. 12.
Severino, M. 1998, *The Australian,* 17 June, p. 6.
Smith, H. 1997, "Industry policy in East Asia". *Asian-Pacifc Economic Literature, 9(1);* pp. 17–39.
Stiglitz, J. 1994, *Whither Socialism?* MIT Press, Cambridge, MA.
Thurow, L. 1980, *The Zero-Sum Society.* Basic Books, New York.
Wade, R. 1990, *Governing the Market: Economic Policy and the Role of Government in East Asian Industrialization.* Princeton University Press, Princeton, NJ.
Wilson T. 1950, *Modern Capitalism and Economic Progress.* Macmillan, London.
—— 1964, *Planning and Growth.* Macmillan, London.
World Bank 1993, *World Development Report.* Washington, DC.
Yergin, D. and J. Stanislaw 1998, *The Commanding Heights: The Battle between Government and Marketplace in Remaking the Modern World.* Simon & Schuster, New York.

Index of Names

For Product Safety Concerns and Information please contact our EU representative GPSR@taylorandfrancis.com
Taylor & Francis Verlag GmbH, Kaufingerstraße 24, 80331 München, Germany

www.ingramcontent.com/pod-product-compliance
Ingram Content Group UK Ltd.
Pitfield, Milton Keynes, MK11 3LW, UK
UKHW011010180926
475701UK00004B/660
9780367249465